THE DEFINITIVE GUIDE TO FUTURES TRADING

VOLUME II

THE DEFINITIVE GUIDE TO FUTURES TRADING

Volume II

by Larry Williams

WINDSOR BOOKS, BRIGHTWATERS, NEW YORK

Published by Windsor Books
P.O. Box 280
Brightwaters, N.Y., 11718

Manufactured in the United States of America

ISBN 0-930233-36-0

## Chapter 1

Introduction

Volume I of the Definitive Guide to Futures Trading received an interesting series of responses: while it drew criticism from some of my fellow investment advisors and authors, it has received acclaim from many others. I have personally been besieged by requests for more information, been begged to hurry up the second volume, and already have had numerous people call to thank me for the many profitable trades they've had from systems outlined in that volume.

Volume II completes, as much as anyone can ever complete, this unending subject of trading commodities. It contains everything I have left to teach at this point in my life.

To me, writing books and teaching has always been synonymous. A good commodity trader, just like a good athlete, may or may not be a good teacher.

I suffer some of those same problems. While at times I'm a pretty decent commodity trader, I'm not always able to communicate or convey exactly how I do what I do. Hopefully, to remedy that, both volumes of this guide have been a painstaking work where I've laboriously gone over what I do, how I do it, and then tried to transmit to you, the poor reader.

Above all, I can tell you this about commodity trading: whether you choose to trade or not to trade, you'll be making a mistake!

9

Yes, once you enter the world of trading commodities, you'll find nothing else quite like it. It is the most thrilling commercial enterprise I've ever encountered. Certainly that has been the commentary of thousands of other people who have begun trading commodities. By the same token, if you start trading commodities you're going to lose money at some point in the game, perhaps all of your money. So, one can say in a cosmic sense that starting to trade commodities is the wrong thing to do.

By the same token, I assure you that it's equally wrong not to trade commodities. I don't see how anyone could live without the thrill, the rush, the exhilaration of trading commodities, let alone the profits that one can make. I certainly believe that trading the markets, whether you win or lose, will add a great deal to you as an individual. It will round out your personality; it will teach you many lessons and a few lessons that will be re-taught to you time after time. Without that background, frankly, I think people are incomplete. After all, this seems to be the only arena left where there is no one there to help when you lose or when you win, no government bail-out programs, no insurance companies.

The only thing that seems to exist are unscrupulous lawyers who, if they find someone who has lost money, are more than willing to bring suits against CTA's or brokerage firms. I do not say this facetiously.

In the summer of 1988, a client who I had made about four hundred fifty thousand dollars for filed an action against me with the Commodity Futures Trading Commission for fifty-four million dollars because one of my personal accounts, traded at a different brokerage firm than where her account was traded, went from ten thousand to a little over a million dollars! Accordingly, she, and apparently her attorney, felt that her account should have had the exact same performance as that personal account of mine which won the World Cup Trading Championship, sponsored by Robbins brokerage firm.

Because it didn't and her fifty thousand dollars only made four hundred fifty thousand dollars, I got slapped with a fifty-four million dollar lawsuit. Ah . . . the price of fame!

This underscores the general tenor that people have towards commodity traders, lawyers in particular and, I'm certain, regulatory agencies, as well.

If there's to become a demise of this business, that's where it's going to come from. I urge you, dear reader, whether you are a registered commodity trading advisor, a money manager, someone who gives your money to other people to manage or even a bureaucrat to realize that trading commodities is not a cakewalk.

Trading commodities is not a Sunday picnic. There are ups and downs to this business, highs and lows. People crash and burn. People kill themselves. The reality of this is that rocks are hard and water is wet. People can, and do, lose substantial amounts of money trading commodities. Because I have been successful one year, does not mean I'll be successful another year. Generally speaking, however, I think it's a correct assumption to say, though, that winners persist through good and bad times. A winner will give better performance than a non-winner. But you are individually responsible for the performance of your account. Whether you have someone manage it for you or not, you know at what point you absolutely must bail out.

Lest one detect any notes of bitterness let me hastily add, as I sit here on the shores of beautiful Big Fork Bay, basking under the big blue Montana sky, that I cannot think of anything that could have elevated my life and lifestyle as much as trading commodities. It has enabled me to go from being a kid from the other side of the tracks to a person of, hopefully, some means and influence.

What else could one ask from a profession?

Also, at the risk of sounding like a pretty old codger, I do want to make note that it seems as though free market believers and entrepreneurs in America are being "caged" by the United States government and its political institutions, to homogenize our lifestyle versus letting us be the free spirits that, I think, made this country and can continue enhancing its greatness.

That's what I like about trading commodities: ultimately, when you're riding on a bucking bronc, about to get tossed off, whether you hang on or not is a function of how good you are, how intelligent you are, what type of balance you have, and your own muscular dexterity.

So it is in trading commodities. You sink or swim based on your own efforts. So, if you can stand that type of "heat," I assure you trading commodities will be the single greatest experience in your life.

People always ask if books I've written earlier, particularly the first book, are still valid.

The question really raises a greater question, which is: do the markets change that much and is there a difference between, say, stocks, a share of IBM and Pork Bellies or Treasury Bonds?

Introduction

What I have come to believe from my experience in the markets is that there are differences between certain markets and certain stocks. But these are explainable differences. Hence, once one understands them, one can trade them, and trade them better.

I start with the assumption that stocks are inert items, like guns, which are totally safe until they come into human interaction. Nothing can take place with IBM or a contract of pork bellies until people start to react.

However, certain types of people are more willing to trade certain types of stocks or commodities.

To wit, IBM is more apt to be traded by substantial mutual funds and fund managers than renegade traders. Two dollar stocks are more apt to be traded by renegade traders, people seeking to make a big killing, than fund mangers.

There's an additional breakdown that will cause a difference in the way one commodity trades than another, and that's who produces the commodities. Certainly, there is a difference in the way cattle trade than the way wheat trades.

What accounts for this difference? I believe it's because it takes a different mentality to grow wheat or soybeans than it does to raise cows and hogs.

Then there's the final difference you need to take into consideration: that is the hours of trading and if the market is traded internationally. A leading example of this would be Swiss Francs, which opens at 5:20 in the morning, California time, and closes later in the day, but reopens and continues trading around the world. Because of this, there tends to be more of an opportunity for gaps to exist between last night's close in the Swiss Franc and the following morning's opening. That gap is not a function of American buyers, as much as it is a function of what took place in the overnight activity. Hence, one needs to look at the mechanics of how the commodity trades, and the psyche of who trades it.

Given those basic understandings, I think it's true that markets do tend to trade with a great deal of similarity, and there is enough similarity that we can capitalize on and make money. The techniques that I've shown in this book, I believe, will be essentially as effective ten or twenty years from now, just as the techniques that I revealed in my earlier books have continued working almost twenty years later.

The final comment that I'd like to make is that as far as I'm concerned there is no mysticism to the market. I've spent almost a quarter of a century tracing down these "mystical," wonderful approaches to the market. Whether it's W. D. Gann, astrology, certain angles of descent and ascent, or configurations, I have not been able to make much use of that approach to the market.

First of all, it's terribly subjective, at least with the precious little understanding I've been able to get of these techniques. I think it would behoove most traders to spend more time in serious "scientific" research than chasing pie-in-the-sky dreams of one hundred percent perfection. The market, by definition, is an imperfect game because it's traded by people. We all have our own imperfections. If you can get to be sixty to seventy percent accurate, that should certainly be good enough. It tips the scales way in your favor and will put you ahead in any game of probability. So, be content with that. I think you will only lose money . . . in substantial amounts . . . when trading on things that are supposedly one hundred percent effective or have some Houdini-like impact on the market. Admittedly, I am surprised, at times, what impact some of these strange and arcane techniques do import to the market. But there is an equal, if not greater, number of times that they simply have no bearing on price direction.

As Sergeant Joe Friday would say, "Just the facts, ma'am . . . just the facts." If you deal with just facts, I think you can quickly become a winner in this game.

In closing, let me say that there is still a great deal to be learned about the markets, about relationships, about price structures, about how momentum works and, particularly, the true relationship of volume and open interest. We have really just scratched the surface of the markets in the past few years. Yet, our knowledge, by comparison with the knowledge we had ten years ago, is much greater. It is my hope that my writings will help you and other traders make sure that ten years from now, what we know about the market today is as equally insignificant.

There are lots of winning trades out there, lots of treasures to be discovered in research. I hope you uncover them. I wish you good luck and good trading.

Larry Williams

## Chapter 2

The Ultimate Oscillator

There is nothing more intriguing to the beginning commodity or stock trader than the discovery of oscillators.

At first oscillators appear to be the perfect trading tool because so often they give excellent buy and sell signals. But, the more one uses oscillators, the more one realizes that oscillators give an equal number of false signals, false indications, and are not stable data on their own.

Since the turn of the century traders have tried to tame their oscillators to develop a new approach that does not give false signals and false divergences, yet provides an insight into the market that no other tool can.

What an oscillator actually does is measure the momentum of the data, whether your data is price, volume, or open interest. An oscillator will help show the speed at which the information is changing . . . it can also define overbought and oversold areas.

Perhaps the pioneer in oscillator work was Owen Taylor, who in the 1920's presented oscillator work based on 7 day data. Taylor looked at price today versus a seven day moving average of price or 7 day moving average of advancing and declining stocks over the last seven days.

15

In the 1940's Woods and Vignolia started their interesting approach to the market measuring volume in what is now known as On Balance Volume.

These two gentlemen, based in San Francisco, started running a cumulative positive-negative volume flow that was later popularized by Joe Granville. But we must not forget that Woods and Vignolia also did a tremendous amount of oscillator work using 20 to 40 day measurements of days that had up volume versus days that had down volume.

Slightly earlier than this the Lowry reports out of Florida were busy running moving averages on advancing and declining stocks or advancing and declining volume under their heading of "buying pressure" and "selling pressure."

In the 1950's, not too much was done in the way of oscillators. It wasn't until 1960, when Securities Market Research, a chart service out of Denver, Colorado, showed an oscillator based on the difference between two moving averages, that the oscillator number crunchers started getting busy again.

The ability to construct oscillators improved substantially with the advent of the computer and especially the small personal computers.

That gave the introduction to a new approach to oscillators going beyond a simple moving average where one takes a total of all the data over the last time period and divides it by that number in the time period. The new trading crowd had been to college, had studied their math, and was suddenly flipping around words like exponentials, supersonic averages, front end weighted moving averages, lagged moving averages, rolling numbers, etc.

Perhaps this all reached its zenith in what has become one of the most widely known oscillators, which I believe has been misnamed. Constructed by Welles Wilder, the relative strength index is not a measure of relative strength because relative strength means in relation to something. What Welles created was an oscillator based on a 14 day time cycle that has a decent record of giving buy and sell signals on the market.

THE OSCILLATOR OPPORTUNITY

The reason people have continued dabbling with oscillators is because they have the capability to give indications in advance of market turning points. I authored an article in 1973 for what was then known as "Commodities Magazine" now "Futures," that showed an approach to oscillators in the Pork Belly and Soybean Oil market that actually led major tops and bottoms in the market.

The trouble for most oscillator users was, and has continued to be, that while frequently oscillators lead, sometimes they lead far too early and instead of buying a bottom you are buying falling daggers and getting sliced up.

Perhaps the oscillator is best in identifying the areas of significant tops and bottoms. Yet, to date, even the best oscillators consistently give premature buy and sell signals. My ultimate oscillator, I believe, corrects this—and is one of the major improvements you are about to learn.

Frequently, however, when divergence occurs, that is price goes to a new high and the oscillator does not or the price goes to a new low and the oscillator doesn't, you are in an area of an important turning point of the market place.

The only problem is that many oscillators will show such divergence 3, 4, 5 or 6 times along the way to the ultimate low, and a person buying on those divergences quickly ends up with a flood of margin calls from his brokerage firm.

Another one of the opportunities of using oscillators is that they are relatively easy to construct and relatively easy to follow. In a time period when most market approaches have more rules than we have commodities, and when some of the rules are more complicated to figure out than Rubik's Cube, it is important that one simplifies his approach to the market so he has more time to actually deal with the market and less time crunching numbers.

Many traders end up having so much work to do that they can't separate the forest from the trees. After all, the question isn't how much work you are doing, the question is how much money you are making.

THE OSCILLATOR PROBLEM

I believe the largest failure of the oscillators is the inability to deal correctly with the time cycles involved.

Let me explain that a bit:

If you use a seven day average, as Taylor did in the 1920's, you will quickly find that the maximum move you are going to catch is one that lasts somewhere in the area of three and one half to nine days. In other words, the type of moves the oscillator speaks of cannot, by definition, be much longer than the time period measured in the oscillator.

By the same token, if you go out to a longer term approach, say something that measures what is taking place in sixty or seventy days, the problem then is a loss of sensitivity in the indicator. By the time your oscillator's identified the trend and the trend then reverses, you may have not made any money at all (and may be net losers on your trades). The markets are so quick anything that has 30, 50 or 80 days built into the data base does not respond quickly enough to get you in and out with a profit.

Some advisors have suggested that oscillators be used as judgmental tools, as opposed to a systematic approach to the market. That may well be correct, but the problem with tools is two different people will come up with two entirely different approaches to using the oscillators. One reading a sell, the other a buy. Perhaps you know the experience.

ALL ABOUT THE ULTIMATE OSCILLATOR

I have wrestled with oscillators since 1965. Initially all of my oscillator work was done on a hand calculator. In the late 60's that was made a little bit easier with the advent of the electronic calculator, and then made even easier with the new and powerful computers.

One thing I noticed through the years is that the traditional short term oscillators, such as those featured in most chart books, will turn very positive at the start of a major upmove in the market but quickly show divergence and overbought readings, causing most traders to sell short somewhere after the first leg of a bull market. They then take a short position on the market and hold that short position in one form or another, actual outright short or afraid to purchase, for the next three or four legs of the bull market. That can be a costly experience.

This happens because the time measurements in the oscillators they are following are too short term in nature to catch a major move.

What is really needed . . . and unfortunately I don't have the mathematical background or understanding to create it . . . is an oscillator that expands as the market gets stronger or weaker.

As an example, if the market shows a tremendous amount of strength your oscillator would continue expanding the time base out, not allowing the short term fluctuations to influence the fact that the market has turned the corner on a long term basis.

What I have done with the ultimate oscillator is an attempt to accommodate the three most important time cycles in the marketplace. Additionally, instead of measuring price I believe it is more profitable to measure the amount of accumulation and distribution taking place in the market.

PRICE IS DECEPTIVE

I say that because I believe price is very deceptive. If you have ever seriously tried to trade commodities, I think you will agree with me. Price action alone, although it can be instrumental and educational, can be equally deceptive. Breaks to new highs are frequently false. Breaks to new lows are also equally frequently false. What looks like very strong price action may end up being very weak price action. In short, you have about as much reliability with price action alone as America has had in collecting loans from the Soviet Union.

IT IS ABOUT TIME

Time is one of the most critical elements in creating your oscillator. I have chosen three different time periods for the oscillator that I am about to show you. What I am actually doing is combining three time cycles that have been the most dominant time cycles in the market.

You will soon learn about the data that we will measure, but first let me tell you that we will use three different measurements of the same data. We will use one which will be based on the seven day measurement, a 14-day and a 28-day measurement. Accordingly then, I am measuring what one could call the short, intermediate and longer term cycles in the market. Obviously, to a very long term trader in the market 28 days is not a gargantuan time period, but in terms of the volatility of the markets I have found that those time periods are generally the ones that give moves most commodity traders wish to trade for.

19

THE GREAT EQUALIZER

One needs to equalize these time periods.

As an example, all of the data for the last seven days gives you a total reading of, let's say 7. If you add that in with all of the data from the last 28 days, let's say 28, you can clearly see that the effect of a short term cycle is far outweighed by the weight of the longer term cycle. In fact, in this case you would only be getting 1/4 the influence of the initial seven days data.

To correct this situation, we will simply multiply the data from the seven day time series by 4 and multiply the data from the 14 day time period by 2, giving equal values for all three cycles. As you can see, you do not need to multiply the end time period, 28, by anything as you are equalizing to that long term measurement.

If one were to use a series of 4 or 5 cyclical measures in the oscillator, which can be done, you would do the same thing . . . you would divide the shorter term time number into the longest time number in your measurement and then multiply the shorter term measurement by the product of the division.

As an example, if your longest term cycle was an 85 day cycle and one of your short term cycles was a 9 day cycle, you would multiply the data arrived from the 9 day measurement by 9.44 to equalize it out to the 85 day time period (9.44 x 9 equals 85).

MEASURING ACCUMULATION AND DISTRIBUTION

To my knowledge no one has spent more time in attempting to measure and study accumulation and distribution than I have. That is not a boast, just a statement of what I believe to be the fact.

I have tried to measure accumulation and distribution in commodities in terms of volume, in terms of open interest, in terms of net change, in terms of volatility factors, and in terms of tick by tick trade. You name it and I have tried to pull accumulation/distribution measures out of the data.

The bottom line of all that effort is that what appears to be the easiest way of measuring accumulation and distribution is to simply define selling pressure as the price movement from the high to close each day, while taking the buying pressure to be the difference between the low and the close.

For this study, one must also incorporate the previous day's closing price if the following day's high is lower than the previous days' closing price, or the following day's low is higher than the previous day's closing price.

In short then, one must fill in the gaps that occur in going from yesterday's price to today's high or low. This creates true highs and true lows.

As an example, if yesterday's closing price was 60 and this morning's low was 61 with a close today of 63, the measure of buying and selling would not be 63 minus 61 but 63 minus 60, or 3 cents of buying.

I think it is quite valid to substitute the buying price ranges for actual buying and selling volume. I say this not only from the practical studies I have done but also from the theoretical view as well.

As an example, on an up limit day we have little if any volume, so if you were just to look at volume studies you would be under the impression that there was not buying for the day. That flies directly in the face of what has happened, because prices were up the maximum amount they could trade.

I think it is a fair statement to say that whenever volume expands in the market the daily trading range expands, and whenever volume contracts in a market the trading range contracts.

TO BEGIN CONSTRUCTING THE OSCILLATOR

You need to set up several columns. First I always post the high, low and close each day. One column to the right I have the buying unit for that day, which will be defined as the close minus the true low. I then skip a couple of columns and have another column to record all of the activity of the day, defined by subtracting the true high from the true low. We have then created, on a daily basis, the amount of buying for the day versus the total amount of activity (buying and selling) for the day.

I next run a 7 day sum of the total amount of buying for the last seven days. This is simply done by adding each day's amount of buying and adding the sum of that buying for the

21

seventh day. The next day I want to drop off the number 7 days ago and add the new number coming in, giving me a new seven day sum.

The next day I will drop off the number seven days ago and add the new number coming in, giving me a new seven day sum, and so on.

I also run a fourteen day sum of the buying figure and finally a twenty-eight day sum of the buying figure.

I then do the same thing with the total activity or range figure by running a seven day sum of the range, fourteen day sum of the range, and a twenty-eight day sum of the range.

Now the fun begins. I then divide the seven day figure of the range, or total activity, into the seven day figure of buying, to give the % of buying in that time period. I next divide the total range of the fourteen days total into the buying of the fourteen days, to give me a percent of buying for the fourteen days. I follow that up with the third step of dividing the total range of the last 28 days into the total buying for the twenty-eight days, giving me a percentage of buying during the time period.

Finally, I multiply the seven day figure by 4 and the 14 day figure by 2 to balance the impact that each time period will have.

If you have followed along with me so far you now realize that I add the final seven, fourteen and twenty-eight day figure into one master percentage figure that reflects the buying and selling pressures of three time periods over the last twenty-eight days, all equalized to give each time period an equal impact.

This data is then plotted as a percentage change underneath price action, resulting in . . . "the Ultimate Oscillator."

RULES FOR USING THE ULTIMATE OSCILLATOR

There will be two requirements for a buy or sell signal to activate a market position using the oscillator. Our first demand is that we have a price divergence from the oscillator.

In the case of a buy we must have had a low in price that was not matched by a lower low in the oscillator.

In the case of a sell we must have had a higher high in price that was not matched by the oscillator.

The chart below depicts the basic configuration we are looking for. The inability of the oscillator to follow prices tells us that accumulation is coming into the market on the buy side or that distribution is taking place on the sell side.

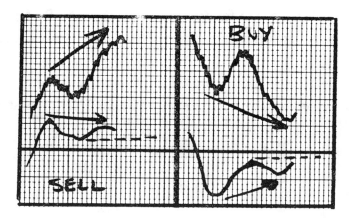

We next await a trend break in the Ultimate Oscillator to produce the actual signal . . . to pull the trigger on the trade. Let me explain this to you.

Once the divergence for a sell signal has occurred note the low in the oscillator prior to the peak that set up the divergence. I have marked this as A on the Feb. 84 Belly chart.

Once the U.O. falls below this peak you can take a short position in the market. The failure in the oscillator is your indication that it is time to sell. Frequently you will see this taking place right at, or very close to, the actual high in price.

Once the divergence for a buy signal has occurred note the high in the oscillator prior to the low that set up the divergence. I have marked this as B on the Feb. 84 Belly chart.

Once the U.O. rises above this peak you can't take a long position. The trend break in the oscillator is your indication that buyers now dominate and an up move will begin. Again, note how close this trend break to the upside occurs to the low in price.

Once you have entered a position you will exit in one of the three following manners:

IF SHORT

1. Exit on an opposite signal occurring. You would also be reversing to the long side.

2. Go flat, not reversing, when the U.O. falls to 30% or less. This go-flat signal will be early at times, but its usage will greatly increase your % of winners and reduce your number of sleepless nights.

3. Once short, close out your position, going flat any time the index rises above 65%. This is your stop loss.

IF LONG

1. Exit on an opposite signal occurring. You would also be reversing to the short side.

2. Go flat, not reversing, when the U.O. rises above 70%. Comments in 2 above apply.

3. Once long, close out your position, going flat any time the index falls below 45% after having risen above 50%. This is your stop loss.

ALL DIVERGENCE SIGNALS MUST FIRST HAVE SEEN THE INDEX RISE ABOVE 50% FOR A SELL AND FALLEN BELOW 30% FOR A BUY. DIVERGENT PATTERNS THAT OCCUR WITHOUT THE INDEX FIRST GOING TO THESE LEVELS ARE NOT TO BE ACTED UPON.

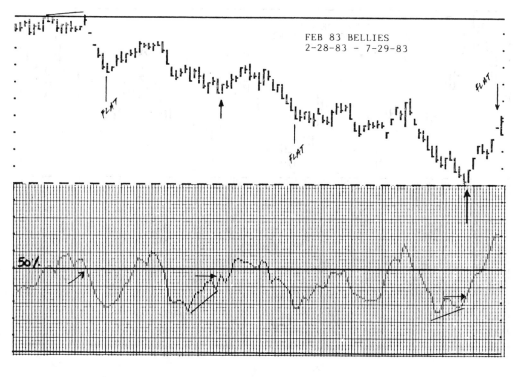

FEB 83 BELLIES
2-28-83 – 7-29-83

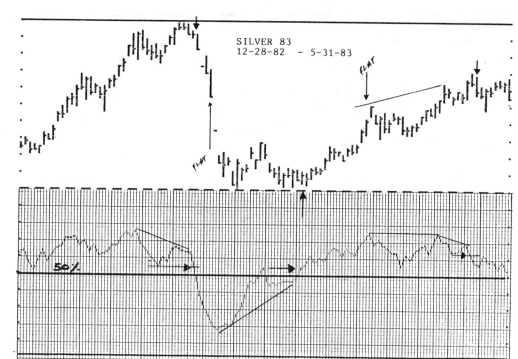

SILVER 83
12-28-82 – 5-31-83

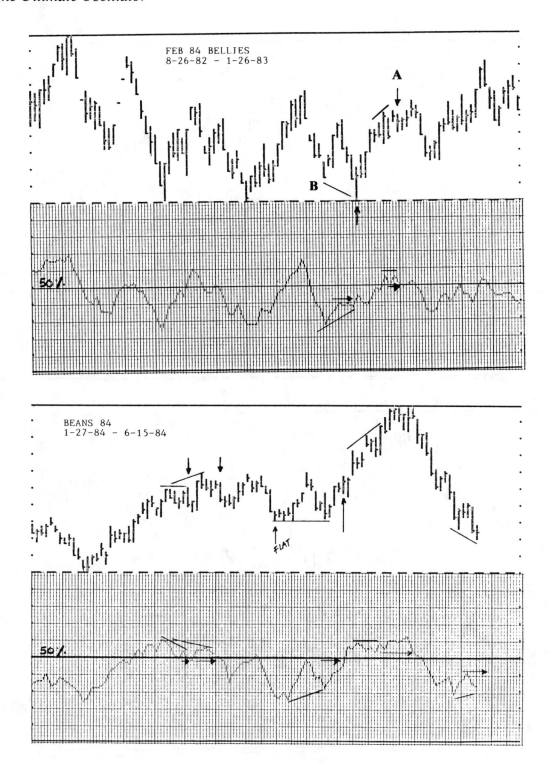

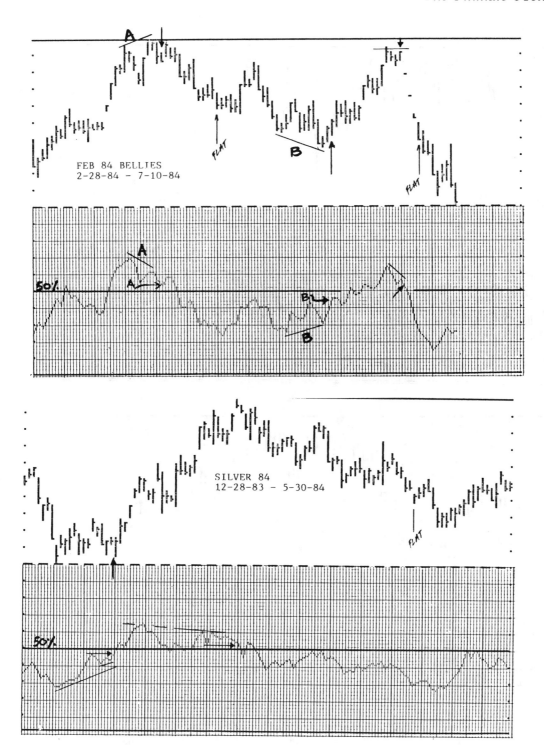

FEB 84 BELLIES
2-28-84 - 7-10-84

50%

SILVER 84
12-28-83 - 5-30-84

50%

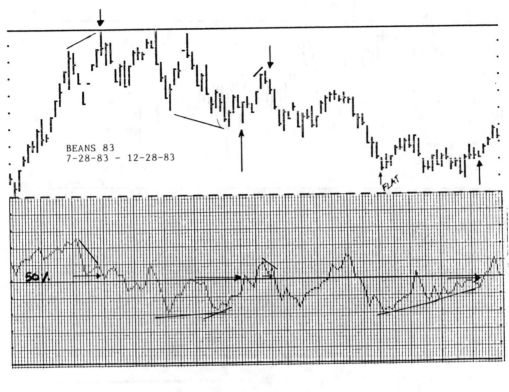

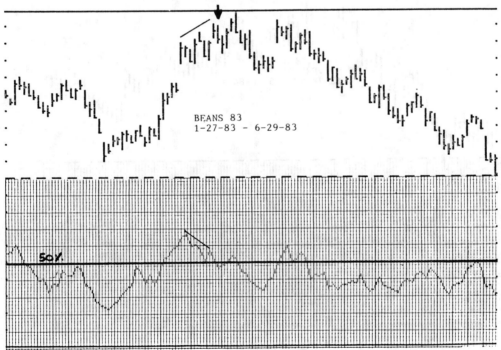

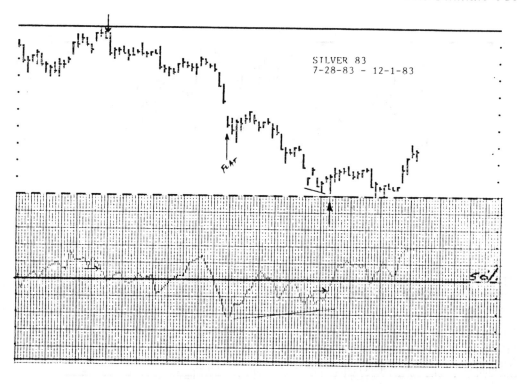

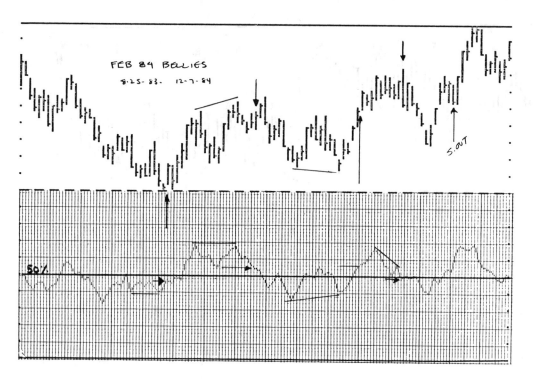

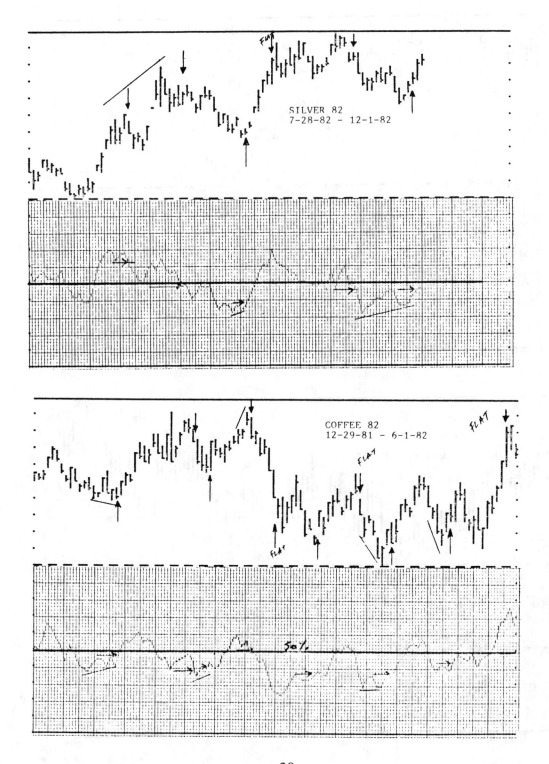

SILVER 82
7-28-82 - 12-1-82

COFFEE 82
12-29-81 - 6-1-82

## Chapter 3

A Weekly Trading Signal

There are two optimum games when it comes to trading commodities. The first, the one most people try, is day trading.

The reason day trading is an optimum game is because in theory you need precious little money to take advantage of major market swings. It is not unusual for a day trader to have positions that would require overnight margin of $20,000 to $30,000 or more—trading a $10,000 account. The other good side of day trading is that you don't have to worry about overnight news, you never have to worry about gap openings against you in the morning. You start every day trading anew, fresh.

The second optimum game of commodity trading is long term position trading. Here the advantage is not lower margins, or large daily returns on small amounts of money. On the contrary, it is quite the reverse, the advantage here is that you have small positions in the market but catch huge and major moves.

One of the first people to teach me anything about the markets, Bill Meehan, repeatedly stressed the importance of having small positions in large major moves as a profitable way of trading. In fact, that was the backbone of my initial success, which inspired my first commodity book, "How I Made One Million Dollars Trading Commodities Last Year."

The problem with this trading approach is that it is very difficult to have a timing indicator that gets you in for these long term major moves.

In recent years, several methods have been developed to allow traders to capitalize on major swings. Usually they consist of buying once price gets above a moving average and holding on until price falls below another long term moving average.

There may be validity to this approach. However, the problem is that most often you are not getting very much out of the move or you are getting in so late that your emotions talk you out of getting in!

Accordingly, I have developed a weekly entry signal that will enable you to get in at some most opportune points in major moves.

THE PROBLEM

First, let's talk about the problems with the entry method I am about to teach you. They are there and they are for real, and they will happen to you in real time market trading. The first problem with the system is that it does not go from long to short to short to long. It does not always give signals.

There may be a major market top wherein the weekly entry signal never gives a signal. Conversely, there can be a major market low that is not indicated by a weekly entry signal.

Also, you may have a weekly entry signal to buy but never get an opposite weekly entry signal to sell. Thus, this chapter has been entitled "A Weekly Trading Signal" because it is simply that, a signal telling you that there is a high probability on a weekly basis . . . a longer term view . . . that the market has turned the corner and a move of some consequence should follow.

Sometimes these will be major moves. Other times it will be a move of just one or two weeks. You have to use other tools, as well as your own intuition and judgement, to determine the difference between the two.

If you are convinced that a market is at an important low point, then you certainly want to be looking for the weekly entry signal that I am about to introduce to you.

Another problem with the weekly entry signal is that you must pay attention to the market closely on one day of the week. Some long term approaches simply give you an entry number.

If prices get above or below that number for the week, that is your signal. This is different. In this instance, you must watch the opening price on Monday to see if the opening price is above or below last week's high or low.

Without paying attention to Monday's opening, you will not be able to correctly follow this system. Hence, another disadvantage to this long term method is that it will force you to take a short term view of the commodity market every Monday. If you have the time and are willing to do that, then you will find this to be an invaluable indicator as an entry point into the marketplace.

Now that we have talked about the potential problems of the method, let's talk about the good sides of it as well.

THE GOOD NEWS

The good news is that the method is explicitly simple. It does not take a computer . . . not even a hand-held calculator . . . to follow the system. It can be backchecked quite easily on the commodity of your choice to see how it has been operating, and will give you the potential of catching some incredible up-moves and down-moves when they occur.

There are two basic approaches to trading the market. One deals with the trend of the market, hoping that you are in phase with the trend. The other is what I would call an anti-trend method. An anti-trend method is something that in some fashion suggests to you that the huge up or downtrend is finished. The weekly entry signal I am teaching here is an anti-trend method as it goes against the trend. While virtually every trend mechanism will show the trend to be down, the weekly entry signal indicates that there is a high probability that the trend has reversed, long before it has actually been seen in the price structure of the market.

WHY THIS SIGNAL WORKS

I believe this signal works because it is based on psychology and human emotions of the marketplace.

The signal, for a buy, demands that Monday's opening be below the lowest point of the previous week. This type of activity occurs because there is a negative article in Barron's, The Wall Street Journal, or some place. Speculators, commercials, floor traders and the public all rush in, causing huge gap openings on Monday morning. The gap is large enough that it is below the previous week's low.

A BUY SIGNAL . . . A SELL SIGNAL

However, the activity in a turnaround is not and cannot be confirmed until prices rally to take out the low of the previous week. So here is the definition of a buy signal: A Monday morning opening that is lower than the previous week's low, then a rally in the market that rallies above the previous week's low, by 1 or 2 ticks. I usually like to see about 3 to 4 ticks on a weekly chart for a buy signal.

A sell signal is going to be just the reverse. Here we are looking for a market that opens higher than last week's high, then starts trading down and trades below the high of last week. That indicates that a substantial sellout is about to come into the marketplace.

The same emotional phenomena takes place; here the shorts are scared out of their wits on Monday and the public rushes in to buy. They end up buying, frequently, at the exact high of a move. Prices then start drifting back, taking out the previous week's high and that is it; it's all over, the market heads South!

I have shown 11 charts of various commodities going back to the late summer of 1983. On the charts I have marked with arrows all of the weekly entry signals that occurred. I have left some charts for you to mark up. Make notations yourself so you can study and create your own signals on the weekly charts.

Once you think you have a handle on the system, turn your attention to the chart of the Swiss Francs. And if you want to see an incredible signal, look at the buy signal that occurred October 1985 on the weekly Coffee chart. Unfortunately, while there are some absolutely phenomenal signals, look at the one that occurred in the Standard and Poor's in July 1984. There was a May 1984 buy signal in Treasury Bonds and for that matter a March 1985 buy signal.

34

Not all of the signals come, as you will see, so perfect. If you like to trade the D-Mark, you might want to look at the sell signals that occurred in late December 1983, and in late April 1984. Both were humdingers. Again, not all signals produce such moves. It is nice to see that the absolute high in Silver was called with this method, and that there had been a buy signal just the previous week. You may want to look at these examples.

On the Silver chart I have marked off exactly what happens during a week where a buy or sell signal develops. As you see, the first requirement is that we open above the previous week's high and then start to drift down, taking out the high of the previous week. That is our sell signal. From there on we are locked into a sell signal. A buy, of course, is just the reverse.

Let's walk through the charts so that we might look at the signals and see how you may have traded each market.

The first thing on the Standard and Poor's chart is typical of a bad signal. What is interesting to know is that while the signal is wrong, it certainly stopped price from going appreciably higher. Following the higher opening, then going below the previous week's high, the market did not immediately respond to the down-move. Hence, one would have had to use a stop.

WHERE SHOULD STOPS BE?

When trading this system, you should use a stop that is below the low of the week that you purchased, or above the high of the week you sell short.

If you wish to use a trailing stop once in the trade, use the low of the week that you buy for the first 3 weeks. Following that, trail up with a stop that is below the lowest low of the last 2 weeks. This trailing system often works quite well, enabling you to catch some major moves.

In the Standard and Poor's chart notice that the next signal, a sell, came in December 1983. Here the market opened higher than the previous week and came down. Unfortunately, this trade was also stopped out in the first week of January 1984. The second week of January 1984 we barely opened higher than the previous week, and in this instance we got a very nice signal. Immediately prices started going down. Three weeks later your stop would have been the highest high of the last 2 weeks and you would have been out in February. You sold short at approximately 170, getting out at about 159.

35

Obviously, if you get an opposite signal you should switch. Let's say you received a weekly sell entry and then a buy signal occurred. You would not continue holding on to your short. You would reverse the trade, trading from signal to signal.

The next signal to occur is one of those all-timers that occurred in July right at the absolute lows. You were home free with a gargantuan up-move in the thousands of dollars over the next 7 weeks. Three weeks later another signal occurred, where prices opened below the previous week's low, leading to a very powerful week. It opened higher the following week to create a sell signal. At that point you would have taken your profit a tick or two below the high of the previous week, because you had the opposite signal.

Prices did not plummet immediately, but notice the impact the signal had on the market. The market then moved down and sideways for 13 weeks!

The next signals occurred prior to the high in July of 1985. Unfortunately, they did not produce any major profits, and in both instances were stopped out with nominal losses.

Equally unfortunately, and this is something that you must learn about the system, is that there was no signal given at the July 1985 low. How one wished there would have been, but there simply wasn't. Nor was there one in the bottom that occurred in September 1985.

This system does not always speak, but when it speaks you should listen.

The Value Line chart produced similar signals, so let's next turn our position to the Bond chart. As I mentioned earlier, the system called the absolute low week in 1984 with the buy as I have marked. Four weeks later another weekly signal was given.

You will find these to be very good signals, one following another, kicking off a huge and gargantuan up-move. There were no other weekly entry signals until January 1985, when the buy signal produced a very strong 3 week rally. Again, no sell signal occurred at the top, but another buy signal was given in late March. This heralded in a second buy signal in April, and one of the largest rallies to ever take place in the Bond market.

Another buy signal came following the correction in July 1985 and a 4 week rally proceeded. In the fall of 1985 a sell signal was given and prices came down for 2 weeks. A buy signal, and then another buy signal, was given 3 weeks after that as the market started shooting for the stars.

You may want to closely study the next chart, which is the Soybean chart. When the market was wild in late '83 and '84, it gave some excellent signals, but as the volatility started to

36

dwindle down in 1985 the signals, while profitable, did not produce such spectacular moves.

When it comes to spectacular moves, take a look at the Pork Belly chart. Some of the buy signals are absolutely incredible. Take a look at the sell signals in 1983, as well as the buy signal in late 1985, which come on the absolute low. Then the system gets choppy, producing an early buy signal and yet another buy signal again in October. This did trigger a nice rally, as did the buy signal coming just prior to the end of 1983. The first week of January produced another excellent buy signal. All of these were profitable up to the sell signal that occurred in 1984. Unfortunately, on the way down a buy signal was given that was not profitable which would have been a losing trade.

Then no trades until June of 1984, when there was a phenomenal buy signal the week of the low. This ran into an equally phenomenal sell signal the week of the high. Unfortunately, in the July-August time period there was a bad sell signal. You should pay attention to what happened here. The market opened higher and came down and it looked like you were home free, but immediately prices turned around and you had a losing trade. The next trade was a very nice sell signal that occurred in September. Prices declined into a buy signal in early October, which was a beautiful buy signal as was the one in late November. Unfortunately, at the 1984 peak there was no sell signal.

There was a sell signal in early 1985 which was profitable for 3 weeks before prices turned around.

In the huge market slide of 1985 there was an early buy signal, then a buy signal in May that saw a very nice 6 week rally. However, prior to the rally starting you may have been stopped out, as prices went below the low of the entry week.

A buy signal was given in late July and a sell signal was given shortly thereafter, leading to the ultimate low of the market.

Bellies are one of the wildest of the markets, as you can see from the chart. While some of the signals were not good, the system did have the unbelievable occurrence of calling some of the major moves of the market. Hence it is something I think we all need to pay attention to.

The Silver chart is equally fascinating. Look at the buy signal given in January 1984, leading up to a sell signal 11 weeks later. The April buy signal was profitable for 4 weeks. Then, without an opposite weekly sell signal, the market declined.

37

As you can see, you obviously need to have another mechanism to get you out or protect your profits. When it comes to creating an absolute trigger mechanism to force you into a long term move I can think of few better than the one I have just shown you.

You may want to study the Crude Oil chart as well as the Live Cattle chart.

The Live Cattle chart is particularly noteworthy, because I was doing a seminar in November of 1985 with Bruce Babcock and Jake Bernstein.

At that seminar we instructed people for 2 days how to trade the markets using Commodity Quotegraphics equipment.

Then on Monday we actually traded, so people could see how we traded the market and how we used the tools we taught. I bought at the arrow point on the Cattle chart, and had an immediate profit of $600 to $700 for the day in that particular trade.

While some analysts' signals always occur in hindsight, here is one that occurred in real-time. Seventy-five or 80 traders watched me put the trade on and watched the Cattle market start a huge run. What is interesting is that I had not traded Cattle . . . at all . . . for 7 or 8 years. It had been that long since I had traded Cattle, but in my analysis of the markets going into Monday's opening, I noticed that of all the markets, Cattle had the potential for this weekly entry signal. I took the signal and made money.

There are few things in life more embarrassing than to have people watching you and not make money when you are supposed to be an expert.

Equally rewarding, however, is to have people watch you trade when you do make money. I will always remember this Cattle signal.

THE BEST USE OF THE WEEKLY ENTRY SIGNAL

The best use of the weekly entry signal comes not from using it on a mechanical basis but from using it as a timing technique once you are convinced, for other reasons, that a market is a buy or sell. If you are a fundamentalist, I believe you will find this to be an excellent entry point. After all, fundamentals don't time trades, they just tell you that "Yes, this commodity should be purchased or sold."

It is then the technicians problem of when to get into that particular market. For long term trades, there are few things that will do a better job for you than this weekly entry rule.

If after running your technical or fundamental indicators you find that the vast majority of them are indicating that you should be buying . . . let's say they show the market as oversold . . . or there is a substantial divergence between oscillators implying a market bottom at hand . . . or your cyclical data shows that you are approaching a cyclical low point . . . or your measure of Accumulation/Distribution shows that the market has started to come under accumulation . . . then you can use this as your entry point to get into the trade. When you get this combination of technical data all happening at once you have a truly outstanding and excellent trading opportunity.

If we traders would simply limit ourselves to selecting these 15 to 20 trades a year, we would do far better and make a tremendous amount of money. If we could only sit back and have the patience to wait for this convergence of Bullishness or Bearishness, we would be excellent traders.

When the convergence occurs in your other work, then turn your attention to the weekly entry signal, using it as your timing mechanism.

GETTING OUT

Getting out, of course, is a problem. Sometimes you may get a weekly entry signal in the opposite direction, which of course will be your entry or exit to get out of the trade and possibly reverse your position (if the convergence of other data shows that the market should be at a significant top or bottom).

However, in the event that a weekly exit signal does not occur, you are still stuck with the problem of what to do now . . . where do you get out . . . and when?

If you are really at a loss for what to do once you take your weekly entry signal, and want to make certain your profits are protected (or the market does not run substantially against you) I suggest the following; Once you have entered a position, take 60% of the true range for the week. Let's say that the range for the week was a high of 58.50 with a low at 47.25. Your range would have been 11.25. If you then take 60% of that range, you have 6.75 points. If you short the market, have a stop 6.75 points above Friday's close as your point to exit the trade.

By the same token, if you are long the market have an exit 6.75 points below Friday's close as your point to exit the trade.

This is certainly not a panacea, nor is it a system within a system, but it will provide you with a point of protection if that is what you are looking for.

Hopefully, one of the readers of this book or someone else will be able to further develop the weekly entry signal, perhaps making a complete system out of it

But for now, if you are looking for protection, use either the trailing stop as discussed in the first part of the chapter, or the 60% of the range signal I have just given you.

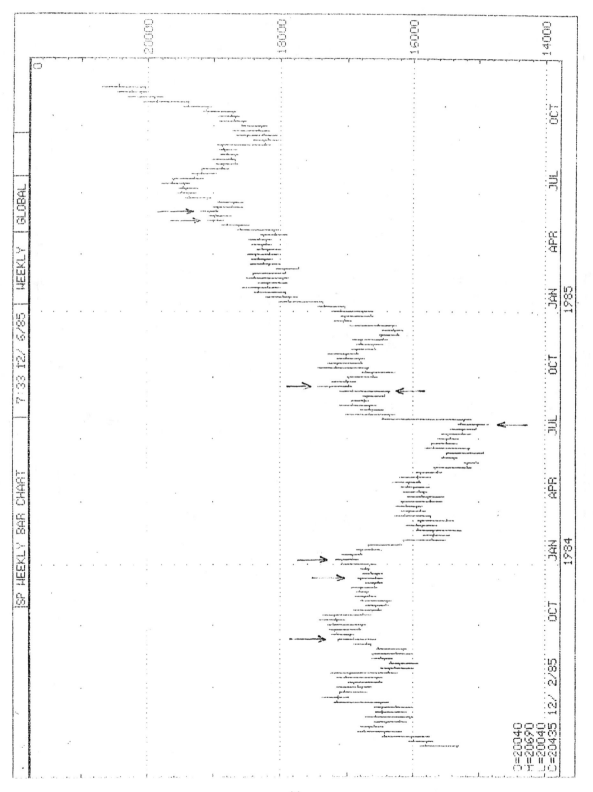

41

A Weekly Trading Signal

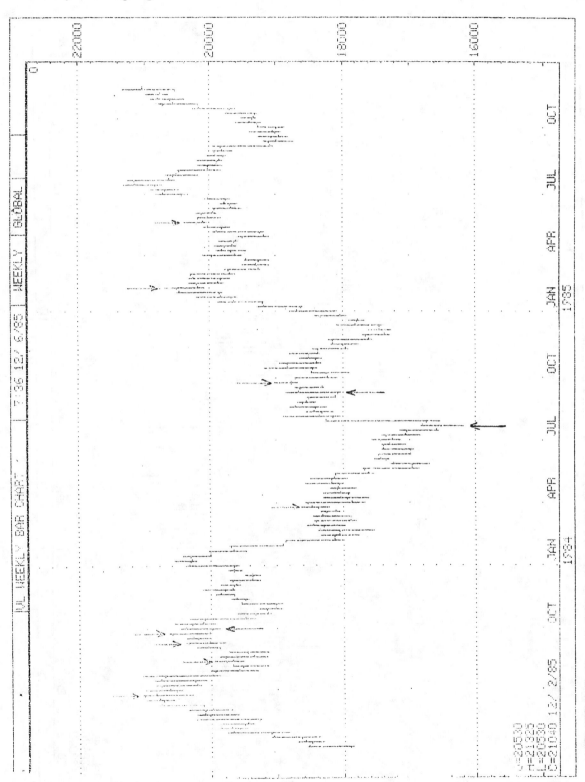

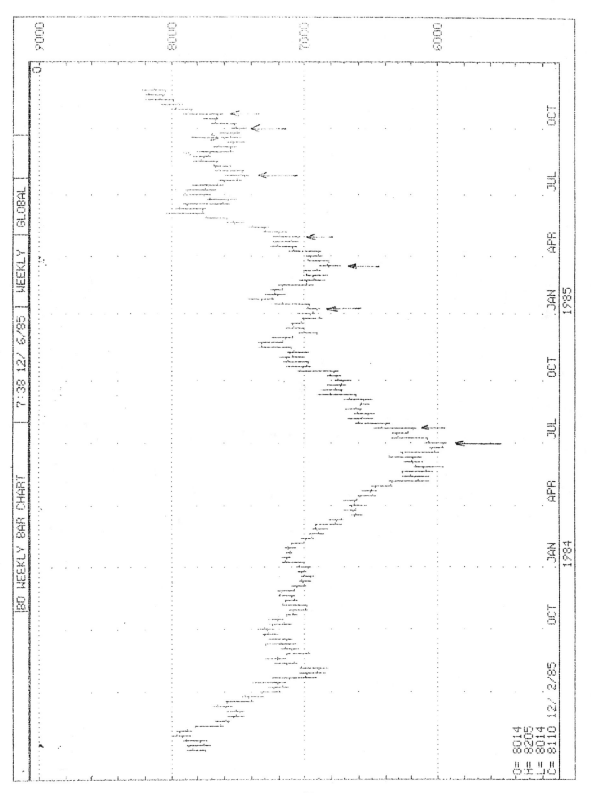

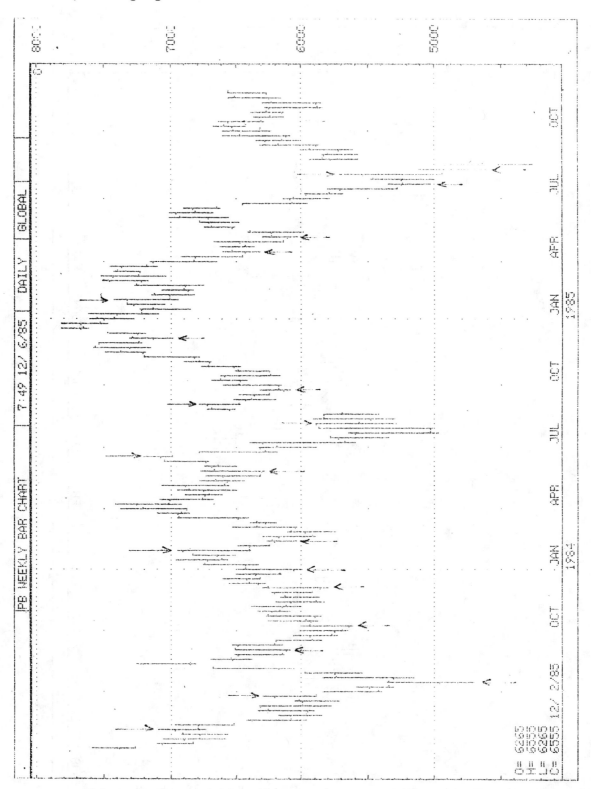

Commodity Quote-Graphics 10-20/20

45

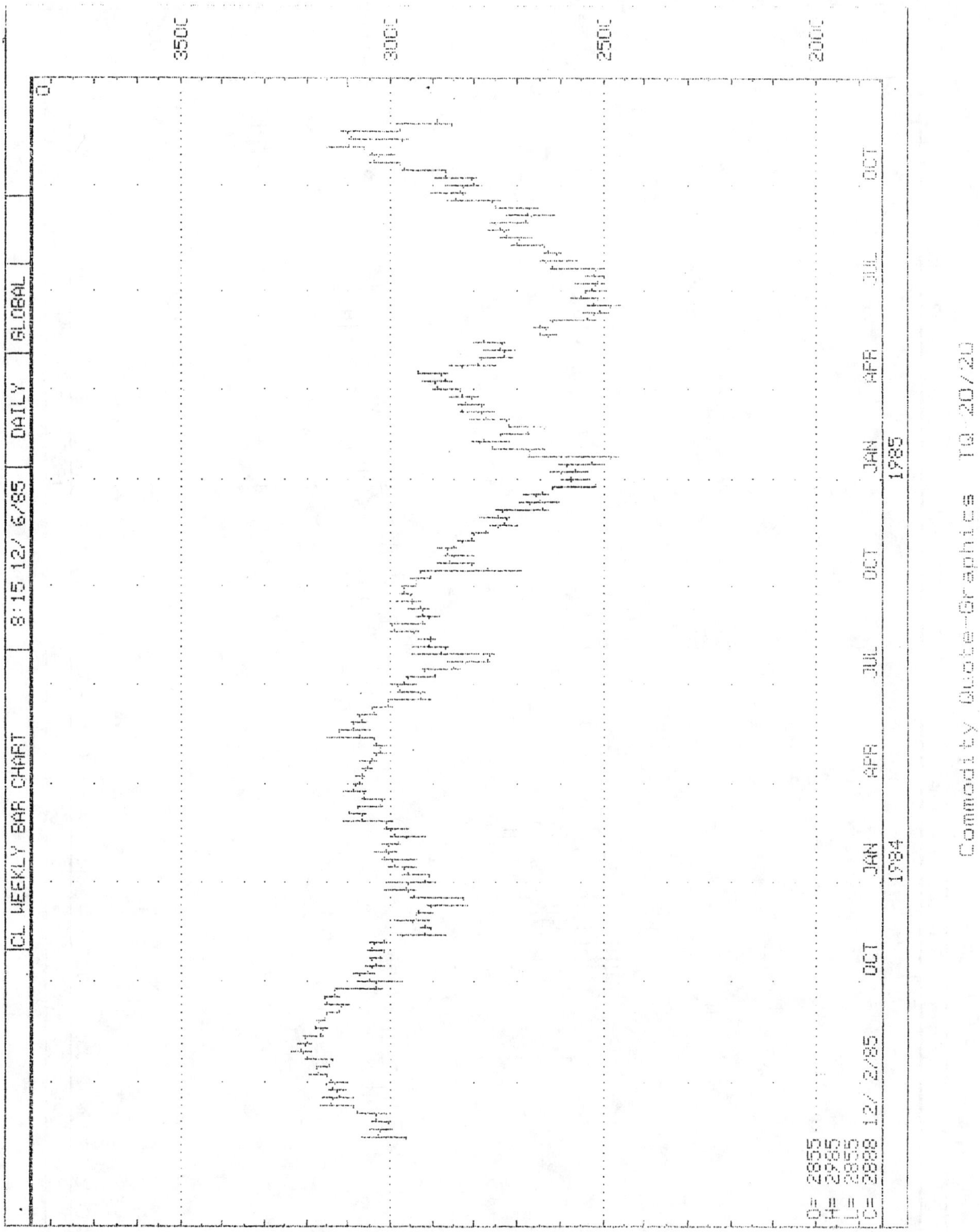
CL WEEKLY BAR CHART
8:15 12/ 6/85
DAILY
GLOBAL
3500
3000
2500
2000
OCT
JAN
APR
JUL
OCT
JAN
APR
JUL
OCT
1984
1985
12/ 2/85
O= 2855
H= 2985
L= 2855
C= 2888
Commodity Quote-Graphics TQ 20/20

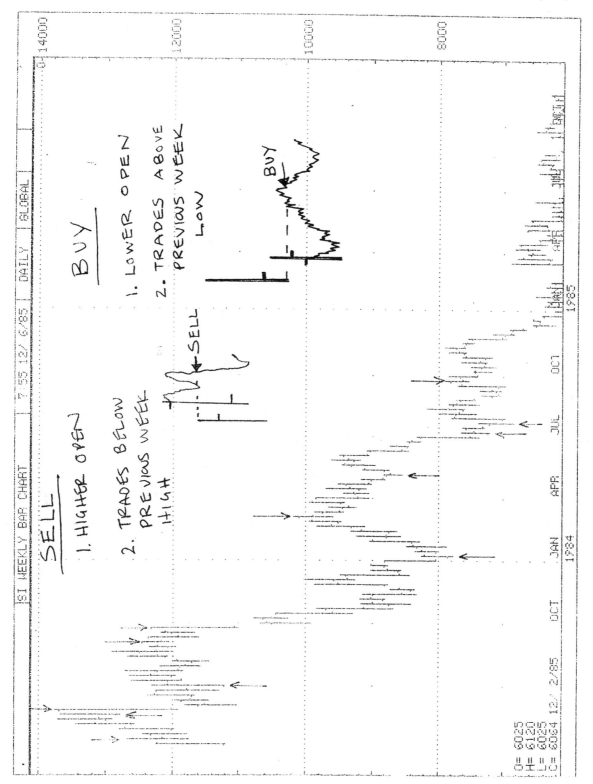

47

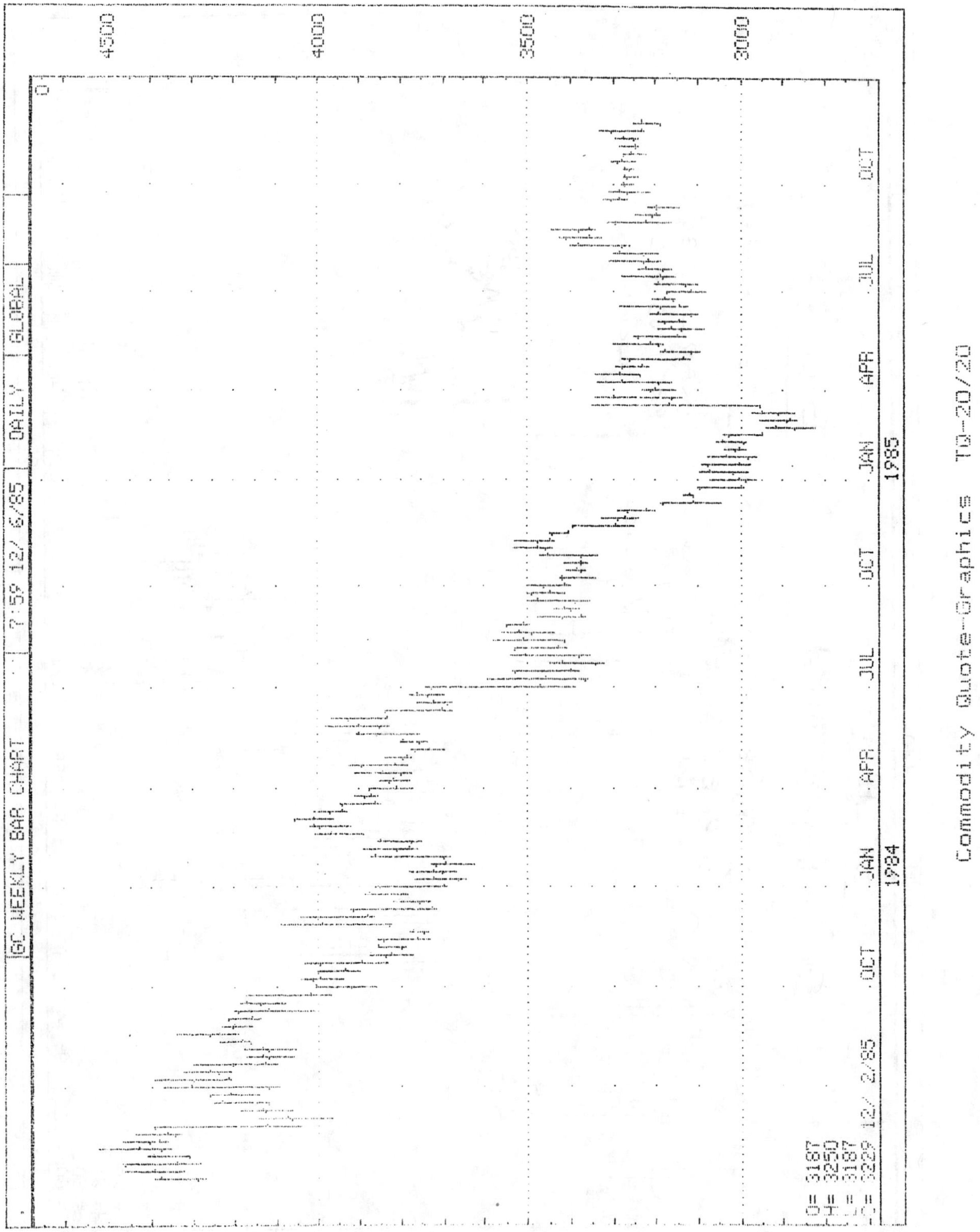

GC WEEKLY BAR CHART   7:57 12/ 6/85   DAILY GLOBAL

4500

4000

3500

3000

O 3187
H 3250
L 3187
C 3229 12/ 2/85

OCT   1984   JAN   APR   JUL   OCT   1985   JAN   APR   JUL   OCT

Commodity Quote-Graphics TQ-20/20

Commodity Quote-Graphics TQ—20/20

Commodity Quote-Graphics TQ-20/20

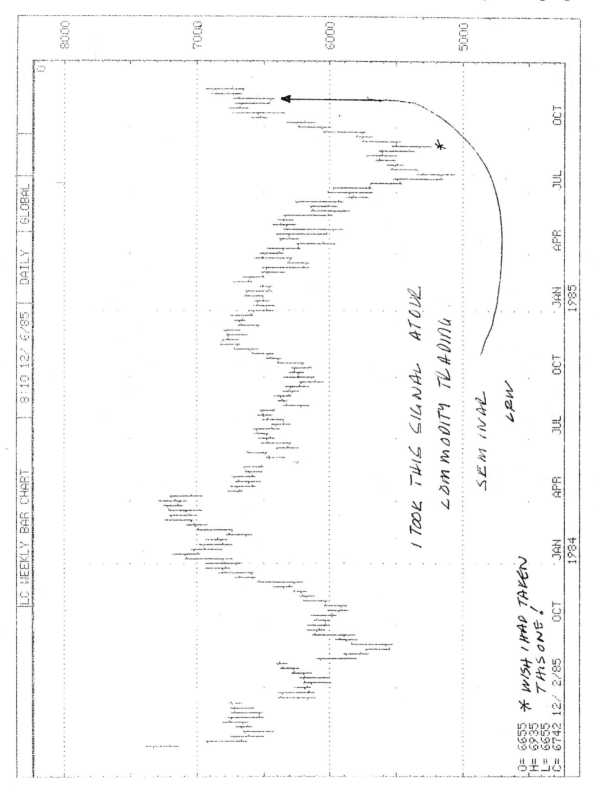

## Chapter 4

Half Cycle Differencing

Aside from Fourier and Maximum Entropy methods of discerning what the dominant cycles are in a given data segment, there is a third method I call Half Cycle Differencing. This technique, though more straightforward than the others, attempts to approximate the dominant cycle(s) by returning a given reliability for every even numbered cycle. For example, if the most reliable cycle returned is 20 days, that is an approximation of the most reliable cycle or one day more than that. In this instance, the dominant cycle can be assumed to be 20-21 days.

If you have experience with trying to mathematically deduce cycles, I think you will find this technique easier to follow than the others.

To begin with you will have to select a data segment to analyze. We'll call this N. The largest cycle we will be able to approximate will be the first even number that is less than or equal to N divided by 2. If N were 43 days, we could approximate cycle reliabilities for 2 to 20 day cycles.

Now for each cycle there is an associated half cycle which equals the cycle divided by 2. If we are looking at a 26 day cycle, the associated half cycle is 13 days. If we are looking at a 2 day cycle the associated half cycle is 1 day, etc. The half cycle is important in that it is the only measurement between 2 points that will measure the full amplitude of the cycle (i.e. peak to trough).

What we will try to do now is measure the cycle's amplitude for each day in N, starting at the most recent day and working backwards. If we are starting with a 2 day cycle (fig. 1) then 1 is our associated half cycle. Now we subtract the day that is one half cycle away from day 1. In other words, we take day 1's close minus day 2's close (We don't have to work with closes, we could work with opens, highs, lows, medians, moving averages, etc.). Now to that sum we will move down to the next day and add the difference of day 2's close minus day 3's close to our running total. All we are doing is summing differences here. The less this sum of the differences is for each cycle, the more reliable the cycle is. Figure 1 bears this out in that there is a perfect 2 day cycle evident. If we continued with our summation of the 2 day cycle differences we would finish with a sum of 0, indicating a very reliable 2 day cycle.

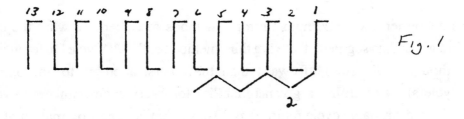

Fig. 1

If we look at figure 2 for a moment, we can see that here is a data set that will also show a very reliable 2 day cycle! It is important to note at this juncture that this technique assumes cycles exist within the data. If no cycles do in fact exist (as is the case in fig. 2) then this technique is of no use to us whatsoever.

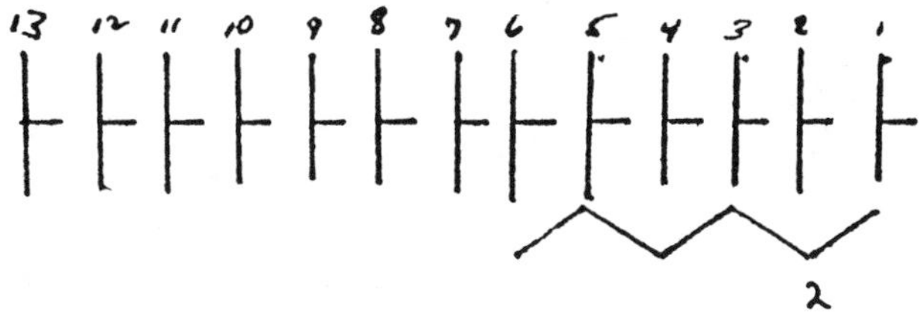

Fig. 2

Once you have completed summing the differences of the 2 day cycle, you then need to proceed to the next half cycle increment. Since we used a half cycle of 1 previously (in looking for the presence of a 2 day cycle) we now go to using a half cycle of 2 and look for the presence of a 4 day cycle.

Refer now to figure 3. Notice that it is very important where, within N, you stop differencing for a given cycle length. In figure 3 notice that there is a perfect 4 day cycle, the same way that there was a perfect 2 day cycle in figure 1. If we difference out to day 10, then our sum will be 0 and we assume we have a perfect 4 day cycle. If, however, we difference out to day 12 (which we could have) then our sum will not be 0 and we will not have readings indicating a perfect 4 day cycle.

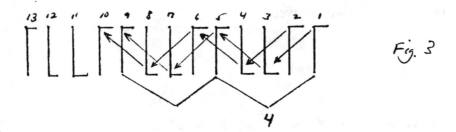

Fig. 3

To alleviate this problem, there is a formula which tells us the maximum number of days to difference to for each cycle length, which we will call maxdays.

$$\text{MAXDAYS} = (\text{Cyclelength} \times Z) + 1$$

Where $Z = (N - 1) / \text{Cyclelength}$
And Z is taken to the next lowest even integer if it is not an integer itself.
If Z is less than 1 then set $Z = 1$.

To plug our problem from fig. 3 into this formula:

$Z = (13 - 1) / 4$
$\quad = 12 / 4$
$\quad = 3$, and taken to the next lowest even integer is 2.

$\text{MAXDAYS} = (4 \times 2) + 1$
$\quad\quad\quad\quad = 8 + 1$
$\quad\quad\quad\quad = 9$

56

We would keep summing the differences of 2 days (4 day cycle) until we came to the difference of day 7 minus day 9. Then we would move on to the next cycle.

What would our MAXDAYS number be for a 2 day cycle where N = 13? If you plug the values into the MAXDAYS equation:

$$Z = (13 - 1) / 2$$
$$= 12 / 2$$
$$= 6 \text{ (since this is an even integer there is no need}$$
$$\text{to round it down to the next lowest even integer)}$$
$$\text{MAXDAYS} = (6 \times 2) + 1$$
$$= 12 + 1$$
$$= 13$$

You would therefore difference out to day 12 minus day 13 in calculating the 2 day cycle.

With N equal to 13, we can deduce cycle lengths of up to the first even integer which is less than or equal to N/2. Since our diagrams show N as 13, we can deduce up to a 6 day cycle (6 being the first even integer which is less than 6.5 or 13/2).

Now assume N to be 12 days, and we are looking to deduce a 6 day cycle:

To find MAXDAYS for the 6 day cycle:

$$Z = (12 - 1) / 6$$
$$= 11 / 6$$
$$= 1.833 \text{ taken to the next lowest even integer is 0.}$$
$$\text{Since Z cannot be less than 1, Z=1.}$$

$$\text{MAXDAYS} = (6 \times 1) + 1$$
$$= 6 + 1$$
$$= 7$$

So the farthest out we can difference a six day cycle with N = 12 is to the difference of day 4 minus day 7. Look now at figure 4 and you will see how this formula makes perfect sense, given a perfect cycle where the sum of the differences should be zero.

57

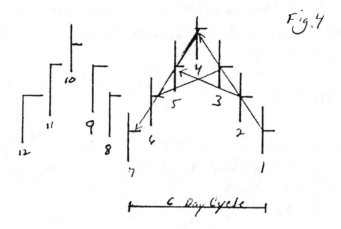

Fig. 4

6 Day Cycle

There is one other preprocessing point we have not yet addressed. Refer to figure 5. Notice that there is a very reliable 6 day cycle present here - more reliable than any other cycles in the figure. Yet, obviously, if we go to difference this type of pattern we will not arrive at a 0 sum of the differences because of the upward trend evident here. Yet there is a very reliable 6 day cycle and we want our technique to reflect the reliability of the cycle in question regardless of trend. Therefore, we must detrend each cycle by an average equal to the cycle itself. When we are differencing to deduce a 2 day cycle, we must run a 2 day moving average through all of the data in N, then subtract the average from its corresponding day to delineate the trend. For a six day cycle, we must detrend the data by a six day moving average prior to differencing it. If we were to detrend figure 5 by a 6 day moving average, we would end up with figure 4 again and the perfect 6 day cycle.

Detrending your data can cause some problems though. It is important that there be enough data points between N and MAXDAYS, inclusive of both, to arrive at a cycle length moving average at the MAXDAYS day.

In most cases this does not pose a problem. In figure 5, where you are looking for a 6 day cycle length with N=12, your MAXDAYS=7. At day 7, however, you are able to calculate a 6 day (the cycle length) moving average (of days 7, 8, 9, 10, 11 and 12).

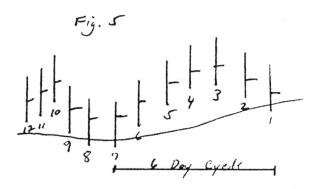

Fig. 5

6 Day Cycle

Once your data is detrended, you can difference it. When you are done differencing for a given cycle length, you must now de-weight that sum. Look at figure 6. If you were to run a full half cycle differencing on a data window like that the longer cycles would inevitably be farther from 0 than the shorter cycles. If you are doing a 1 day differencing (for a 2 day cycle) then the difference between any 2 consecutive closes is accounted for only once in the differencing process. If you are doing differencing on a longer cycle length, then the difference between 2 consecutive closes is accounted for only once in the differencing process. If you are doing differencing on a longer cycle length, then the difference between 2 consecutive closes is accounted for more than 1 time. This bias must be removed if our results are to be correct. After you have summed up the differences for a cycle, out to its MAXDAYS, you de-weight the sum by the following equation:

59

Fig 6

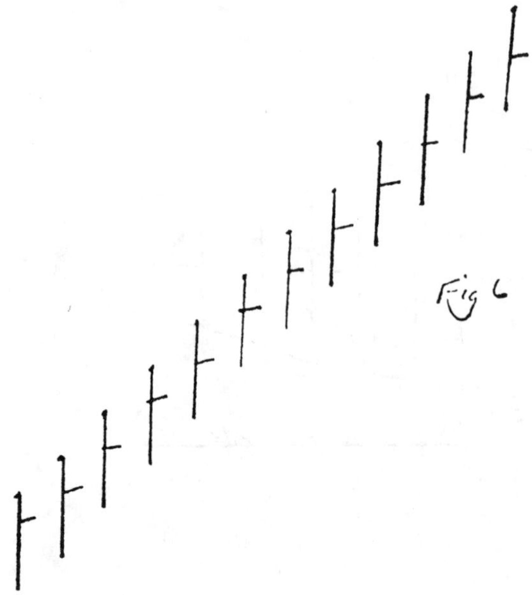

DE-WEIGHTED SUM = Raw Sum / ((MAX DAYS - Q) * Q)

Where Q=cycle length divided by 2 (the differencing amount).

To sum up the process thus far:

1.) Choose a data window, the longer the better. The length of this window we will call N.
2.) Begin differencing, starting with the 2 day cycle.
   A.) First detrend the raw data by a moving average equal to the cycle length.
   B.) Difference the detrended data starting at day 1 and work back, summing up the differences that are 1/2 the cycle length apart. Continue differencing until the number that you are subtracting is the MAXDAYS number.

C.) De-weight the sum by the de-weighting equation.

3.) Save the last sum (e.g. there is a sum for the 2 day cycle, 4 day cycle, etc.). Add 2 to the cycle length, recalculate a new MAXDAYS number, and go back and do step 2 over again for the new cycle length until you are working with a cycle length equal to the first even integer that is less than or equal to N/2. That will be your last cycle length.

Once you are finished with the last cycle length, you are finished. For each even numbered cycle you now have a relative measure of that cycle's reliability. The numerical value of this number associated with each cycle is meaningless. What does have meaning is what the numbers are with respect to each other. The lower a number is to 0, the more reliable that cycle length is relative to the other cycle lengths in the spectrum. You may want to multiply all of the final de-weighted sums by -1 so that the higher the resultant de-weighted sum is, the more reliable the cycle length.

Finally, remember that these measures of relative reliability are only approximations for that time period, i.e. the 6 day cycle is really the 6 to 7 day cycle estimation, the 8 day cycle is the 8 to 9 day cycle estimation, etc.

This chapter is the product of my friend and programmer, Ralph Vince.

Half Cycle Differencing

HERE IS A GENERIC BASIC LISTING FOR A PROGRAM THAT DISCERNS THE MOST RELIABLE
CYCLES BY THE HALF CYCLE DIFFERENCING TECHNIQUE. THE PROGRAM TAKES AS INPUT
THE ARRAY C(X), WHERE THE LOWER X IS THE MORE RECENT THE DATA (E.G. C(1)
IS 1 PERIOD MORE RECENT THAN C(2), ETC.). THE PROGRAM PROVIDES AS OUTPUT
THE ARRAY SUMMA(X), THE DE-WEIGHTED SUM OF THE HALF CYCLE X (OR RATHER THE
DE-WEIGHTED SUM OF THE CYCLE X TIMES 2).

NO INPUT OR OUTPUT ROUTINE IS PROVIDED, BUT RATHER IS LEFT TO THE USER.

```
100 N=60  : REM MAXIMUM LENGTH OF WINDOW
110 MXCYCLE=29  : REM THIS IS THE MAXIMUM CYCLE WE WILL OBSERVE
120 CYCLEN=2 : REM START LOOKING AT CYCLE LENGTHS OF 2 DAYS
130 WHILE CYCLEN<=MXCYCLE
140 FOR X=1 TO 100
150 XTWIN(X)=C(X)
160 NEXT  : REM MOVE DATA INTO XTWIN ARRAY & DETREND
170 FOR X=1 TO N
180 FOR Y=(X+1) TO (X+CYCLEN)
190 XTWIN(X)=XTWIN(X)+XTWIN(Y)
200 NEXT
210 XTWIN(X)=C(X)-(XTWIN(X)/CYCLEN)
220 NEXT
230 MAXDAYS=INT((N-2)/CYCLEN)
240 IF (MAXDAYS MOD 2)>0 THEN MAXDAYS=MAXDAYS-1
250 IF MAXDAYS=0 THEN MAXDAYS=1
260 MAXDAYS=(CYCLEN*MAXDAYS)+1
270 HCY=CYCLEN/2 :REM HCY IS HALFCYCLE WHICH IS CYCLEN/2
280 SUMMA(HCY)=0
290 FOR X=1 TO (MAXDAYS-HCY)
300 SUMMA(HCY)=SUMMA(HCY)+((C(X)-XTWIN(X))-(C(X+HCY)-XTWIN(X+HCY)))
310 NEXT
320 SUMMA(HCY)=SUMMA(HCY)/(HCY*(MAXDAYS-HCY))     .
330 CYCLEN=CYCLEN+2
340 WEND
```

HERE IS THE SAME PROGRAM AS A C FUNCTION :

```
static void halfcyc()
{
    int cyclen, hcy, maxdays, mxcycle, n, x, y = 0;

    n = 60;     /* MAXIMUM LENGTH OF WINDOW   */
    mxcycle = 29;     /* THIS IS THE MAXIMUM CYCLE WE WILL OBSERVE */
    cyclen  = 2;      /* START LOOKING AT CYCLE LENGTHS OF 2 DAYS  */
    while ( cyclen  <=  mxcycle )
        {
            for ( x=1;  x <=  100;  x++ )
                    xtwin( x ) = c( x ); /* MOVE DATA INTO XTWIN ARRAY & DETREND */
            for ( x=1;  x <=  n;  x++ )
                {
                    for ( y=( x + 1 );  y <=  ( x + cyclen  );  y++ )
                        xtwin( x ) = xtwin( x ) + xtwin( y ) ;
                    xtwin( x ) =   c( x ) - ( xtwin( x ) / cyclen ) ;
                }
            maxdays = ( n - 2 ) / cyclen ;
            if  ( ( round(  maxdays ) % 2 ) > 0 )
                    maxdays =  maxdays - 1 ;
            if  ( maxdays ==  0 )
                    maxdays = 1;
            maxdays = ( cyclen  * maxdays ) + 1 ;
            hcy =   cyclen  / 2 ;     /* HCY IS HALFCYCLE WHICH IS CYCLEN/2  */
            summa( hcy ) = 0 ;
            for ( x=1; x <= ( maxdays - hcy ); x++ )
                    summa(hcy)=summa(hcy)+((c(x)-xtwin(x))-(c(x+hcy)-xtwin(x+hcy)));
            summa(hcy) =   summa(hcy) / ( hcy *( maxdays - hcy  )   ) ;
        cyclen  =   cyclen  + 2 ;
        }
}
```

63

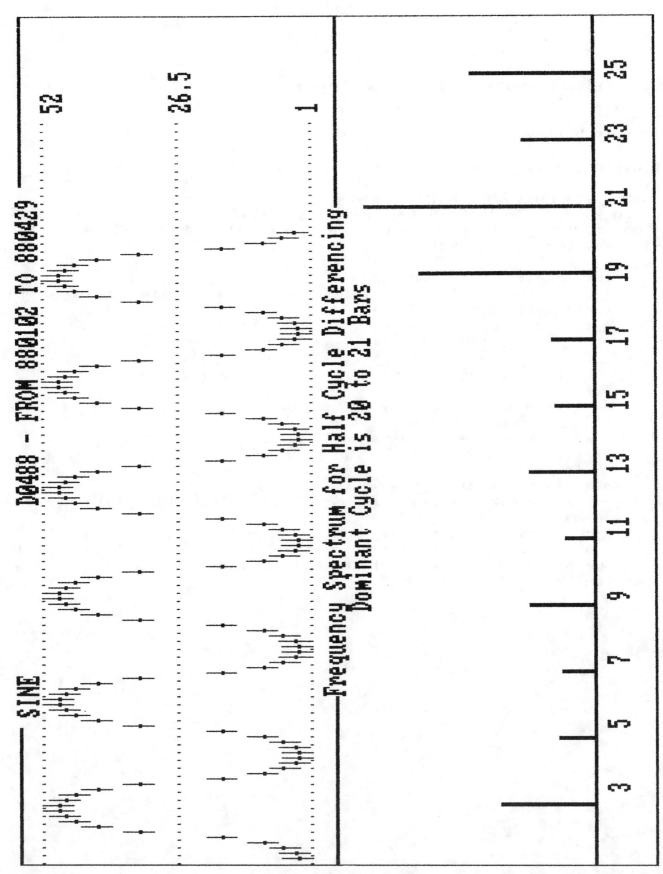

D0488 - FROM 880102 TO 880429

Frequency Spectrum for Half Cycle Differencing
Dominant Cycle is 20 to 21 Bars

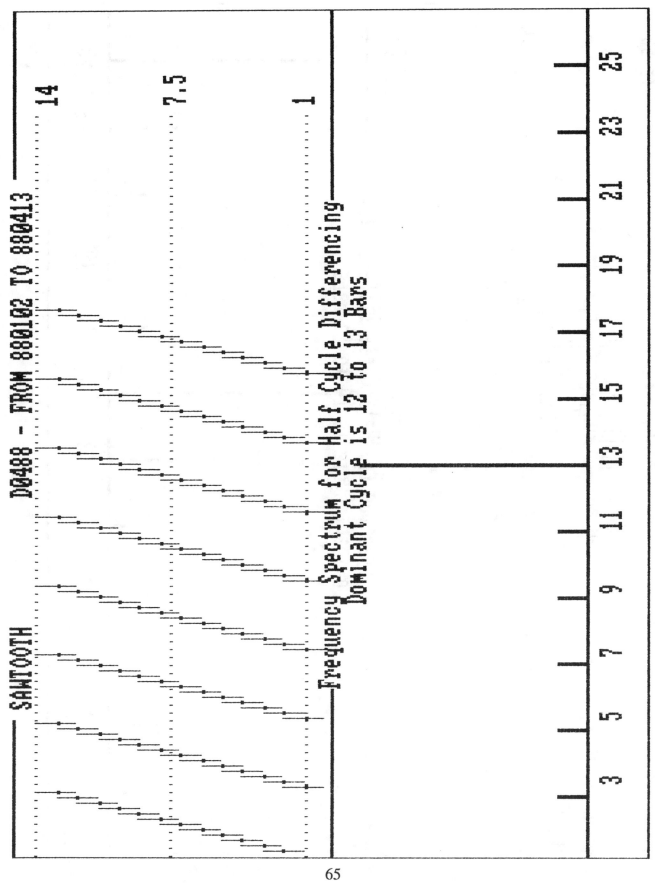

SAWTOOTH   DO488 — FROM 880102 TO 880413

Frequency Spectrum for Half Cycle Differencing
Dominant Cycle is 12 to 13 Bars

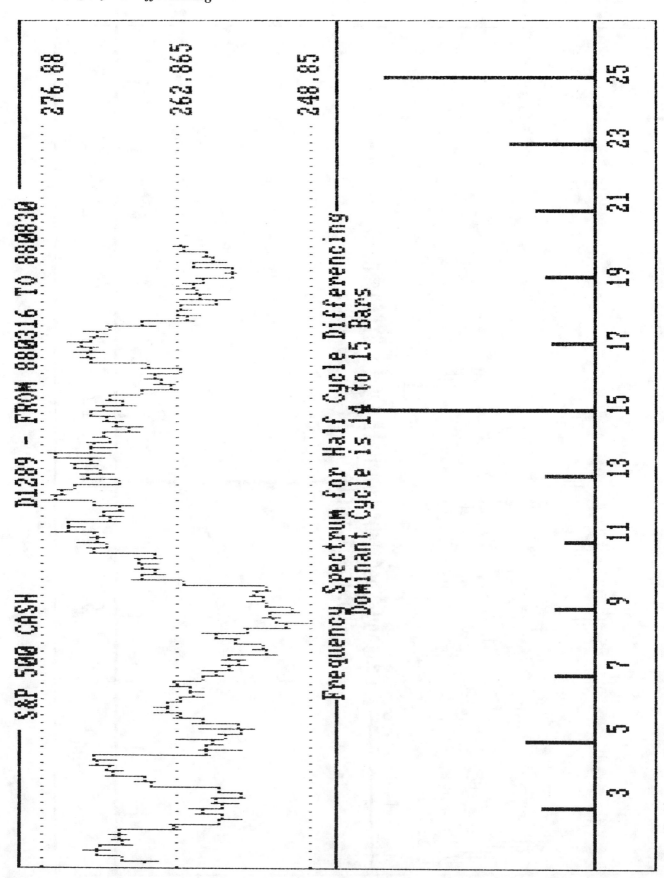

S&P 500 CASH   D1289 - FROM 880316 TO 880830

276.88

262.865

248.85

Frequency Spectrum for Half Cycle Differencing
Dominant Cycle is 14 to 15 Bars

3   5   7   9   11   13   15   17   19   21   23   25

## Chapter 5

Zero Balance

Only in the concept of change can we find opportunity; for in a static situation, there is no possibility for improvement. Gains or losses in the market can only result from a change in price. It is the heart of change at which zero balance is directed, and thus the essence of its value.

Zero Balance is essentially a targeting method designed to determine where the terminus of future cyclical price swings *should* be. In this application of defining targets, you will find the method inaccurate; but in this inaccuracy, you will discover the valuable use of Zero Balance. You'll understand what I mean shortly.

DEFINITION OF SWING POINTS

The concept and applications of Zero Balance are predicated upon the analysis of the establishment of price swings in the market. We wish to analyze prices as they fluctuate from high to low to high to low, etc. Consequently, we need to begin with some definition or method of mechanically designating at which points prices "record" highs and lows. The following method is very easy and is uncanny in identifying the important highs and lows in the market.

IMPORTANT RECORDED HIGH (IR HIGH)

If today's intra-day low is lower than the lowest intra-day low in the past seven market days, an IR High has formed and is the highest intra-day high since the last IR low.

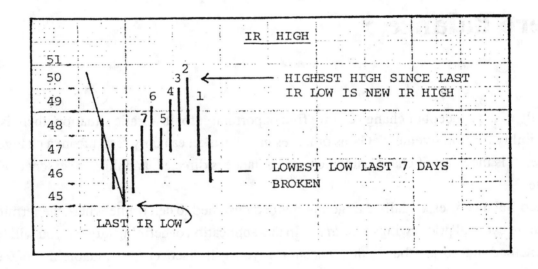

IMPORTANT RECORDED LOW (IR LOW)

If today's intra-day high is higher than the highest intra-day high during the past seven market days, an IR Low has formed and is the lowest intra-day low since the last IR High.

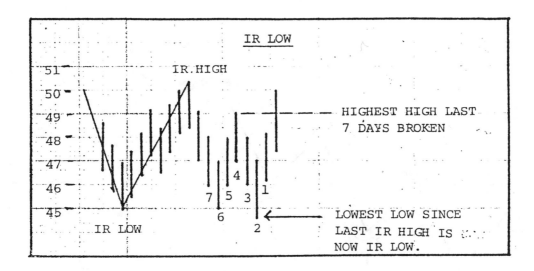

That's all there is to it. Just remember — once you have found an IR High, look for an IR Low until one forms. Then look for an IR High until one forms, and so on. We have connected the IR Highs and Lows by solid lines in our examples in order to assist you in seeing where these points have formed.

ZERO BALANCE DEFINED

If we consider a succession of cyclical market swings, prices always move from IR Low to IR High to IR Low, etc., as in the following example:

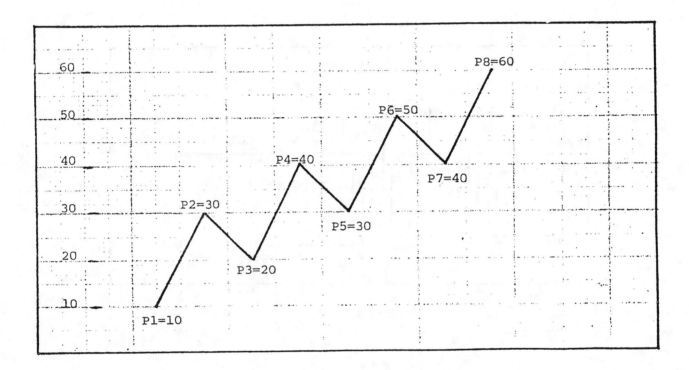

We can determine the price level at which each high and low point *should be* in order for the succession of swings to be in perfect rhythmic balance.

Notice, above, that prices move from 10 at point #1, up to 30 at point #2, then down to 20 at point #3, then up to 40 at point #4, and so on. In our example, we will assume these are where prices actually occurred in the past, and the points are IR Highs and IR Lows determined by our *swing* point rules. What we next want to determine is where prices should have been in order for the sequence of prices (or the sequence of highs and lows) to be in perfect balance.

THE FORMULA

The ideal level, or Zero Balance level, for each point is determined by the following formula:

$$ZB_8 = P^6 + P^5 - P^3 \text{ Or:}$$

ZERO BALANCE for point #8 equals the price at point #6 plus the price at point #5 minus the price at point #3.

Another way of stating this might be . . . the ideal Zero Balance level at point #8 (which is 60 in our example) is determined by adding the actual price at point #6 (50) to the actual price at point #5 (30); and from this total, subtracting the actual price at point #3 (20).

$$
\begin{aligned}
\text{Thus:} \quad & ZB_8 = P^6 + P^5 - P^3 \\
\text{OR:} \quad & ZB_8 = 50 + 30 - 20 \\
\text{OR:} \quad & ZB_8 = 80 - 20 \\
& ZB_8 = 60
\end{aligned}
$$

We have found in our example that the Zero Balance level at point #8 = 60. Consequently, in this situation, actual price at point #8 is the same as the Zero Balance level at point #8; and thus at point #8, prices are in perfect balance.

To summarize, in order to determine the Zero Balance level for a given high or low, consider that high or low as point #8. Now, count back in time or to the left labelling the next point #7, then #6, etc. . . . always moving from high to low to high to low.

Then apply the formula to those prices for points #6, #5, and #3. Your Zero Balance result will always be less than, greater than, or equal to the actual price at point #8.

71

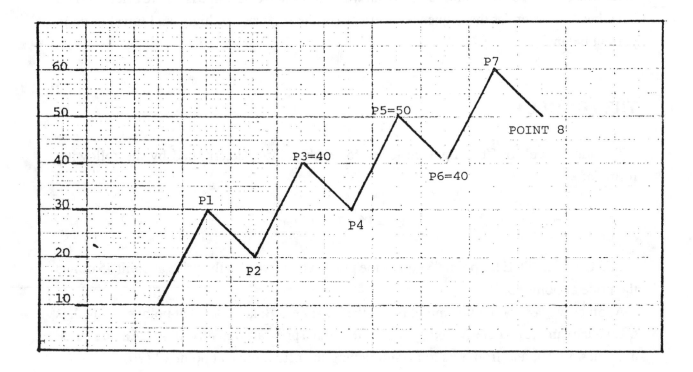

When the next point occurs in our example, due to the move from 60 to 50, we will label this most recent point, point #8, and work back, labelling the points #7, #6, etc., in succession. Note that what was point #8 before is now point #7; the old point #7 is now point #6, etc.

Applying the Zero Balance formula at our new point:

$$ZB_8 = P^6 + P^5 - P^3$$
$$\text{OR:} \quad ZB_8 = 40 + 50 - 40$$
$$ZB_8 = 90 - 40$$
$$ZB_8 = 50$$

Well, the Zero Balance level for the new point is 50, and price at point #8 is also 50. And in this admittedly ideal example, prices are still in perfect balance.

72

ZERO BALANCE IN REAL LIFE —
AN INSIGHT AS TO WHERE YOU ARE

The price pattern that we have been working with is ideal inasmuch as all points are in harmonic balance. In real situations, this is rarely the case. Occasionally, prices will match the Zero Balance level at one individual point, but usually prices are either greater than or less than the Zero Balance level. It is precisely this reality that provides the amazing power of this tool. It is this delicate difference that provides predictive value.

Let's consider the following example, where the price pattern represents what actually occurred in the Dow Jones Industrial Average from May through October 1979. We have marked the swing pattern and the Zero Balance line in for you.

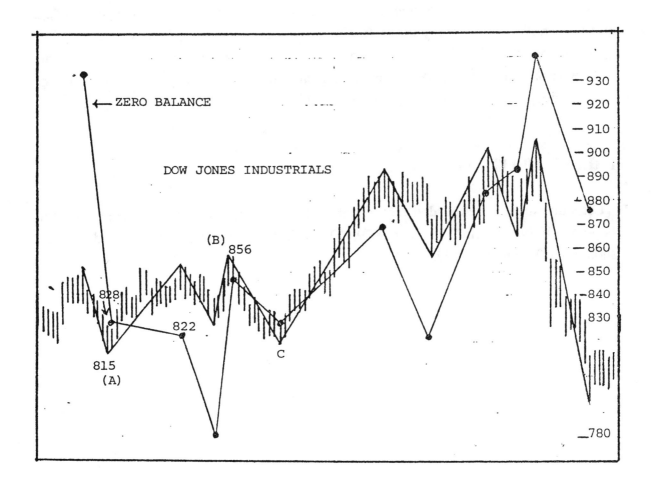

Note that the low point at 815 (A) is below the Zero Balance point at 828, and hence is negative. However, the next Zero Balance point is 822. Consequently, once prices traded above that level, we knew Zero Balance was telling us the market had turned positive. The Dow rallied to 856 (B); but in pulling back again, dropped below Zero Balance at point C, warning us that the market was weakening. In this case, prices rallied and again went over Zero Balance, turning positive. The rally ultimately carried to 905 in October 1979, wherein prices again were under Zero Balance, indicating weakness.

Now, at this point, let's not worry about Zero Balance's predictive value (we will get to that). But, I want you to understand how to calculate Zero Balance points and to see what occurs in reality in terms of Zero Balance's relationship to prices.

What is happening is that as prices are weak and running below the Zero Balance, or below their ideal level, a negative variance builds up that must be corrected. Yin changes to Yang, and prices rally. As prices rally and are trading above Zero Balance, a positive variance builds up and is corrected. This is all well and good in terms of insight into what type of footing the market is on (strong or weak) at any particular time, but not very helpful in terms of predictability. Let's look into that aspect next.

PREDICTABILITY

Let's investigate an expanded example of the Dow Jones, covering the time period from February 1979 through November 1979. The swing points have been indicated and you should verify their accuracy.

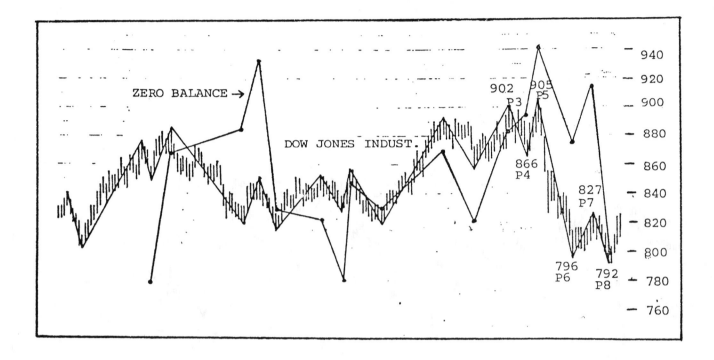

Furthermore, we have plotted the corresponding Zero Balance points which you should also work out on your own and verify.

The last point plotted is the IR Low at 792. We determine that this is point #8; and by using our formula, can calculate that Zero Balance for this point is 799.

The next thing to occur is for prices to move up from the 792 low. In fact, they already have, of course, or we wouldn't know that 792 is a low. What we don't know yet is where prices will actually move to from 792, but that doesn't matter for the moment. Let's just assume they move to some point which will become our new point #8. And, 792 will then become point #7; 827, point #6; and so on. (See Dow Jones Chart II).

75

Zero Balance

Well, we can determine the Zero Balance point for our next high now, before the high actually occurs. The new high will be point #8 as follows:

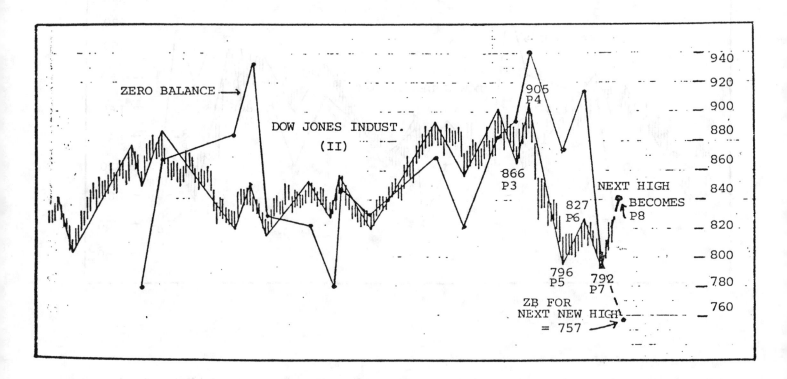

Thus: $ZB_8 = P^6 + P^5 - P^3$

$\qquad\qquad = 827 + 796 - 866$

$\qquad ZB_8 = 757$

Our new Zero Balance point for the now developing high will be 757. Prices are presently over this level and, thus, have turned positive.

Let's go one step further. After the high occurs, which we are now waiting on, prices will then move to some future new low (see Dow Jones Chart III which follows).

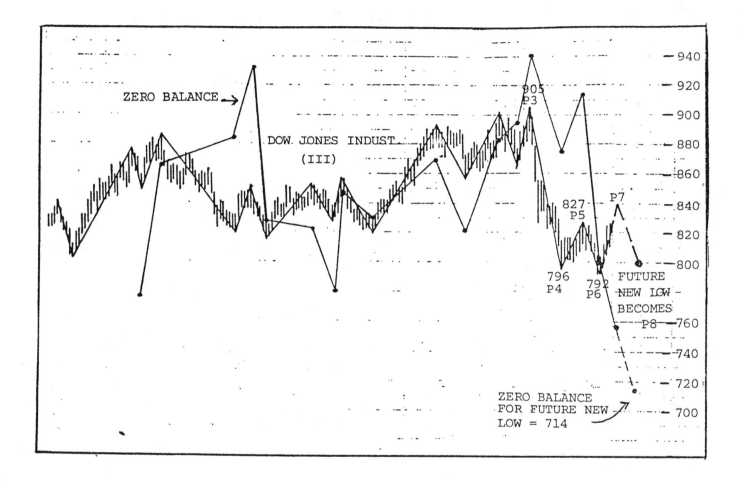

At some time in the future, this new low will become point #8 for our formula; but since we only use points #6, #5 and #3, we needn't wait for this low to actually occur. Again, we can determine its Zero Balance point now.

Zero Balance

$$P^6 = 792 \qquad P^5 = 827 \qquad P^3 = 905$$

So Again: $\quad ZB_8 = P^6 + P^5 - P^3$

$$= 792 + 827 - 905$$

$$ZB_8 = 714$$

At this point, then, we have been able to project the next two Zero Balance points into the future.

THE ULTIMATE

We can go one step further; we can get a peak at the third projected Zero Balance point out into the future. Here's how:

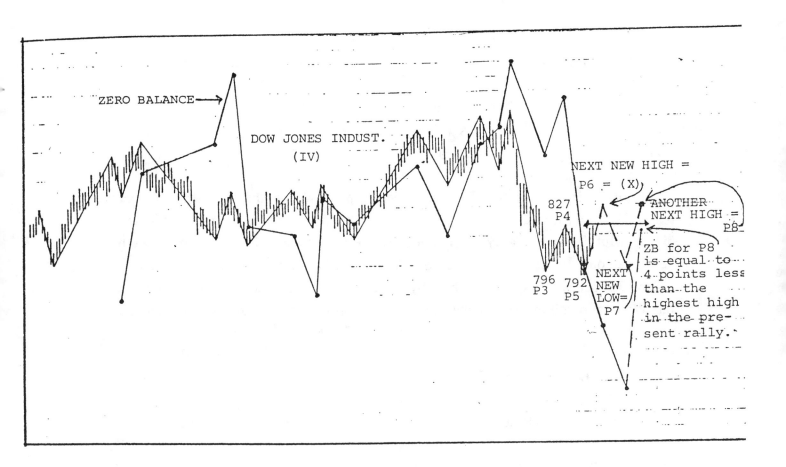

In our example, we determined a point for the next new high; then the next new low.

Now, what about another next new high as we have pictured (See Dow Jones Chart IV)? Well, if this is point #8, point #6 becomes the first new high we assume occurred. This is the high that will occur after our last known point — the low at 792. It is the high which will occur in the rally we are presently in. The low at 792 has been made, and we know it's a low because prices are presently rallying. So, the high is unknown as yet, but points #5 and #3 are known.

Our formula says:

$$ZB_8 = P^6 + P^5 - P^3$$

Where P6 is unknown (x) and P5 = 792 and P3 = 796

$$ZB_8 = X + P^5 - P^3$$
$$= X + 792 - 796$$
$$= X - 4$$

Thus, our third distant Zero Balance projected point will be the highest level we have reached in the current rally less 4 points. And, as we move higher, this projection will move higher. But we have a fairly accurate idea where it is at any given time. Well, we have developed our projected targets or Zero Balance points for the next 3 swings in the market.

Zero Balance was first written about by a Dr. Heiser, pretty much as presented to you so far. What follows is my development of the tool — presented here publicly for the first time.

THE BIG THREE-STEP RULE

The Big Three-Step Rule is the most important predictive element in Zero Balance. This is what alerts you to the big turns in the market — the October 1979 crash; October 1978 crash; the November 1978 rally; the December 1979 rally; right through the October 1987 crash and beyond.

Again, we present the Dow Jones Industrial and the Zero Balance points for the period February 1979, through February 1980.

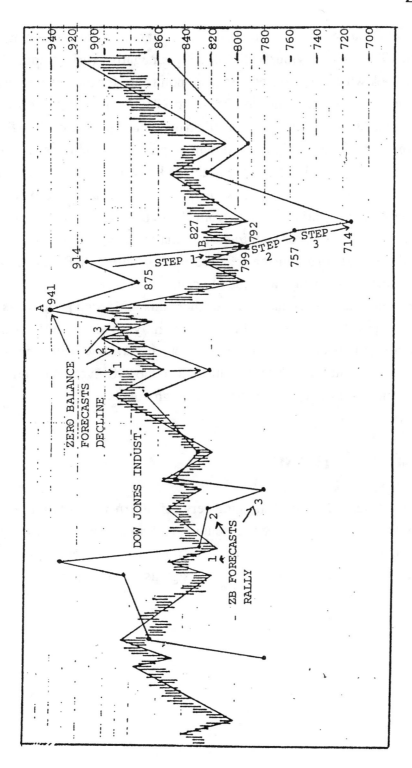

Note that Zero Balance made a high at 941 at A that corresponds to a market high at 905 on October 5, 1979. We previously discussed this negative (prices under Zero Balance) situation. But look what the next Zero Balance points are for the ensuing decline.

Zero Balance goes from 941 down to 875; up to 914; down to 799 (Step 1); down to 757 (Step 2); down again to 714 (Step 3). Rather than the typical pattern of Zero Balance moving up, then down, then up again, it moves down in three successive steps. Since *prices* by definition must move from high to low to high, we know that this decline *must* move back over Zero Balance, indicating strength. Remember, we were able to project this three-step sequence in Zero Balance during the rally from 792 to 827 (b). We knew well ahead of time that this decline was going to form an *important* market low. We knew ahead of time that prices wouldn't be able to maintain the negative position with Zero Balance. We knew ahead of time that an important change was due to occur.

Just look back in time on the chart and see where this three-step pattern has set up before. The February to April 1979 market decline forecast a rally which moved from the 820-30 area to 905, culminating in the October 1979 crash. Note this crash was also forewarned by Zero Balance's three-step sequence. The resulting slide to the 790 level again indicated a rally by Zero Balance; and that rally is now into the 918 high area.

FINE TUNING YOUR TIMING

Up to now, we haven't discussed anything very definite in terms of timing. We know how to use Zero Balance to understand the present underlayment (weak or strong) of the market or commodity under analysis. And we have seen how the three-step rule points to important changes. Let's now see how we can generate "signals" to prompt us to action.

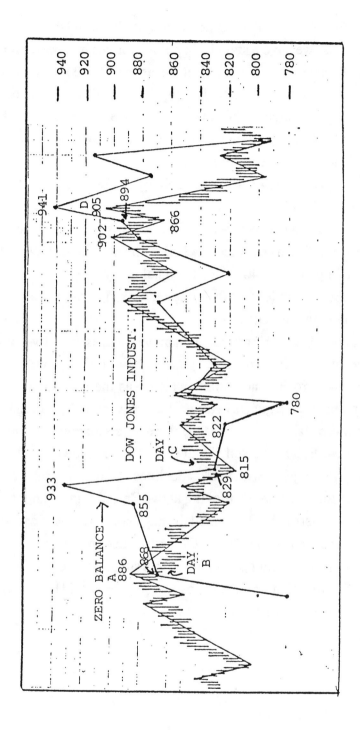

Zero Balance

Simplistically, any time prices penetrate a Zero Balance level and thus change from positive to negative, or vice versa, we have a signal. At point A prices had been running above Zero Balance in the rally. Then at about the 860 level, we have a day (B) breaking the lowest intraday low of the last seven days, and thus indicating 886 as an IR High. The high is positive in relation to its 868 Zero Balance, but the next Zero Balance point is 885, which will correspond to the next low, moving down from the 886 high. We obviously are now negative in terms of Zero Balance and have a sell signal.

A signal then occurs at the very earliest time that you discover you have changed from running above to below Zero Balance, or vice versa.

As prices moved down from 886 to 815, Zero Balance was negative. The 815 low indicated on day C was below the 829 Zero Balance level. But, the next Zero Balance level is 822, and prices are already trading at 830-840 — a buy signal is given.

Note also in both these examples that the three-step configuration was present, indicating important turning points in the market.

My favorite situation is discovering a last ditch move, such as the rally from 866 to 905 (D). Notice that once we had identified the IR High at 902 for the Dow, we were trading at 866 — well below the 894 Zero Balance point (which was the second step in the three-step sequence). At this point, a sell signal is in effect, but we were lucky enough to get a last ditch rally. We are under Zero Balance; we have the three-step sequence; we need to rally to 941 to go positive with Zero Balance; a sell signal is in effect . . . the perfect rally to sell.

This same situation will happen with market declines where Zero Balance sets up its three-step sequence. Prices turn positive by moving above Zero Balance; and thus a buy signal is given. And, you get that last ditch effort to sell the market where prices can fall some distance before going under Zero Balance again . . . the perfect decline to buy.

Look at the chart on the preceding page and see this situation after the October 1979 crash. Prices decline from 827 to 793 after turning positive. Prices would have had to go below 714 to turn negative — a nice decline to buy.

APPLICATION

Zero Balance will serve you well when applied to any cyclical data — individual stock issues, market averages, commodities, and one of my favorite applications . . . to oscillators.

The concept of oscillation is incomplete in itself, as the mere fact of being overbought or oversold is not enough. The markets can stay overbought or oversold for a long time. What is predictive is determining when the overbought or oversold condition has run its course and is going to change. Zero Balance is very useful in determining this.

I am sure these are only a few possible examples of Zero Balance application. The technique is now yours and its application up to you, limited only by your imagination. Therein, may my technique be your continued discovery.

Much of this chapter was written by one of my former brokers who went on to be a protege, eventually buying out my stock advisory service, Professional Timing. While I taught this Zero Balance to Curt Hesler, he has refined it, added to my techniques and produces one of the better stock newsletters. Write him at Box 7483, Missoula, Montana 59807.

## Chapter 6

Spread Trading With
Seasonal Tables

Spread trading is really no more difficult than trading net positions, yet most of the time there is less risk. The margins for spreads can be as much as 85% less than for a net position, thereby allowing a person without much capital to trade commodities, and providing a person with more capital an opportunity to increase his diversification.

In order to understand what is to follow, it is necessary to know the industry standard for constructing a spread chart. As you no doubt already know, a spread is <u>simultaneously</u> buying one commodity and selling another; or buying one contract month of a commodity and selling another contract month of the same commodity. The standard method of constructing a spread chart for different commodities is to name the commodity that historically has the greatest value first and the commodity that has the lesser value second. Example: Corn-Oats. The second named commodity is always subtracted from the first named commodity. Therefore, the daily price of Oats would be subtracted from the daily price of Corn to obtain the daily spread price. (There is slightly different treatment of a Corn/Oats spread than other different commodity spreads. Since the price of Corn is historically about twice the price of

Oats the normal Corn/Oats spread is 1 Corn minus 2 Oats.) This brings the two into a more normal price relationship. Other different commodity spreads are traded on a one-to-one basis. For a spread of the same commodity the contract month closest to expiration is named first and the one further from expiration second. Example: March Corn/July Corn. Again the second named commodity is subtracted from the first. The seasonal spread table and the Spread Scope charts that follow were constructed as described in this paragraph.

The next thing to understand before we describe an actual trade is the construction of the Averages and Ranges of the Seasonal Spread Table. For the Averages, the highest spread price of the month is added to the lowest spread price of the month and the result is then divided by 2. This gives us the median monthly price. The Range is simply the lowest price of the month subtracted from the highest price. For convenience, all Ranges have been converted into dollars, rather than cents or points.

Right under the averages in the middle of the Table on the right side you will note % Hi and % Lo. The % Hi and % Lo figures are very important and are the preliminary factor in determining whether a trade will be taken or not. The % Hi or Lo must be 70% or more for us to consider the trade. The other factor in our initial determination is the Average Range (at the bottom of the page). The Average Range must at least equal the margin for the trade to be considered.

The % Hi and % Lo are constructed by comparing a month against the prior month. If the value of the month is higher than the value of the prior month, a plus is placed after the month; if lower a minus. Example: (Comparing Oct. 1974 to September 1974) Oct. is lower so a minus is placed after Oct. Caution must be used in comparing negative numbers. A high negative number has a lower value than a low negative number. Therefore, Oct. with a -400 is lower than Sept. with a -38. Pluses are Hi and minuses are Low. The % Hi is the percentage of pluses in the column and the % Lo is the percentage of minuses in the column.

You will note that in the table all of the % Hi's and % Lo's do not add up to 100%. Example: A plus or minus could not be placed after July 1974 because there was no value for June to compare it to. July 1985 could not be compared to June because the values were the same. Since the percentage is based on the total number of years and there were only ten years with a plus or minus instead of 12, we get 42% and 42% instead of 50% and 50%. Computers at times just don't understand.

To get the plus or minus for the first month of the year, the figure is compared to the last month of the prior year. Example: May 1984 (the last month of 1984) was a -1238. June 1985 (the first month of 1985) was a -5475. Since -5475 is lower than -1238, a minus is placed after June 1985.

One last bit of information you must understand before we consider the May Corn/2 May Oats spread table is that when we say the curve is going up we mean that Corn is gaining on Oats and you would want to be long the Corn and short the Oats. If the curve is going down you would want to be long the Oats and short the Corn. Remember what was said earlier about constructing a spread chart. If you forget and subtract Corn from Oats you will find your curve going South when it should be going North.

You have made an initial decision to trade the May Corn/2 May Oats spread in March of 1985, since in March 1984 it had a 73% (rounded) probability of an up move and the average range was $1007, twice the required margin. You could have made that decision any time after receiving an updated table about mid-May 1984.

You now decide to see what the exact up move range is, since the average range at the bottom of the Range Table is for both up and down moves. You transfer the pluses and minuses from the Average Table down to the Range Table. Example: Mar. 1974 in the Average Table was a plus, so you put a plus for Mar. 1974 in the Range Table. Mar. 1975 was a plus in the Average Table, so a plus is placed after Mar. 1975 in the Range Table. You now add all the dollars that have pluses after them and divide by the number of additions to determine the average dollar range — which you find is $1014. Note: all of 1985 is shown in the Table, but none of the 1985 figures were used in the calculations since they were not in existence when you were making your decisions.

You now know that the criteria for a good trade has been met. You have a 73% probability of an up move and an up move dollar range of twice the margin ($1014). The rule is that the range must at least equal the margin, so the $1014 makes the trade look even more attractive.

It is now June 1984, what do you do now? May Corn and Oats are trading, so spread prices can be calculated. Calculate the spread price each day and write it down in columnar form with the corresponding date. Don't want to go to that much trouble calculating the spread price each day? Clip the prices from whatever source you use to get commodity prices and on a rainy Saturday afternoon calculate nine months worth of prices. Should take you about two hours with a simple calculator.

89

What are you going to do with these prices you have put in nice neat columns with the dates? You are going to determine some pluses and minuses. Remember how we said the averages were calculated in the Table? Well, you are going to construct the Table for the present year (in this case 1985) to determine whether a similar year(s) exists. Add the highest price of the month and the lowest price of the month and divide the result by 2. Each month's median price compared to the previous month's median price will give you a plus or minus.

When you have completed the pluses and minuses right up to Feb. 1985 you can check to see if one or more similar year(s) exist. The rule for similar years is that the prior years must have two or more months with pluses or minuses the same as the year under consideration to be a similar year. Example: Looking at Feb. 1985 we find there was a plus in Feb., a plus in Jan., a minus in Dec., etc. (for the balance you can look at the Table). Now look at the other years in the Average Table and see if there are other years with a plus in Feb., a plus in Jan., etc. 1978 has a plus in Feb., a plus in Jan., and a minus in Dec. 1979 has a plus in Feb. and a plus in Jan. 1980 has a plus in Feb. and a plus in Jan. 1983 has a plus in Feb. and a plus in Jan. 1984 has a plus in Feb. and a plus in Jan. 1985 has a plus in Feb., a plus in Jan., and a minus in Dec. You are now ready to make your projection for Mar. 1978 is a similar year and it indicates a down move in Mar., but it is outweighed by 1979, 1980, 1983, 1984 and most importantly 1985, which all indicate an up move in Mar. So you feel safe in assuming the spread will move up in Mar.

In addition to making the similar year determinations, you started to actually plot the spread in Jan. Here again you do not necessarily have to make each plot each day, but can save your plotting for another rainy Saturday. Of course, you use the spread values you already calculated (for the similar year determination) as your plot points. Toward the middle of Feb. you make sure your plots are up to date, because you want to study the spread to get a "feel" for it and to make some money management determinations.

Toward the end of Feb. you are ready to calculate your stop point. You do this by calculating the longest move between one day's close and the next (marked A through F on the chart). When you add A through F and take an average (A+B+C+D+E+F = 6) you find your stop point is 3¢ (rounded). You can now determine your profit/loss ratio. The Range Table shows an average range of $1014, which is 20¢ (rounded), so your potential profit is 20¢ (we will now call this the Target) and your potential loss is 3¢ (we will now call this the Stop). A 20¢

profit and a 3¢ loss is roughly a 7 to 1 ratio. Very acceptable. All ratios of 3 to 1 or better are acceptable.

Mar. is here. You now know much about this May Corn/Oats spread. All that is left to do is wait for an entry point. It does not come on Mar. 1st, because the spread curve is moving against the direction you wish to take. The settlement prices on Mar. 4th indicate the spread is now moving in the direction you wish to take, so on Mar. 5th you take a position long May Corn short 2 May Oats and are filled at a spread price of 70.25¢ (indicated on the chart as E). Again it's good to remember that large negative numbers have less value than small negative numbers. That is the reason the -80.0 is at the bottom of the chart and the -49.0 is at the top of the chart.

Once you know your entry point you can plot your stop point (indicated on the chart as S). Since you know the Target is 20¢ you can plot the Target (-70.25 + 20¢ = -50.25) marked as T on the chart.

Since all the other % Hi's and % Lo's in the Table are less than 70%, you call Mar. your prime trading time.

Another rule that you are going to follow is that you will not move your stop from its original position until the spread has a profit of at least 1/2 the margin. When, or if, the 1/2 margin point is reached, you will start trailing your stop, keeping it at 3¢, to protect your profit.

Now that you have taken your position, only four things can happen to you. 1) You can be stopped out with a loss of $150 plus commissions; 2) you can be stopped out at one of the trailing stops with a profit; 3) you can reach the Target at which point you would get out with $1,000 profit less commissions; or 4) you could run out of prime trading time, causing the spread to start moving against you at which time you would get out with a profit.

Another rule you must remember: if the trade goes past the prime trading time and at some point past the prime trading time (in this case Mar.) the spread turns and starts to go in a direction opposite to the desired direction, you exit the position on the next trading day.

Since you did your homework well and followed all the rules, you exit the trade at -54.0. -70.25 - 54.00 = 16.25¢ x 50 = $812.50. You missed the Target by $187.50, but since the Target is an average of a number of years you consider that pretty close.

You always keep uppermost in your mind that the exchanges will not accept stops on spreads. If the settlement prices indicate the stop has been hit you get out the next day. No fudging. You may check prices several times during the day you are to get out looking for the best price, <u>but you will be out by the end of that day.</u> The same holds true if you have run out of prime trading time and the spread moves against you.

You probably put in a total of five hours of calculations on this spread over a period of nine months and you made $812.50.

Let's take a look at what our spread looked like in Spread Scope. You will note we missed a down move in Nov. because the Table did not indicate a favorable % Hi or % Lo for Nov. We missed an up move in Jan. for the same reason. Feb. looks more like what we normally see with % Hi's and % Lo's in the 40 to 60% area.

Some questions you may ask: Do you take every position if the Table indicates a 70% or more % Hi or % Lo? No, not even if the % Hi or Lo is 100%. It depends on whether the Range is equal to the margin. What if later, after tracking the spread, we find that the stop is quite large and the profit to loss ratio is less than 3 to 1? What do you consider an acceptable stop? Of course the answer to that depends on the size of the account and the number of other positions that have already been taken prior to the new position you are considering. For a modest account, 3¢ - 5¢ in the grains and no more than 100 points in anything else, preferably less. Are there many good trades in a year? Of course much of the answer to that depends on market conditions, but in general probably more than any but a large account can handle. The Tables allow you to pick and choose. Generally, as your work progresses it becomes apparent that for any given time frame one spread will appear to have a better potential than another spread. In most cases all you will lose is the time you spent with the spread. We would rather lose some time than money.

How many months do you plot in your chart prior to the prime trading time? Always 2.

You have now made $812.50 less commissions on a Corn/Oats spread — on to the next spread. Just follow this example as you practice one yourself.

You can use these same rules on virtually any spread — agricultural or financial. The principle is a general one and can be applied to any commodity.

For more information contact Spread Scope, Box 5841, Mission Hills, CA 91345.

MAY CORN minus MAY OATS(X2) SEASONAL SPREAD TABLE

CNOA02

AVERAGE

YEAR	MAY	JUN	JUL	AUG	SEP	OCT	NOV	DEC	JAN	FEB	MAR	APR	MAY
1974		-2438	-1250	337	-38	-400	-100	-25	-2750	-2388	1825	1937	-113
1975		-2913	-2775	-375	812	425	1050	1125	812	-925	-225	-3063	-6938
1976		-6925	-3250	-1500	-650	-363	-1913	-2113	-2500	-3763	-3875	-4188	-2588
1977			-6000	-4700	-5275	-5238	-6313	-6900	-8588	-9250	-8363	-9500	-10375
1978			-2800	-3613	-4913	-4738	-4700	-4788	-4000	-2888	-2938	-3350	-2388
1979		-3638	-3700	-4825	-6275	-6575	-5750	-4963	-4450	-4238	-2925	-2313	-3163
1980	-5200	-5400	-4025	-4963	-5263	-4175	-3875	-3463	-2813	-1875	-1600	-1413	-4900
1981	-5688	-5788	-7100	-6313	-7163	-6525	-5800	-7425	-6813	-7775	-7063	-7288	-8375
1982	-5425	-7138	-5488	-6313	-4625	-7425	-11200	-10713	-12063	-12450	-12525	-14263	-14713
1983	-8100	-6888	-6063	-7138	-8688	-8800	-10650	-10388	-8525	-4400	-1975	-788	-663
1984	-7763		-6113	-5100	-4850	-5138	-3688	-3613	-3250	-1550	-1213	-538	-1238
1985	-6688	-5475	-5475	-5750	-5313	-6638	-7025	-7700	-7013	-6650	-6275	-4663	-3975
1986													
1987													
1988													
Avg	-6477	-5267	-4551	-4188	-4353	-4633	-4997	-5081	-5163	-4846	-3929	-4119	-4952
# Hi		2	5	6	5	5	7	7	7	7	9	6	4
# Lo		4	5	6	7	7	5	5	5	5	3	6	8
% Hi		33	42	50	42	42	58	58	58	58	75	50	33
% Lo		67	58	50	58	58	42	42	42	42	25	50	67

RANGE (In dollars)

YEAR	MAY	JUN	JUL	AUG	SEP	OCT	NOV	DEC	JAN	FEB	MAR	APR	MAY
1974			900	1688	1213	400	1200	1075	1250	1513	825	863	2513
1975			825	2625	1288	775	900	475	1013	1275	1525	2213	3363
1976		1975	525	1000	700	613	713	1113	625	663	875	1088	988
1977			1300	700	875	1188	388	375	1588	500	938	1250	1225
1978		1188	400	1763	613	613	800	538	525	1238	688	1100	538
1979		1000	1100	775	775	1100	800	913	750	1363	675	1038	1163
1980	700	788	750	938	388	975	975	263	638	975	1150	1313	1725
1981	288	738	1100	1088	638	900	1325	1450	788	1925	1238	1663	3375
1982	525	838	713	788	850	2025	2300	1938	938	1375	1400	1463	1338
1983	275	888	1038	1888	563	825	875	838	1325	2700	1200	1813	1563
1984	413	1275	1513	1100	1125	663	1138	538	525	1200	563	1188	1388
1985	513		825	850	763	513	325	575	838	275	850	888	675
1986													
1987													
1988													
Avg	452	921	916	1267	816	882	978	841	900	1250	994	1323	1654

1014↑ 988↓

(C) 1985 ComFutures   2509 Thousand Oaks Blvd., Thousand Oaks, CA 91362   (805) 492-4270
Data from sources believed to be reliable, but is not guaranteed.

93

MAY CORN / 2 MAY OATS

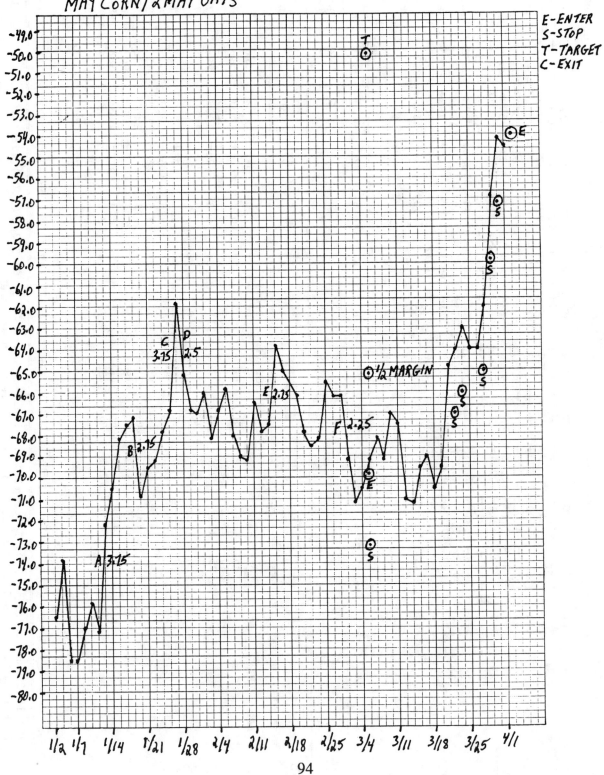

E - ENTER
S - STOP
T - TARGET
C - EXIT

CORN/OATS

MAY85 CORN/MAY85 OATS

5¢ = $250

JUL85 CORN/JUL85 OATS

CORN/(2) OATS

MAY85 CORN/(2) MAY85 OATS

JUL85 CORN/(2) JUL85 OATS

5   19   3   17   7   21   4   18   4   18   1   15   6   20
NOV   DEC   JAN   FEB   MAR   APR   MAY
              1986

## Chapter 7

Sure Thing Commodity Trading
An Update of How Seasonal Tendencies Influence Commodity Prices

In one of my previous books I commented a great deal about seasonal tendencies. I perhaps need to touch briefly again on seasonal tendencies. To do that, I am showing seasonal charts which are available in the TECHVIEW newsletter, a market publication of Stotler & Company, Board of Trade Building, Chicago, IL 60604. What is shown here are several charts which depict the ten year seasonal tendency of the market. First is the December Bean Oil contract. Here you can see that the strongest opportunity for this market to rally, in the last 10 years, has been on the June time period, with market tops coming in early August.

In terms of Sugar, the strongest time period for rallies to come during the last ten years has been on the July time period, with declines starting somewhere in mid-May. When it comes to trading the D-Mark, these rally periods start around the first week of June and go into late August. At this point the declines, during the last 9 years, have predominated the marketplace. Study the other charts to learn for yourself the seasonal tendencies, but they are something that should not be overlooked. For some good ideas on how to use these, see my earlier book, "Sure Thing Commodity Trading." For a more complete view of seasonal patterns, buy any of Jake Bernstein's excellent seasonal books. All of these books are available from Windsor Books.

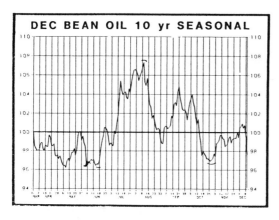

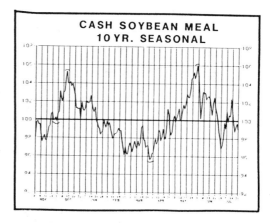

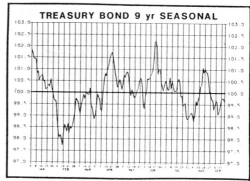

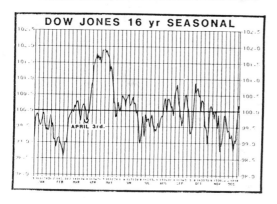

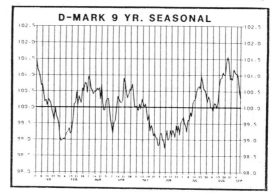

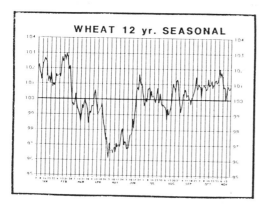

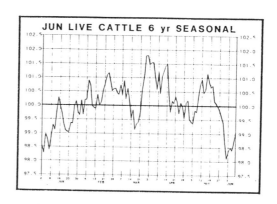

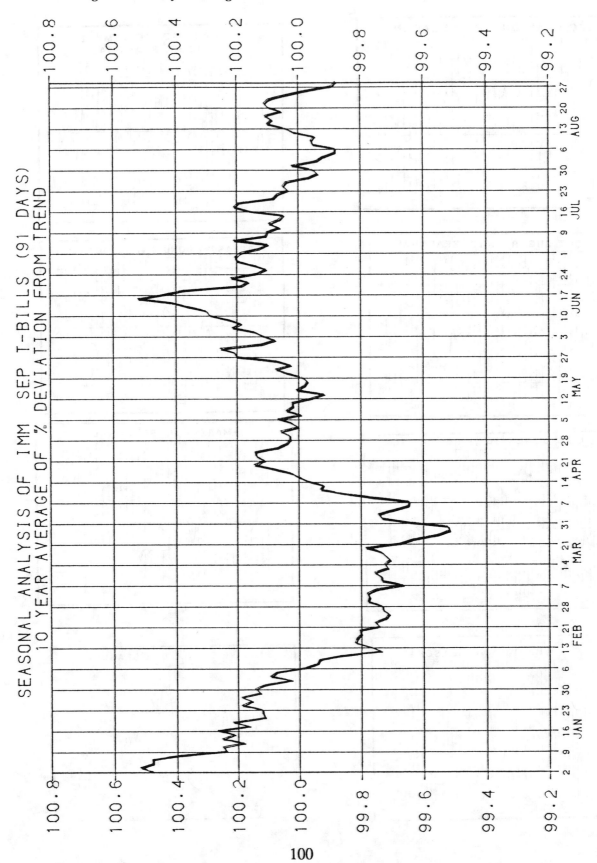

SEASONAL ANALYSIS OF IMM SEP T-BILLS (91 DAYS)
10 YEAR AVERAGE OF % DEVIATION FROM TREND

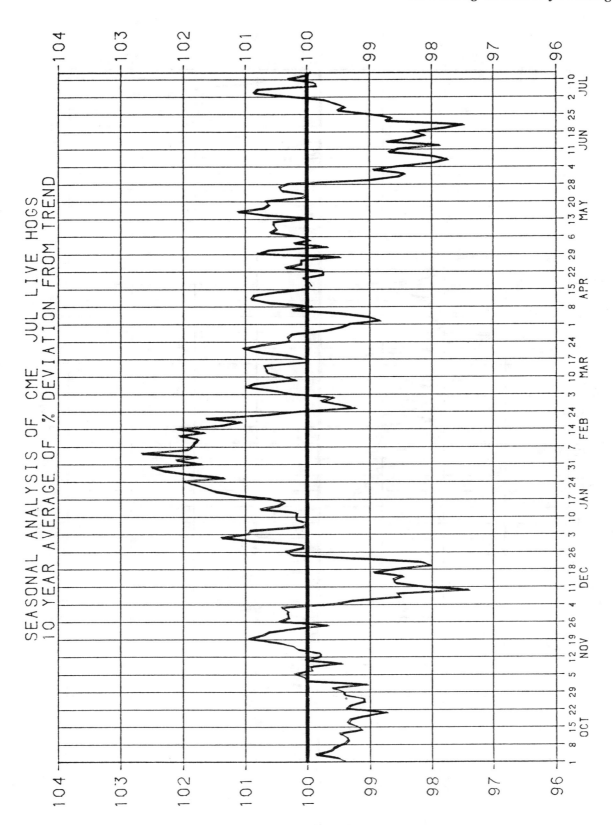

SEASONAL ANALYSIS OF CME JUL LIVE HOGS
10 YEAR AVERAGE OF % DEVIATION FROM TREND

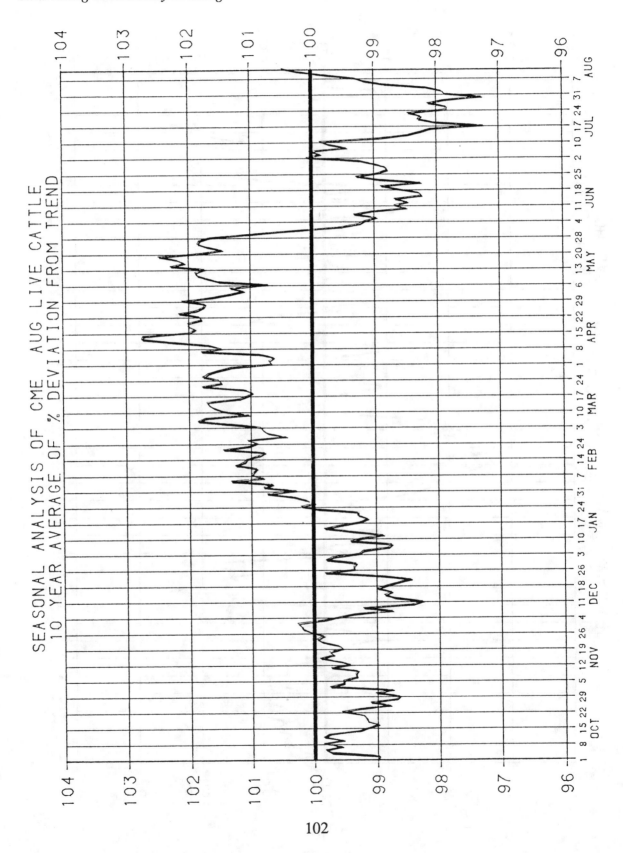

SEASONAL ANALYSIS OF CME AUG LIVE CATTLE
10 YEAR AVERAGE OF % DEVIATION FROM TREND

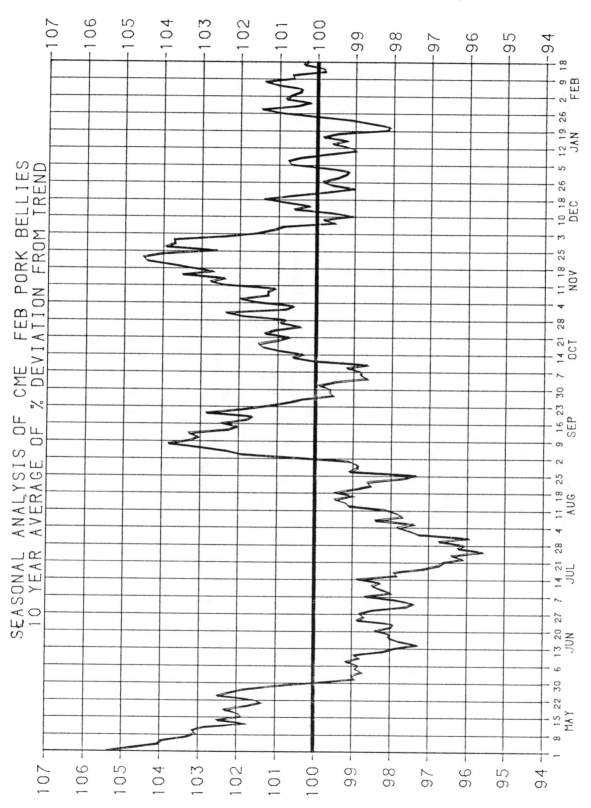

SEASONAL ANALYSIS OF CME FEB PORK BELLIES
10 YEAR AVERAGE OF % DEVIATION FROM TREND

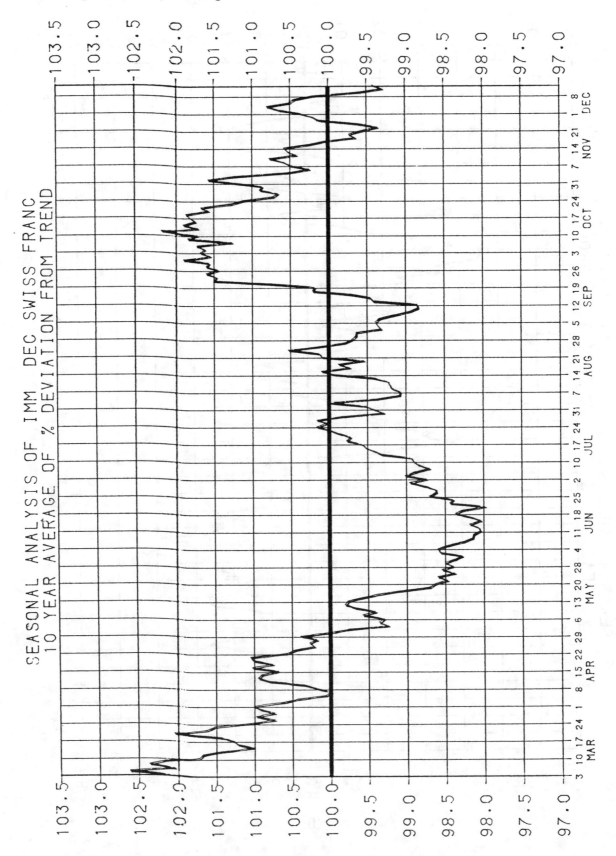

SEASONAL ANALYSIS OF IMM DEC SWISS FRANC
10 YEAR AVERAGE OF % DEVIATION FROM TREND

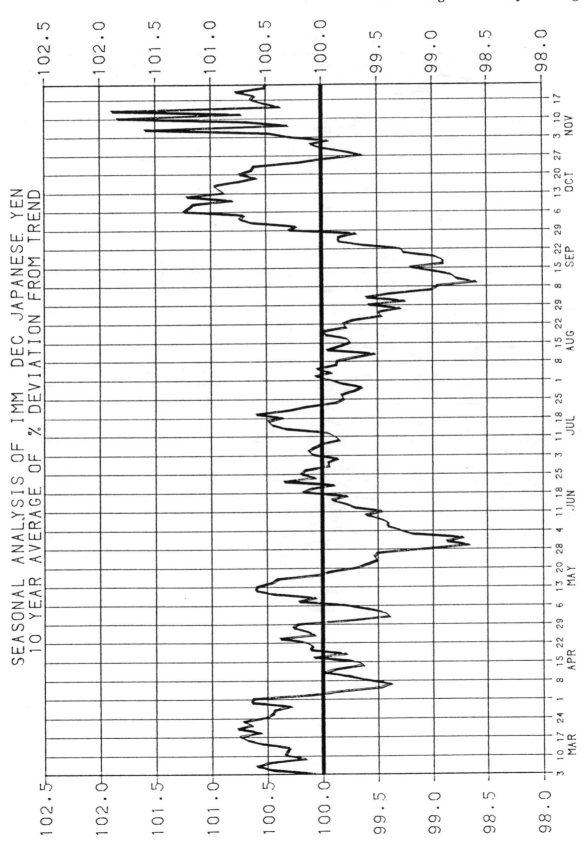

SEASONAL ANALYSIS OF IMM DEC JAPANESE YEN
10 YEAR AVERAGE OF % DEVIATION FROM TREND

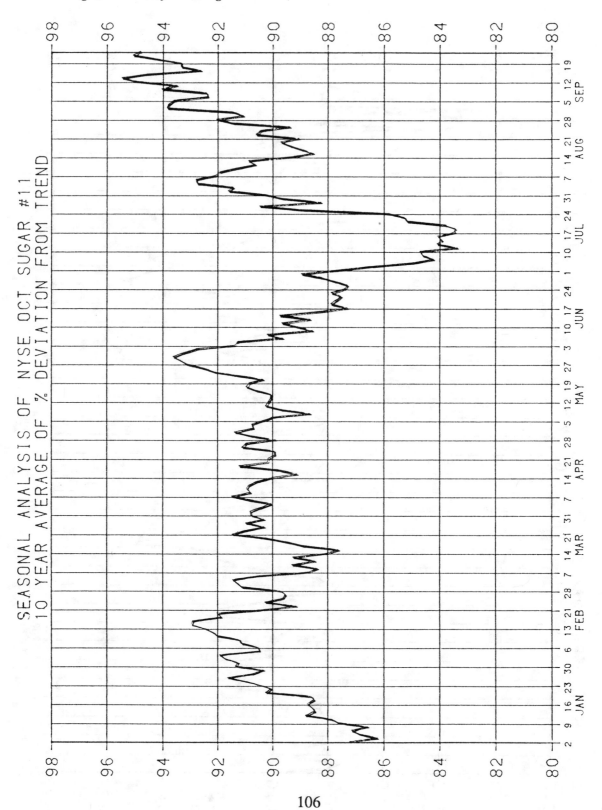

SEASONAL ANALYSIS OF NYSE OCT SUGAR #11
10 YEAR AVERAGE OF % DEVIATION FROM TREND

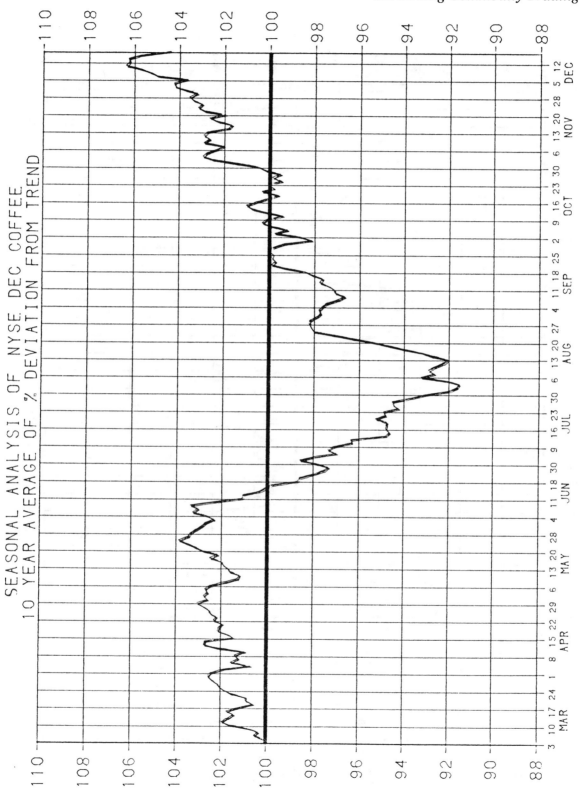

SEASONAL ANALYSIS OF NYSE DEC COFFEE.
10 YEAR AVERAGE OF % DEVIATION FROM TREND

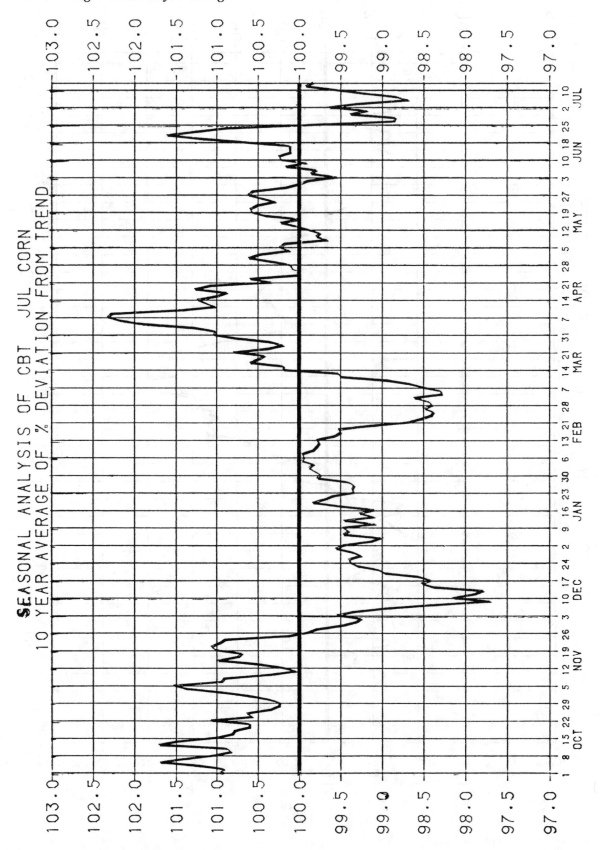

SEASONAL ANALYSIS OF CBT   JUL CORN
10 YEAR AVERAGE OF % DEVIATION FROM TREND

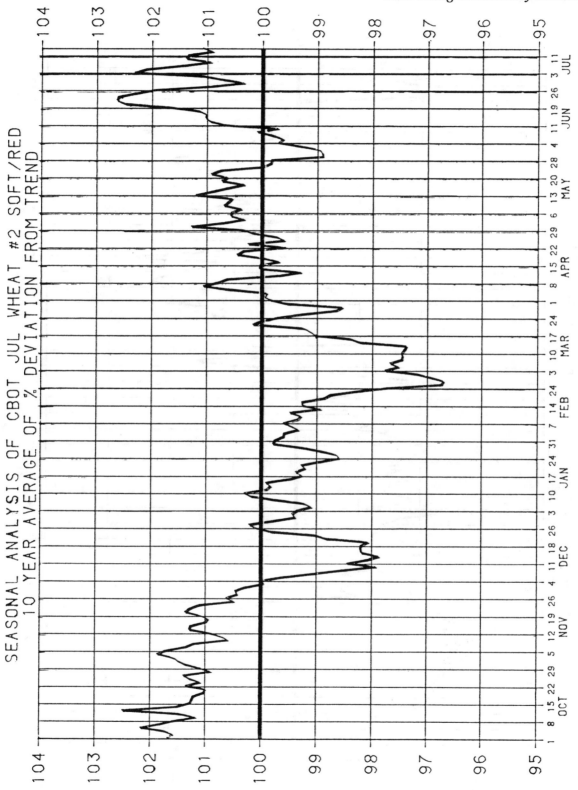

SEASONAL ANALYSIS OF CBOT JUL WHEAT #2 SOFT/RED
10 YEAR AVERAGE OF % DEVIATION FROM TREND

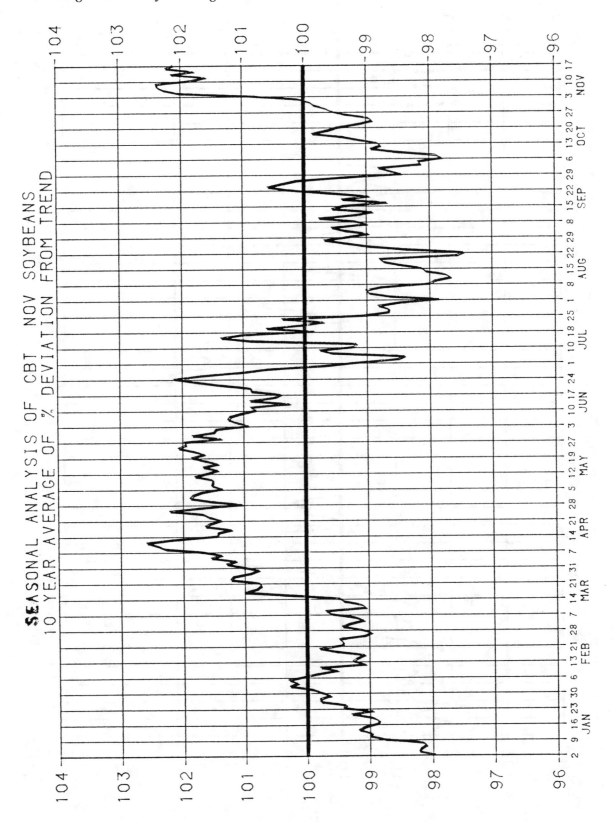

SEASONAL ANALYSIS OF CBT NOV SOYBEANS
10 YEAR AVERAGE OF % DEVIATION FROM TREND

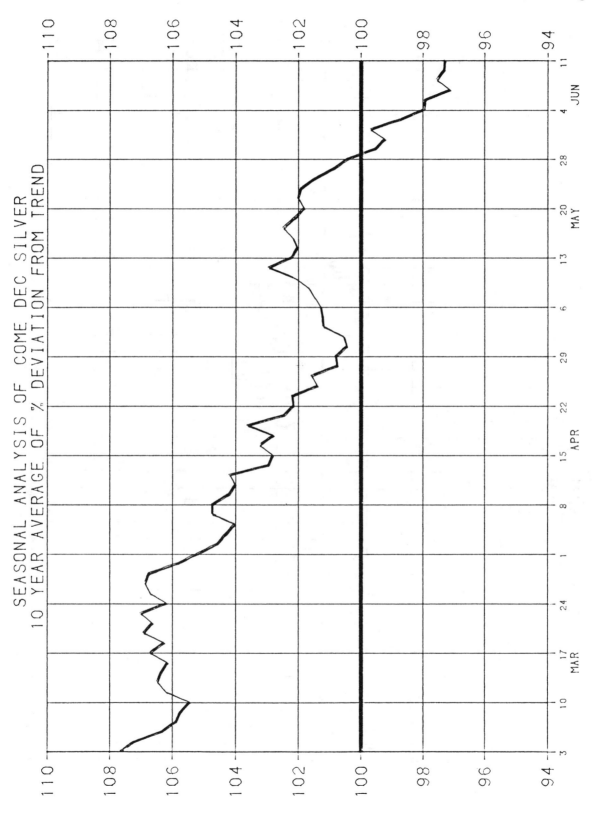

SEASONAL ANALYSIS OF COME DEC SILVER
10 YEAR AVERAGE OF % DEVIATION FROM TREND

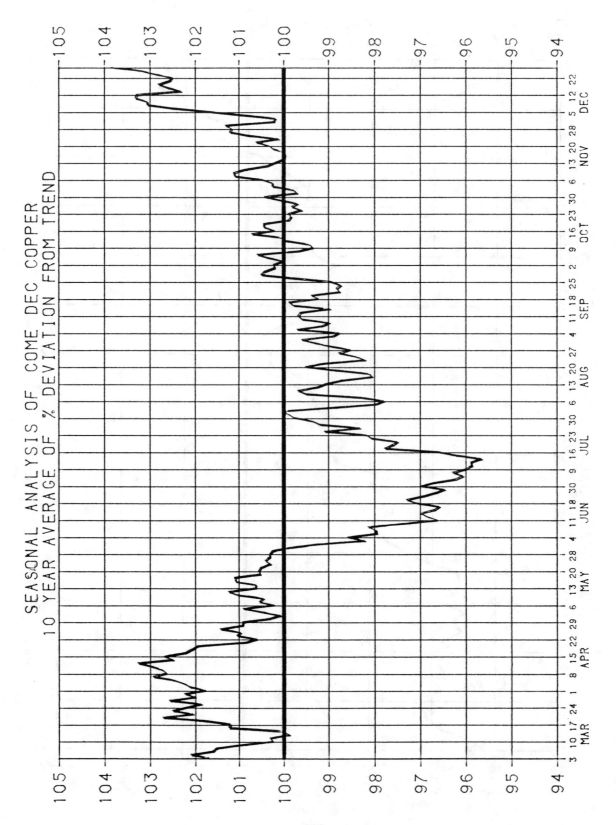

SEASONAL ANALYSIS OF COME DEC COPPER
10 YEAR AVERAGE OF % DEVIATION FROM TREND

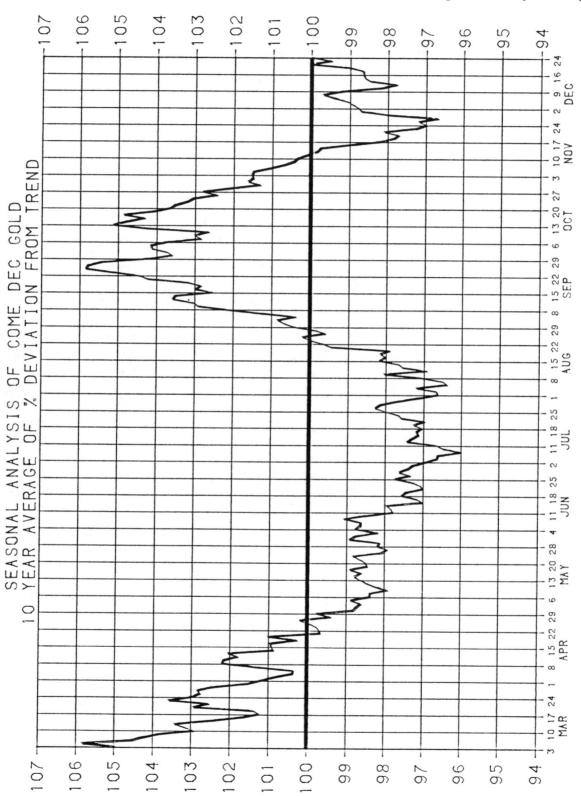

SEASONAL ANALYSIS OF COME DEC GOLD
10 YEAR AVERAGE OF % DEVIATION FROM TREND

## Chapter 8

The Art of Day Trading: Tools, Techniques, and a Profitable System

What follows is a transcript of a 4 hour seminar I taught on day trading in July of 1985.

Seminar Attendees were taught a specific approach to day trading the Standard and Poor's and Value Line, which has been quite profitable in real-time trading.

The system continues working in current time as well as it did in past time.

Hopefully, this chapter will give readers not only a sense of how the markets work on shorter term fluctuations, but also a reliable day trading system they can use for their own trading. I am also providing you with computer printouts of how the system has done on a daily basis in the active contract months since the inception of the Standard and Poor's contract.

This chapter may be a bit difficult to read because, remember, it was not written for reading. It has been edited to make for easier comprehension.

Inasmuch as there were questions asked during the presentation, those questions have been kept in the transcript. Some of these questions you may have in your own mind. Hopefully they will be answered for you.

The good news . . . the big news . . . is that it is possible to make money day trading. We have now proven that, on a consistent basis, I have taught other people to day trade who have also gone out into the marketplace and made money from our day trading methodology. We have had day trading Hot Lines that have averaged over $2,000 a month of profits in real time trading, which are no longer available.

If you are interested in my day trading system developments, drop me a note. Should we reactivate the hot lines or offer a system you will be advised.

A quick glance at the equity from my day trading account shows this is serious business . . . this account began at $3,000 on 8/1/86. By 12/1/86 it had generated over $300,000 of profits. 98% of these came from day trading. When it's all said and done, if there is anything I've proven in 20 years of writing, teaching, and trading it is that anyone can make money day trading.

Now . . . here is how you can do it too!

DAY TRADING SEMINAR

I want to talk to you a great deal about tools, techniques and little insights into day trading. I want to show you how to forecast tops and bottoms and I am going to show you indicators that tell you when you have a better probability of success, based on market patterns. I will tell you a lot about patterns. I am also going to tell you about what doesn't work. I am convinced the problems that most of us have is that we have been told, "THIS WORKS," and when we start trading we say, "How come we are losing money if this works?" There are things that flat out don't work, but that you have been told work.

I am here today to tell you what some of those things are, as well as to say which things work. In the second part of this session I will teach you a specific system for day trading the Standard and Poor's and Value Line. We don't use it on any other markets . . . it is not my very best day trading system. My very best day trading system I don't give away at seminars. What you will get here is a good systematic approach to day trading the Standard and Poor's.

WHAT DOESN'T WORK

I feel this is as important as what does work. I have probably had the privilege of seeing most every day trading system that has come along over the years. The first day trading

116

system that I recall seeing was in 1964. That was based on moving averages. It was a theory that if a three day moving average got above a seven day moving average during a market session, you could be a buyer. It worked for a short time period, but that was about all.

The traditional moving average approach would say that you are going to buy when price breaks above a moving average and sell when it falls below the moving average. It looks pretty good when you get a trending market, but markets usually don't trend often enough.

Not only do you get too many signals that occur too often, but in actuality, your fills make your trades even worse, as there is so much slippage. Just because it is on the chart or just because the price is printed in the Wall Street Journal, don't believe for one minute that you can get that price. Slippage is a terribly important part of day trading. I want to tell you what you can do to avoid slippage. For now, just notice that here is something that really doesn't work; moving averages. The moving average approach has as many faults with it as it has opportunities. Interestingly enough, a study was done at the University of Chicago around 1957. They looked at a lot of moving averages on stock prices, and the bottom line conclusion was that it was impossible to develop a consistent moving average of the market that made money. In other words, using the same 1 or 2 moving averages all the time did not make money. I did a similar study when I had a stock market letter, The Williams Report, back in 1967-68. We looked at stocks and commodities at that time and reached the same conclusion. I had all sorts of fancy guys from Stanford help me do it. Yet we could not construct a successful trend following method for stocks or commodities that always worked with the exact same moving average parameters.

Another thing that is very popular because it is on Commodity Quotegraphics is the Parabolic. The Parabolic Index is something that Welles Wilder developed which may have some value for trading on a daily basis. But on an intra-day, or day trading, basis I haven't been able to find any value. The problem with the Parabolic approach, and I am not being derogatory but hopefully explaining, is simply that by the time, on a day trading basis, the market has had its move and starts to react, the distance between your entrance and exit is just too large. Accordingly, you are not going to be making any money. So if you happen to be enamored with that I suggest — if the market hasn't already suggested it to you — to be very careful in the application of Parabolic.

It may or may not be successful for you. Someone might say, "Well Larry, that is kind of a choppy trading range market so let's look at it on a wider range market." This happens to be Standard and Poor's. (Note: visual chart shown to audience.) We had a good run in the market, let's see how it did there. If you look real quickly, though we had a nice run in the market, we had 2, 3 winning trades out of about 10 or 11. It just doesn't work for day trading. It can be of great value to assist you with trend trading over a longer time period, but for day trading we are going to scratch this one too.

One of the very old approaches to day trading is simply to buy breakouts. When the market's going to run it is going to have to break out above a support/resistance level, where you can be a buyer.

The record suggests that just acting on breakouts, for the downside or the upside, is in fact not good.

How many of you actually day trade? How many have never day traded? Day trading is something that everyone wants to do, but very few people know how. There are a couple of logical problems in the day trading systems I have seen. The greatest logic problem is the systems don't know which side of the market to trade. Most day trading systems try to take a lot of trades during the day. What I am going to show you is how you can determine if you are going to be a buyer or a seller. That way you will be isolated to one and only one trade.

You are going to be buying on Monday or you are going to be selling on Monday, based on one criteria that I will give you that shows, about 60% of the time, whether the market will close up or down for that day.

Conventional wisdom says buy at yesterday's high and sell at yesterday's low. That may be right some of the time, but our actual statistics indicate that trading above yesterday's high really shows that the market is overbought and you can get a good sell signal there. It is interesting that the people I have found to have the most trouble trading the market are lawyers and doctors, because they use a very strong logic system, but normal everyday logic. When the light is red you stop and when it is green you go.

But in the marketplace what looks bad is good, and what looks good is bad. It is very difficult on people who come from a logical background.

OK, those are some of the things that don't work. Yesterday's highs and lows, ranges, breakouts. I have found that oscillators don't work very well either. I have been enamored with oscillators and I am going to show you one oscillator that I have found to be of some value. But for the most part, oscillators don't work because they are composed of time and price. You may have a situation where price is nothing but the time is moving so the oscillator moves up and down. It looks like a buy signal, but in fact there is no price movement.

Price is going nowhere yet the oscillator is moving and you think you should have a buy signal. The other problem with oscillators is that a 10 minute oscillator can only monitor a 10 minute move for you. A 10-day moving average can only catch a 10-day move. You can't catch the 30 or 40 day big move. A 30-day oscillator can only catch the 30 day movement. It can't catch the first 5 or 10 days that are so explosive in the market.

AN OSCILLATOR THAT WORKS

My experience with oscillators is that they are very attractive, but you probably don't want to trade them all on their own. There are some tools you can use with oscillators and I want to show them to you. One of the tools we can construct is a combination of 2 oscillators, called dual oscillators. Construct a 5 bar moving average of the high, low and the close and a 20 bar moving average of the high, low and close. What we are doing is taking the difference between a 5 bar moving average and a 20 bar moving average. What actually will happen is that when one crosses over the other, when the short term cycle crosses and rises above the longer term, we get a buy signal. This works particularly well when you get a big gap down opening or a big gap up opening and you want to ride with the opening. You gap down and immediately know you are not going to go much lower.

We can ride this buy signal until we start to top out. When does a rally end? When we get above and then cross down. This is a tool, it is not a system. You cannot take every crossing in it. It is a subjective tool, but it is a heck of a good tool.

There are only 2 kinds of day traders, the quick and the dead. If you are not quick, you will be dead. They aren't going to let you play the game very long. You have got to learn to respond very quickly to these signals when they do occur. The idea of 2 momentum time periods crossing one another is one that I have been working with since 1966. I used to work with it on weekly data in stocks. When I got my Commodity Quotegraphics I started fooling around with this and kind of stumbled into it. I am not certain yet that these are in fact the very best time periods. I am still playing around, but they are the best that I can tell you about right now. This is not a bad little tool to help you with the ebb and flow of the marketplace.

You see, what's causing the signals is short term momentum breaking above the long term momentum: that's a buy. A sell signal would be the short term momentum breaking below the longer term momentum. It doesn't have to reach a certain overbought or oversold position. However, we have found the best ones occur when you get into the 40% to 50% area. Then your crossings are more significant than crossings around the 0 level.

WEEDING OUT GOOD SIGNALS FROM THE BAD

One thing that will help day traders would be the ability to know when tomorrow will close up, 60% of the time. Then you would only take buy signals. I will tell you how a little later. That would probably be as good a filter as anything you could get. You may also want to consider that if contrary opinion is rising you would only be taking buy signals. If it was declining you would only be interested in taking sell signals. I think that is going to weed out some sell signals for you.

Q. Do you use divergence in day trading?

A. I don't use divergence in my own day trading system. I will look at something and say, "Gee, we have a lot of divergence here," higher highs, and a pretty Bullish situation. I will observe that and notice it. I recall buying divergence in a Bellies Bear market one time. I bought because there was divergence. There was more divergence, and more divergence as I lost about 10 to 15¢ in Bellies. All the way down there was supposedly Bullish divergence and I was catching falling daggers. Now I try to wait until that falling dagger stops and sticks in the ground. When it stops quivering then I try to pick it up. Just divergence alone isn't enough. It looks like you have everything there and pow . . . divergence alone can kill you in a hurry. It may be there at a good signal, but its appearance alone guarantees nothing.

LET'S TALK ABOUT SOME THINGS THAT DO WORK

I don't want to be a negative type of person and say that nothing works. There are things that do work in the marketplace. Just for the official record, to let you know that it is possible to make money day trading, in Feb. of 1985 I began day trading a $2,000 account at the brokerage firm of Ira Epstein. This can all be confirmed by them. The $2,000 account, without adding any capital, grew to $37,900 within 3 months. Most every trade in that account was a day trade although I have held a few positions overnight. (I took winners home overnight.) The reason I am saying that is not to pound my chest, but to let you know that, in fact, you can make money day trading. A lot of people, myself included, have always believed it was impossible to make money day trading. I believed that for a long, long time, but no more. My experience is that you can in fact, make money day trading.

But to do that you have to know what works. There are patterns in the market that we have been able to analyze that give us a better idea if a market will rally or not. I will show you what some of those patterns are.

4 Day ++--
% Chance Tomorrow Up

	SAP	VAL	BONDS	SILVER	BELLIES	BEANS
---	64.6	58.6	51.2	49.3	52.5	51.4
--+	48.5	36.8	47.1	46.4	51.4	52.5
-+-	62.5	50.9	46.4	53.5	50.2	51.2
-++	54.7	53.9	45.6	50.8	51.2	46.5
+--	52.8	53.5	54.2	49.3	47.3	53.7
+-+	37.2	44.8	49.3	47.9	48.1	52.3
++-	61.3	62.3	47.2	56.9	53.5	56.0
+++	45.3	46.2	52.5	51.7	49.0	45.5

5 Day ++--
% Chance Tomorrow Up

	SAP	VAL	BONDS	SILVER	BELLIES	BEANS
----	62.5	62.1	56.2	51.8	48.2	47.6
---+	54.8	38.1	50.9	42.9	50.8	47.7
--+-	67.6	50.0	52.8	55.0	52.1	46.7
--++	63.6	62.1	40.7	49.1	51.6	46.7
-+--	55.8	48.2	54.0	50.8	42.5	58.5
-+-+	34.8	45.8	47.3	53.8	50.8	49.2
-++-	64.7	62.9	50.8	57.4	53.2	57.4
-+++	50.0	42.9	58.6	48.8	53.8	47.2
+---	65.6	56.1	46.3	46.9	56.2	56.1
+--+	43.2	35.6	43.8	50.0	52.1	61.9
+-+-	60.0	51.7	38.7	52.3	48.6	53.3
+-++	47.6	48.9	51.0	52.2	50.8	43.9
++--	48.3	63.3	54.4	47.6	52.5	53.4
++-+	40.4	43.5	51.5	42.0	45.6	49.0
+++-	58.5	61.9	42.7	56.3	53.8	56.3
++++	39.4	50.0	46.7	54.3	43.8	44.1

PROFITABLE DAY TRADE PATTERNS

We can ask the computer "What % of the time is the next day up?" Or we might say if we have minus, plus, minus what % of the time is the next day up or down? Fortunately, the computer can come back and give us an answer. If we have 3 consecutive down closes in the S&P, you have a 64.6% probability of an up day tomorrow. If we have minus, minus, plus, we only have a 48% probability. If we have minus, plus, minus we have a 62% probability. That is one of my favorite patterns. The best day-trading commodities, by and large, are the ones I have given you the numbers for; Silver, Beans and even Bellies are not bad for day trading. I have also broken it down for the 4-day pattern. Whatever the patterns, you can look at it and know the probability that tomorrow will be up or down. You now have an insight into the market that nobody else has. The market structure itself is telling you what should take place. As an example, on Thursday of this week, we had a 40% probability of a down close Friday, which we got, and in the Value Line we had about 45% probability of a down close and we got the down close. How many of you watch FNN? On FNN from time to time you will hear me say we have a 60% probability of an up close today. If you have wondered where I get that number from, I get it from these tables. These tables, for those of you who are interested, include data from the inception of trading in the Standard and Poor's and Value Line and the last 5 years in the Bonds, Bellies, Beans, and Silver, so it is a pretty good data base to look at these patterns.

If the number in Beans says 37, that means that we only have a 37% probability of an up close, which means we have a heck of a probability of a down close. Subtracting that number from 100 will tell you the probability of a down close. I supplement this with the five day pattern. Bruce Babcock developed a system using just the 3 or 4 day pattern. The system using just that has done well in real time.

We try to jump on those days that are going to be good for us . . . the days with high probabilities.

We all have this impression that IT is going to happen tomorrow. Whatever it is, it isn't going to happen tomorrow, it only happens 3 or 4 times a year. But because we turn on FNN, read the Wall Street Journal, subscribe to my commodity letter, or someone else's commodity letter, we get excited about tomorrow. When I first started trading commodities I thought the depression of 1929 was going to start . . . then. The old guys in the brokerage firms scared me to death. I was so nervous, and it stayed with me for 4 or 5 years. I thought it had to happen . . . NOW. It does not happen now.

I will show you when the depression is going to happen. You have a long time, you don't have to worry about it now. Notice what we have done with pattern analysis? In the old days, when we first started trading this stuff, we said there is the head and shoulder, a wing and a wedge, and an upper-case outer-Mongolian box car, that looks like a buy signal.

In fact, I can remember when an analyst at a now defunct brokerage firm came out and said he had a buy signal because he had a horizontal duplex breakout!

I am a little kid from Billings, Montana. A duplex is a place I thought you lived. I have never yet heard anyone that can explain the term horizontal duplex breakout. I would like to know what the heck he was talking about. It's phenomenal, the terminology that we have brought up in the marketplaces. I don't know if you happened to see Joe Granville when he was talking to Ted Koppel. Koppel just shook his head because Joe was using all our terms, all the different jargon we have. The average person just doesn't understand our language.

There are other things that we can do to give us some insight into the marketplace. I will show you one of those right now. The most significant thing I can tell you about day trading, bar none, is this: If today's close is higher than yesterday's close, be a seller tomorrow. If today closes below yesterday's close, be a buyer tomorrow. An up close begets down closes. Down closes beget up closes.

Look at the numbers here. Given a down close, 59% of the time I am going to change direction the next day.

In the case of Gold, 62% or 63% of the time if you have an up close in Gold today, you are going to close lower tomorrow. If you have a lower close tomorrow in Gold, 60% of the time you hare going to have a higher close. Gold is the strongest of them. This is the background you need for a good day trading system!

In fact, let me give you a number to support that. Trade the Standard and Poor's and the Value Line, trading only one contract not 5 or 10. Every time you have a down close you buy the opening the next morning. With a 200 point stop, or exit on the close. If you have an up close, sell the opening in the morning, with a 200 point stop, or exit on the close. You would have made about $180,000 since the Standard and Poor's started trading in 1982. You had to wait 2 1/2 years to collect all your $180,000, but that's not a bad salary! Again, on a down close you buy the opening, on an up close you sell the opening. A 200 pt. stop is placed, and you get out on the close. If you had just done that you would have made a lot of money.

None of you can do this, incidentally. I tried to do it, but the equity drawdown is too erratic. But if you have plenty of capital . . . you'll need about $20,000 for each contract . . . you can do this. You are going to have 7 or 8 losing trades in a row. I don't believe a day trader can handle 3 losses in a row. If they get 3 losses in a row they are looking for a new system. Or look to renew their real estate license and get in the station wagon and get into a new business. The method I just told you about has had something like 11 losses in a row, 3 times more consecutive losses than most traders can handle.

What I think happens is that the public goes home and reads the Wall Street Journal or the New York Times, or LA Times and they read that Gold goes up for the day. The public's mind gets Bullish on that. The public, as a group of traders, thinks Gold is strong. But as I mentioned earlier, there is an inversion of logic in the marketplace. Strength is weakness. That is why I think an up close is so significant. It gears the public to do a certain thing.

The professional is probably doing the opposite. Certainly the records indicate that to be true. Next let's look at this problem; if price closes down for the day and below the opening, then the next day also opens lower, what percent of the time will that day close up?

If you stop and think logically about it, (logic will kill you in the marketplace) you would expect the market will continue going down, especially since it opened lower, and your broker says it is going to open lower, so you get out of your long position. 57% of the time, that is almost 60%, price closes *above* the opening. Those are tremendous odds for trading. 57% of the time you are going to close higher if you are coming down. If you are going up, 57% of the time you will be going lower. 59% of the time in an up trend you will reverse it in Value Line, 58% in Bonds, 57% in Silver, while Bellies and Beans are about a 50/50 deal. This is the first step towards getting you into a day trading system. That is all that it is.

Q. The question is does this apply to up limit moves?

A. Yes, all data for 5 years has been looked at by the computer and there were up limits, down limits, and all kinds of things in it. It does apply.

Q. Is the S&P set up for a potential buy signal Monday because it was down on Friday?

Yes, on the buy on the opening method you should be buying on the opening, but again, nobody can trade that. It is the best of any day trading system I have in terms of gross dollars of profit. Huge amounts of money can be made, but I don't think anyone can follow it.

The beauty of this is that you now have direction. Remember when I talked about the problem that most day traders have, they don't know what to do. The market opens up and we are blurry eyed anyway, especially in California, where the Swiss Franc opens at 5:20 in the morning.

You get up and your mind isn't thinking real well and you don't know whether to be a buyer or a seller, so you are trying to buy and sell three or four times during the day. Heck, with commissions, you can't do that folks. One trend trade a day is plenty. Now you know the direction to trade.

Those of you who look on oscillator and ask about filtering out with the oscillator — if you have an up day then you can be looking for only sell signals in your oscillator or whatever other tools you happen to use. You can now start to combine these materials with your old systems if you want to.

After you have been day trading a little bit, I know what is going to happen to you people, you are going to have a position and near the day's close you are going to have a profit and will say "Hey, I am gonna take this baby home, I am going to take this home and show it to my wife and kids. They haven't seen a whole lot of these to begin with." And the next morning it will open lower. You will say, "Why did I take that home, why didn't I get out on the close and be a day trader like Larry said to do?"

WILLIAMS' OVERNIGHT FORMULA

Well if you really have to take the position home I am going to give you a formula to take the position home. If the formula says hold overnight, you can. As long as it says don't hold it overnight, don't hold it overnight. The formula is something that was written about in my book, *The Secret of Selecting Stocks*, about 18 years ago. It has been around quite awhile. The formula is going to look at buying and selling. We are going to take the high minus the opening and are going to take the close minus the low. Add those 2 numbers together calling that A. We will also take the high minus the low and then we will call this number B. We will divide A by B. That will give us a percentage. This is the formula, but before you can apply that I have to show you something.

126

How many of you know what I mean when I talk about a true high or a true low? Up until now those of you who didn't raise your hand have been missing out on about 15% of all market activity. Please bear with me, I am going to give you a little formula here. There is 15% of the market you didn't even know about. That is a very important part of the market. Here's an example: Close yesterday at 61, you call up your broker and he says the high is 68, the low is 63 and it closed at 66. Look at this for just a minute. What happened from 61 to 63? What happened to those 2 points? We need an accounting of those 2 points. Where did they go? Prices did move from 61 to 63, didn't they? It's just that they gapped. The quote low (the first price that occurred during the day) was probably 63. That is the quote low, the chart low is 63, or the Wall Street Journal low, but we will call it the true low.

What about 61 to 63? Didn't it really start trading at 61? That is the last price that it closed on the previous day. This is, in fact, the true low, 61. All this time you people have been using 63. The true low is 61. The same holds for the true high. I will give you a formula that you can write down for the true high and the true low: *True high* equals whichever is greater, Yesterday's close or today's quote high. *True low* equals whichever is less, yesterday's close or today's quote low. There is the formula. It is very, very important that you use true ranges. It is like when you have a radio and you start to tune in a station, there is all that static and then it comes in clearer. This is going to give you clarity in the marketplace. It will drop out a lot of points that your mind is looking at. There are only these key points in the marketplace.

Okay, we have true highs and true lows. Now using true highs and true lows we can then get back to the formula that is related to the overnight formula. We are going to subtract high minus the opening, close minus the low. That has got to be true high and true low. You are going to take true high minus true low to calculate A and B, then divide A by B and arrive at a percentage.

I am going to give you an example. Let's assume you had been short the Standard and Poor's for Thursday. It opened at 193.55 . . . High of 194.25 . . . a Low of 192.65 . . . it settled at 193.95. Open, high, low, close. Now you are going to need to run this formula about 5 to 10 minutes before the close. You'll get an idea of where we are going to close in that market. Obviously, we can't run it when it is after the close, because then it is too late to decide if you want to hold it overnight or not. You can then decide whether to hold the trade overnight. On that basis we say well, what do we have here? Today's high minus the open is 355 minus 425, or 70. The close minus the low, 265 minus 395, is 130. Added together makes 200. These are both true highs and true lows, so 425 minus 265 equals 160. We divide B into A, to get 125%. Would we have held the long position? NO. If we were short and if the value was 56% or lower, we would have held the short position. You can run this just about the time the market is starting to close. Then ask yourself, "How good is the number, is it a number I can hold overnight, or is it a number not to hold overnight?" I use true range figures in absolutely every single calculation. Otherwise you are missing out on 15% of the market activities. Can you imagine if you took 1 1/2 days out of every 10 and pretended it wasn't there? If you subscribed to a chart book that only showed 9 out of every 10 days, you wouldn't subscribe to it very much longer.

The rules are to hold a short with a reading of 56% or less. Hold longs with a 144% or greater reading. We will hold over only about 20% of the time.

Now this the final thing for me to tell you about; it doesn't say the market will be higher an hour after the opening, or 2 hours after the opening, or 15 minutes after the opening. You have to get out on the opening. It also doesn't say how much higher the opening will be. It says it will be higher. Hopefully, 1 tick is at least going to pay for your overnight commission. I had a situation last fall in Beans where I sold Beans during the day, ran the formula, and got a real good value to hold overnight. I held, and Beans opened down 29 points. I said, Oh, heck, I'll hold for limit. Then I thought; now wait, this overnight formula says get out on the opening, I got out on the opening. Beans never went down limit, they actually ended almost up limit for the day! You would have thought they would have gone down one more tick, but they didn't. So it is an overnight formula from the close to the opening. It doesn't talk about anything past the opening. If you want to hold it past the opening, go ahead and do that. It is fine by me, except I am not responsible then. You are, not me.

I now want to talk to you about forecasting. I want to show you how you can find points in time when the market is going to top or bottom. If you will take the time period from one high to the next high (the number of days from a high to a high), multiply that by 1.28 and extend that from the low in between, that is about where the next low should occur. By the same token, if I want to know where the next high will occur, I take the low to low, count the number of days, multiply by 1.28, and extend that from the high in between. That is going to tell me approximately where the next high is going to occur. This formula works on five minute charts, 60 minute charts, day charts, hour charts. It is kind of uncanny how you can see reversal points ahead of time. The formula works on any time frame . . . weekly charts,

128

daily charts, everything. But I think it works best on 5 minute and daily charts. Again, what you are doing is taking a high to a high, multiplying by 1.28 for a low to low, multiplying and extending from a high. Take 2 highs, multiply, and extend from a low. It is totally confusing to some people I know.

Q. How reliable is it?

A. It is about 80% reliable.

Q. How much leeway do you give the forecast?

A. A day either side of the actual call.

Q. Do you use highs, lows or closes?

A. I actually have been using the closing highs, usually but not always. Not on the five minute charts though. Let's look at a couple of things here. We are just going to count time bars now. It is a little boring to do this, but I find it pays off. Ok, we have a nice low where we said in Commodity Timing that on the 19th of June the market is going to bottom. Be a buyer . . . do I have any Commodity Timing subscribers here? Do you remember when we said on the 19th of June and we talked about that about 1/2 month in advance. We arrived at that by taking the high to high, which is 16 days, times 1.28 equals 19 days. The 19th day we made a new low in the Standard and Poor's. You can check it on your charts if you want to. That was the 19th of the month, which happened to be the 19th day. That was the buy point.

Q. When you have markets that are moving limit on a daily basis, do you feel it would be less likely to work?

A. It works just as well.

Q. Will this work on all charts or some commodities better than others?

A. It seems to work on everything equally well. Cattle, Grains, we looked at one last night on Cattle. I don't know what is happening in Cattle, but the last was only off by 1 day. It will usually be within a day or so. The low occurred in the first part of May. We knew back in December and said in our yearly forecast that the low of the year, the technical low, will occur in the early part of May. There were so many clusters of counts in this time period that we could see back then what was going to happen.

If you take low to low it's 18 days. 18 times 1.28 gives 23 days in the the general area of a market top. Generally speaking, it is going to call the short term swings of the market. You may, at times, get what I call an inversion. Let's say we have a time schedule for the market to top, but the market is coming down. I would expect an inversion . . . for the market to rally at that point. That would be the only exception, the only caveat to the method. If the market is going down to what should be a top it is going to be a low. If the market is rallying up to what should be a low, it is going to be a reversal to the downside.

Q. Where do you start the count from?

A. The first day counts as day one.

Q. Did you say this could be applied to any bar chart 5 minutes, 30 minutes, 47 minutes?

A. I don't know about a 47 minute bar chart, but the others yes. You are going to catch that time cycle.

Q. Have you ever worked with it on a weekly?

A. Yes. Go home and work it yourself on weekly charts and you'll see that most times you are catching the highs and the lows in the marketplace. Again, it is a tool. It won't be perfect for you, but it is generally going to predict when a top or a bottom should occur.

I would like to briefly show you one more forecasting tool that predicts where the economy in the U.S. and the stock market is going. Then we will get to that day trading method.

First, let's look at another approach that was first written about by Investment Educators in London, England in about 1951-1952. Their approach to forecasting is different than my 1.28. They basically said that if you multiply the time between two market highs by 1.618, the good Fibonacci number, and extend that out from the second high you will get a market reversal at that time. If you had 20 days, 16 days after this peak you would go out in time expecting a market reversal. If the market had been going up it would now go down. If the market was going down, it would now go up.

Now, before we get into day trading I want to show you a couple of more things that do work that will help you tell whether you should be buying or selling. One is the spread relationship between the Value Line and Standard and Poor's. In this relationship, when the Value Line in the spread is strong, that is the Value Line is stronger than the S&P, nice Bull moves develop. Once it tops out the market comes down!

As the spread improves you get a buy signal, and as the spread falls apart, you get a sell signal. Prior to the big rally which produced the all time new 1983 highs in the Dow Jones Industrial Average the spread turned around and gave a beautiful buy signal. It is not just a timing indicator, it will also tell you, on a short term basis, the strength and weakness of the market. It will tell you if your other timing signals are good or not. This can help you filter out technical signals. I looked through other spread relationships, Value Line to Bonds, Value Line to S&P cash. Out of all these this is the one that gives the best information.

There is another interesting one which is Value Line Cash to Standard and Poor's cash. go with me if you will back to 1982, those bleak cold winters when America was supposed to fall apart, we had no speculation in the stock market, and the Value Line premium to Standard and Poor's was very, very low. Then we had a huge runaway Bull market and the premium got very, very high. Too much speculation and look what happened. You want a rally to be led by the Value Line, not the Standard and Poor's. That is the summation of it all.

WILLIAMS DAY TRADING SYSTEM

There are as many ways to day trade the market as there are day traders.

In 1987 I began what I think will be a legendary feat in the Robbin's Trading Company "World Cup Trading Championship" when I opened an account with $10,000, in this world champion class competition, and ran the $10,000 to $650,000 by the middle of April of 1987. This feat was accomplished using several different techniques, but almost all of the trades in the account were day trades. I will reveal to you next one of the general approaches to day trading that was used for that performance.

The overall success of all my day trading systems is based on one of two phenomena. The first is pattern recognition, such as you have already read about in this chapter, which may also include opening relationships.

As you can see in the chapter on the relationship of opening prices, they are extremely important for day trading. Usually, though not always, it is to our advantage to fade the opening. That is, if markets open higher they're probably going to sell off during the day; if they open lower they're probably going to rally during the day. While this is not always true, it is an extremely good operating rule for day traders to use. It is my belief that the majority of gaps are caused by the public and the public usually does the wrong thing. The people on the floor and professional traders take advantage of this opportunity on almost a daily basis.

As one example of this gap phenomenon, you should look at what happens when prices open above a three day moving average of the high, or open below a three day moving average of the low. Usually, that type of activity shows there's too much strength/weakness in the market and a reversal is imminent most of the time. I suggest you study these gaps to devise your own trading strategy, as I have; it is a most worthwhile study.

The second approach I use to day trading is one that is based on the concept of momentum. Simply stated it is this, "Once a market starts to move in a direction, it will continue moving in that direction until it makes an equal move in the opposite direction."

Now I know that sounds rather rudimentary, but that is the overall secret of my day trading successes!

Once a market indicates it's going to move in a direction by moving a certain amount of points, I buy it and continue holding that position until prices reverse, or the day comes to an end and prices close. Part of this approach is that once a market starts moving, if you're going to have a large range runaway day, the probabilities are much greater that it will close near its high (if moving to the upside) or near its low (if moving to the downside).

Hence, we know that the majority of the times, on a runaway day, (which is where day traders really clean up and make their money) it's best to hold our positions until the close. Most day traders go in and out of the market trying to pick up 50 or 100 points here and there. I believe that is totally wrong and is why most day traders lose money. The approach I use is to take a position, then hold on to it through hell and high water waiting for the close, at which point I exit. I can't call the high of the day and neither can you. I doubt seriously if anyone can do it with any consistency. Thus, it has been shown in my trading account that the best approach is to simply hold on to your day trade positions until the close hoping . . . maybe even praying . . . for one of those big runaway days which are tremendously rewarding.

Just before writing this part of the book, day trading in this fashion, I made well over $1,000,000 in two consecutive days. So I guess we can change the title of the old book "How I made $1,000,000 Trading Last Year" to "How I Made $1,000,000 Day Trading Last Week." The reason this happened was because of the "hold to the close" philosophy. There will be times when you wish you had not held to the close. But by and large, the most profit will be made by holding until the markets close (unless, of course, you know how to consistently call the exact highs and lows of the day). If you do, call me . . . call collect!

Of course, you do need a stop loss of some significant amount, to make certain you are not totally blown away by a trade. In the old days I would use approximately 200 points in the Standard & Poor's, though I deviate from that now because the S&P is trading at a higher level. You determine your stops. The system I am about to show you, however, was arrived at without using any stops in any way whatsoever.

The system I am about to teach you, as the computer printout below shows, made $69,700 from the inception of trading in the Standard & Poor's through January 1987. With 520 trades, 55.8% of the trades were successful. The largest drawdown was $5,000 — had you come in at the worst possible time, that's how much you would have lost prior to making a new high in equity. Note that we did not use stops in this system, but you may choose to do so. If so, I would make them at least two to three hundred points in the S&P. But again, these results are without any stops in the market at all. You can see, even though your stop is essentially getting out on the close, that at no point are you tagged too severely. The risk/reward ratio is 1.55, which means for every $1 lost you made $1.55. Several of my private day trading systems have much better numbers than these, but this is not a bad day trading system. Ones with worse numbers have been sold for thousands of dollars!

(06/01/82-01/23/87)

PCT	PROFIT	TRADES	WIN	LOSS	PCTACC	MAXDRAW	PROFIT/TRADE	P/L RATIO
.0105	$69,700	520	290	230	55.9%	$5,000	$135	1.65/1

HOW THE METHOD WORKS — The method is quite simple, here's all you have to do: At the close of each day in the Standard & Poor's multiply that day's close by .0105. As an example, the Standard and Poor's closed an April 21, 1987 at 295.00. If I multiply that by .0105 I have an answer of 3.0975, which we'll round off at 3.10 S&P 500 points.

I will then add 3.10 points to the close at 295.00, giving me 298.10, and subtract it from 295.00 which would give me 291.90. I then become a buyer at the higher number, a seller at the lower number, exiting the position on the close. If you want to play it closer to the vest, you may want to reverse in the event the market hits one number and then goes back to the other number. This is fine, if you prefer to do that.

To enable you to get a feel for how the system performs, following the recap of the system I'm showing you, on a trade by trade basis, all of the signals that occurred from December of 1985 through January 26, 1987. You can see that during that time period the system had 132 trades and made a net profit of $25,775 with an accuracy of 58%.

Q. Does this work on Bonds?

A. The basic approach will work in trading the Bond market. However, you will need a different percentage figure.

Q. How about the Value Line?

A. Same thing there. You can use it on the Value Line, although you will have to arrive at your own percentage figures. But the answer is yes, it will make money trading the Value Line.

DATE	B/S	PRICE	PROFIT	CUMPROFIT
85.1204	B	205.99	0.00	0.00
85.1204	S	207.35	1.36	1.36
85.1205	B	209.53	0.00	1.36
85.1205	S	207.05	-2.48	-1.12
85.1211	B	210.03	0.00	-1.12
85.1211	S	209.95	-0.08	-1.20
85.1213	B	212.36	0.00	-1.20
85.1213	S	213.40	1.04	-0.16
85.1216	B	215.64	0.00	-0.16
85.1216	S	215.15	-0.49	-0.65
85.1220	B	215.08	0.00	-0.65
85.1220	S	213.70	-1.38	-2.03
85.1223	S	211.46	0.00	-2.03
85.1223	B	210.45	1.01	-1.03
86.0107	B	215.49	0.00	-1.03
86.0107	S	216.05	0.56	-0.47
86.0108	S	213.78	0.00	-0.47
86.0108	B	208.25	5.53	5.07

86.0109	S	206.06	0.00	5.07
86.0109	B	206.85	-0.79	4.28
86.0115	B	209.38	0.00	4.28
86.0115	S	208.95	-0.43	3.85
86.0117	S	207.55	0.00	3.85
86.0117	B	208.10	-0.55	3.30
86.0121	S	206.16	0.00	3.30
86.0121	B	205.55	0.61	3.91
86.0122	S	203.39	0.00	3.91
86.0122	B	202.80	0.59	4.51
86.0124	B	206.80	0.00	4.51
86.0124	S	206.80	0.00	4.51
86.0128	B	209.98	0.00	4.51
86.0128	S	212.05	2.07	6.57
86.0130	S	209.23	0.00	6.57
86.0130	B	210.30	-1.07	5.50
86.0131	B	212.51	0.00	5.50
86.0131	S	213.05	0.54	6.05
86.0203	B	215.29	0.00	6.05
86.0203	S	215.55	0.26	6.31
86.0204	S	213.29	0.00	6.31
86.0204	B	213.70	-0.41	5.90
86.0207	B	216.25	0.00	5.90
86.0207	S	216.15	-0.10	5.80
86.0214	B	220.74	0.00	5.80
86.0214	S	220.65	-0.09	5.71
86.0218	B	222.97	0.00	5.71
86.0218	S	223.20	0.23	5.94
86.0219	S	220.86	0.00	5.94
86.0219	B	220.90	-0.04	5.90
86.0220	B	223.22	0.00	5.90
86.0220	S	223.85	0.63	6.53

86.0225	S	223.33	0.00	6.53
86.0225	B	224.30	-0.97	5.56
86.0227	B	227.01	0.00	5.56
86.0227	S	227.30	0.29	5.85
86.0304	B	230.70	0.00	5.85
86.0304	S	227.10	-3.60	2.25
86.0311	B	232.82	0.00	2.25
86.0311	S	236.25	3.43	5.68
86.0318	B	239.19	0.00	5.68
86.0318	B	239.45	0.26	5.95
86.0320	B	241.00	0.00	5.95
86.0320	S	239.75	-1.25	4.69
86.0321	S	237.23	0.00	4.69
86.0321	B	237.20	0.03	4.72
86.0326	B	240.70	0.00	4.72
86.0326	S	241.50	0.80	5.52
86.0401	S	238.47	0.00	5.52
86.0401	B	236.50	1.97	7.49
86.0403	S	234.96	0.00	7.49
86.0403	B	232.75	2.21	9.70
86.0404	S	230.31	0.00	9.70
86.0404	B	228.90	1.41	11.11
86.0408	B	231.71	0.00	11.11
86.0408	S	235.60	3.89	15.00
86.0409	S	233.13	0.00	15.00
86.0409	B	235.35	-2.22	12.77
86.0410	B	237.82	0.00	12.77
86.0410	S	238.05	0.23	13.00
86.0411	S	235.55	0.00	13.00
86.0411	B	236.65	-1.10	11.90
86.0414	B	239.13	0.00	11.90
86.0414	S	239.05	-0.08	11.82

86.0416	B	241.36	0.00	11.82
86.0416	S	244.20	2.84	14.66
86.0421	B	245.85	0.00	14.66
86.0421	S	246.25	0.40	15.06
86.0422	S	243.66	0.00	15.06
86.0422	B	242.90	0.76	15.82
86.0423	S	240.35	0.00	15.82
86.0423	B	243.30	-2.95	12.87
86.0429	S	242.13	0.00	12.87
86.0429	B	240.45	1.68	14.55
86.0430	S	237.93	0.00	14.55
86.0430	B	234.80	3.13	17.68
86.0505	B	237.21	0.00	17.68
86.0505	S	237.85	0.64	18.31
86.0507	S	234.76	0.00	18.31
86.0507	B	236.95	-2.19	16.12
86.0515	S	234.66	0.00	16.12
86.0515	B	233.40	1.26	17.38
86.0520	B	235.24	0.00	17.38
86.0520	S	236.85	1.61	18.98
86.0522	B	238.88	0.00	18.98
86.0522	S	241.60	2.72	21.70
86.0527	B	245.00	0.00	21.70
86.0527	S	246.35	1.35	23.06
86.0602	S	247.23	0.00	23.06
86.0602	B	247.15	0.08	23.13
86.0604	S	245.84	0.00	23.13
86.0604	B	246.55	-0.71	22.42
86.0609	S	245.05	0.00	22.42
86.0609	B	240.80	4.25	26.67
86.0613	B	245.60	0.00	26.67
86.0613	S	248.15	2.55	29.22

86.0617	S	245.99	0.00	29.22
86.0617	B	245.95	0.04	29.26
86.0620	B	248.08	0.00	29.26
86.0620	S	247.90	-0.18	29.08
86.0623	S	245.30	0.00	29.08
86.0623	B	245.55	-0.25	28.83
86.0624	B	248.13	0.00	28.83
86.0624	S	248.55	0.42	29.25
86.0625	B	251.16	0.00	29.25
86.0625	S	249.60	-1.56	27.69
86.0630	B	252.73	0.00	27.69
86.0630	S	252.25	-0.48	27.22
86.0703	S	251.83	0.00	27.22
86.0703	B	252.00	-0.17	27.05
86.0707	S	249.35	0.00	27.05
86.0707	B	243.55	5.80	32.85
86.0708	S	240.99	0.00	32.85
86.0708	B	241.65	-0.66	32.19
86.0710	S	240.30	0.00	32.19
86.0710	B	244.15	-3.85	28.34
86.0714	S	239.71	0.00	28.34
86.0714	B	238.30	1.41	29.75
86.0715	S	235.80	0.00	29.75
86.0715	B	235.05	0.75	30.50
86.0717	B	237.57	0.00	30.50
86.0717	S	236.15	-1.42	29.08
86.0718	B	238.63	0.00	29.08
86.0718	S	236.85	-1.78	27.30
86.0722	B	238.83	0.00	27.30
86.0722	S	238.40	-0.43	26.87
86.0725	B	240.90	0.00	26.87
86.0725	S	240.90	0.00	26.86

86.0728	S	238.37	0.00	26.86
86.0728	B	234.85	3.52	30.38
86.0730	B	237.57	0.00	30.38
86.0730	S	237.70	0.13	30.52
86.0801	S	233.47	0.00	30.52
86.0801	B	233.15	0.32	30.84
86.0804	B	235.60	0.00	30.84
86.0804	S	237.05	1.45	32.29
86.0811	B	239.79	0.00	32.29
86.0811	S	241.30	1.51	33.80
86.0812	B	243.83	0.00	33.80
86.0812	S	244.20	0.37	34.16
86.0813	B	246.76	0.00	34.16
86.0813	S	246.45	-0.31	33.85
86.0820	B	250.00	0.00	33.85
86.0820	S	250.75	0.75	34.60
86.0826	B	252.22	0.00	34.60
86.0826	S	253.75	1.53	36.13
86.0902	S	251.68	0.00	36.13
86.0902	B	249.40	2.28	38.41
86.0903	B	252.02	0.00	38.41
86.0903	S	252.35	0.33	38.74
86.0904	B	255.00	0.00	38.74
86.0904	S	255.90	0.90	39.64
86.0905	S	253.21	0.00	39.64
86.0905	B	251.45	1.76	41.41
86.0908	S	248.81	0.00	41.41
86.0908	B	250.45	-1.64	39.77
86.0911	S	246.00	0.00	39.77
86.0911	B	234.90	11.10	50.87
86.0912	S	232.43	0.00	50.87
86.0912	B	229.70	2.73	53.60

86.0915	B	232.11	0.00	53.60
86.0915	S	231.15	-0.96	52.64
86.0916	S	228.45	0.00	52.64
86.0916	B	230.85	-2.40	50.24
86.0917	B	233.27	0.00	50.24
86.0917	S	230.35	-2.92	47.31
86.0918	B	232.77	0.00	47.31
86.0918	S	230.95	-1.82	45.49
86.0922	B	232.92	0.00	45.49
86.0922	S	234.60	1.68	47.17
86.0925	S	233.42	0.00	47.17
86.0925	B	231.35	2.07	49.25
86.0926	B	233.78	0.00	49.25
86.0926	S	231.95	-1.83	47.42
86.0929	S	229.00	0.00	47.42
86.0929	B	229.55	-0.55	46.87
86.0930	B	231.96	0.00	46.87
86.0930	S	230.60	-1.36	45.51
86.1001	B	233.02	0.00	45.51
86.1001	S	233.60	0.58	46.09
86.1003	S	232.29	0.00	46.09
86.1003	B	232.40	-0.11	45.97
86.1006	B	234.84	0.00	45.97
86.1006	S	234.10	-0.74	45.23
86.1008	B	237.01	0.00	45.23
86.1008	S	236.70	-0.31	44.92
86.1014	S	234.31	0.00	44.92
86.1014	B	234.75	-0.44	44.48
86.1015	B	237.21	0.00	44.48
86.1015	S	239.70	2.49	46.97
86.1020	S	235.45	0.00	46.97
86.1020	B	235.50	-0.05	46.92

86.1023	B	237.62	0.00	46.92
86.1023	S	239.60	1.98	48.90
86.1030	B	243.23	0.00	48.90
86.1030	S	243.80	0.57	49.47
86.1106	S	244.60	0.00	49.47
86.1106	B	246.20	-1.60	47.88
86.1113	S	244.36	0.00	47.88
86.1113	B	241.55	2.81	50.68
86.1114	B	244.09	0.00	50.68
86.1114	S	245.30	1.21	51.90
86.1118	S	240.79	0.00	51.90
86.1118	B	237.05	3.74	55.64
86.1120	B	240.60	0.00	55.64
86.1120	S	242.20	1.60	57.24
86.1121	B	244.74	0.00	57.24
86.1121	S	244.85	0.11	57.35
86.1124	B	247.42	0.00	57.35
86.1124	S	248.20	0.78	58.13
86.1201	S	246.04	0.00	58.13
86.1201	B	251.05	-5.01	53.12
86.1202	B	254.24	0.00	53.12
86.1202	S	255.30	1.06	54.18
86.1205	S	253.06	0.00	54.18
86.1205	B	252.85	0.21	54.39
86.1208	S	250.20	0.00	54.39
86.1208	B	252.95	-2.75	51.64
86.1210	B	253.53	0.00	51.64
86.1210	S	252.15	-1.38	50.25
86.1211	S	249.50	0.00	50.25
86.1211	B	249.10	0.40	50.65
86.1229	S	245.10	0.00	50.65
86.1229	B	243.65	1.45	52.10

86.1231	S	240.89	0.00	52.10
86.1231	B	242.15	-1.26	50.85
87.0102	B	244.69	0.00	50.85
87.0102	S	246.75	2.06	52.90
87.0105	B	249.34	0.00	52.90
87.0105	S	253.25	3.91	56.81
87.0107	B	256.21	0.00	56.81
87.0107	S	256.25	0.04	56.85
87.0109	B	260.00	0.00	56.85
87.0109	S	259.50	-0.50	56.35
87.0112	B	262.22	0.00	56.35
87.0112	S	260.75	-1.47	54.87
87.0114	B	264.09	0.00	54.87
87.0114	S	263.30	-0.79	54.08
87.0115	B	266.06	0.00	54.08
87.0115	S	266.95	0.89	54.97
87.0119	B	269.50	0.00	54.97
87.0119	S	271.40	1.90	56.87
87.0122	B	271.72	0.00	56.87
87.0122	S	276.40	4.68	61.54
87.0123	B	279.30	0.00	61.54
87.0123	S	269.30	-10.00	51.54

(12/04/85-01/23/87)

PCT	PROFIT	TRADES	WIN	LOSS	PCTACC	MAXDRAW	PROFIT/TRADE	P/L RATIO
.0105	$25,775	132	77	55	58.3%	$5,000	$195	1.70/1

MONEY SUPPLY AS A FORECASTER

(Note: In the 1987-88 time period money supply numbers did not have as strong an impact on the market.)

We have an interesting phenomena called money supply. When does money supply come out now? Thursday. What day in the market do you think money supply affects? If affects Thursday. It really affects Wednesday but rolls over into Thursday. Let me show you how it does.

I bet, but can't prove it, that this is what happens: somebody some place gets a basic idea of what money supply is going to be on Wednesday. They start getting in the market a little bit on Wednesday and the market closes in the direction that they think money supply is going to be.

On Thursday, a few more people know about that and the market continues what Wednesday was doing.

In fact, in the Treasury Bill market, about 80% of the time this year, if Wednesday closed higher, Thursday closed higher. If Wednesday closed lower, Thursday closed lower. Treasury Bonds is about a 70% shot as I recall.

Whatever happens on Wednesday will be duplicated on Thursday.

If Wednesday's Bonds/Bills are up, Thursday's are up. If down, Thursday is down. Look at your charts and you will see what I am talking to you about. This week Bills were right on target. They are a little more consistent, but Bonds aren't bad.

Q. Does it work on both?

A. Yes, it works on both. Now this can help you as a trader, because if you want to day trade the Bonds or the Bills just one day a week, you can isolate the best day. It is going to be Thursday. Now here is the really fascinating thing. Remember, we are looking at, on average between Bills and Bonds, about a 75% probability of duplicating Wednesday's direction on Thursday.

Q. Has it always been a Wednesday/Thursday relationship?

A. No. Only since we started getting money supply figures on Thursday. It used to be that it was on a Friday. The same thing happened with the 2 days before then.

Recall when I went over the plus, plus, minus patterns. What do we know about a plus day? You are usually down the next day. 50 to 60% of the time. This relationship is an aberration

We really have an aberration. Again, look at your charts and see the validity of the system.

Q. How about Stock Indexes?

A. No, I haven't been able to notice a correlation in the Indexes based on the Bonds. People think if the Bonds go up the markets are going to go up. That isn't necessarily so. Many times the Bonds have gone down and the markets have gone up.

If I have a higher close on Wednesday, I expect a higher close on Thursday. You can use this as a day trading system. You're really getting three day trading sytems here. 1). The buy on the opening, sell on the opening. 2). The .0105 method, which is selective and trades a lot less frequently. And finally, 3). The one on Treasury Bonds.

Do you know what I suspect? I suspect that given all the day trading systems I've given you — and they all make money and have made money in the past, I'll bet there's not a cotton pickin' one of you who can make any money day trading . . . until you learn what I'm about to tell you.

First of all, the greatest losses that you will have will not be because of the system. It won't be because you're following my system or your system or anybody else's system. The greatest losses will be because of human error. You will call your broker and say "buy" when you meant "sell." You will actually do that! You will calculate a wrong number in your euphoria of calculating your numbers and do your mathematics wrong. That is going to be your greatest error. Or you will say, "Oh, I'm not going to take that signal, I've had three losers in a row." That will be your greatest error. The emotions of this marketplace get to us. Our greatest errors are human errors, not system errors. Now I say that because that's what my experience has been.

Two weeks ago, I was just floating in seventh heaven and $2,000 had gone to $38,000. We started trading a new silver system I've come up with for day trading. One contract day trading made $450,000 in the last three years. I think I have got *the* system for day trading silver. We started trading it and I lost money. Not because of the system but because we did some dumb things. We decided to hold some positions overnight one time. That's not in the system. Then instead of getting out of half of our position, we held all of it. We gave the wrong order on the close. We ended up going home net long ten, instead of being net long five. That rattled us. We didn't get out on the opening in the morning. We wished and prayed, went to church that night, that it would open higher. It didn't open higher, of course. Then we didn't know what the heck to do. Human error is tahe problem. Not the system. You've got to follow the system.

Anybody here see Star Wars? For those of you who didn't, and bear with me those of you who did, what happens in Star Wars is a lie . . . a lie that's been perpetuated in our society. The lie of Star Wars is that Luke Skywalker hops in his plane . . . he's got to destroy an asteroid in outer space. The other pilots, fighter pilots, are going ahead of him, and they're looking at their computers, when the computer says, "pull your triggers," BOOM! They miss the target. Not only do they miss the target, some other planes come up and blow them away. Really unpleasant to see these guys splattered all over the screen.

But along flies Luke Skywalker. When he looks at his computer, (his market system if you will) he hears the voice of the Force, and it says, "Let the Force be with you. Throw away the system! Don't have stop losses! You're an all-American hero. You don't need this stuff, Luke. Just do it when it feels right." So Luke just waits and he says, "Now!" BOOM! The Asteroid blows up, Luke comes home the hero! The Princess kisses him, and who knows what else they did.

We've learned that process in the movies and in our society. Go on your emotions, throw away the system of life.

But I'm telling you if you're going to try to make money trading commodities, you've got to follow the system, you can't be Luke Skywalker. Stick with your system, not your guns!

A WORD ON OVERTRADING

One of the ways that you can stick with your system is to not overtrade. This is how you violate your system, and I see a couple heads nodding in the room. You say, "Oh, hey, I'm gonna be Jesse Livermore or Larry Williams or whoever. I'm gonna trade 500 Bellies on this signal, I'll show 'em." You hop in with 500 Bellies and Bellies move two ticks. You say, "Oh my gosh! I want to get out. I can't stand the pressure."

Trade one little measly, lousy contract. Don't be greedy. Trading one contract, you won't have any pressure. Especially day trading. The maximum loss you can have day trading with the Standard and Poor's method I gave you is a thousand dollars on your worst possible day. Most of you can probably live through that. If you can't you shouldn't be trading commodities.

145

But if you have ten or fifteen contracts, you can lose $10,000 or more in a day. Now it's a different ball game and you can't follow the system because of the emotions and the pressure. The market doesn't create pressures on you. You create pressures by overextending your position in the market.

The greatest thrill in life, at least in the market, is making money. The second greatest thrill is losing money.* The pulse is very thrilling . . . just don't get into the thrill of the marketplace. (*This presents a psychological problem; we are rewarded, win or lose.)

Those of you who want to develop your own day trading systems, or carry my work farther, should know that the basis of my day trading success has come from big stops and big profits. Most of the day trading systems have little stops and little profits. When you stop and think about it, the day trading system I just gave you, the .0105 method, really is a money management technique. There's no mysticism to .0105 of the range. But it says that I'll always limit my losses to $1,000, and I may have those big booming days where I catch 2 or 3 or 4 hundred point moves. That is the essence of the method.

Most other day trading systems are going to have a little tiny stop and they're going to automatically go for a fifty point profit and cannot be successful. We have beaten the numbers to death with the computer to find out what the optimum stops are. It's interesting . . . for most all of the markets it's about $500 (with the exception of the S&P and Value Line), Bonds, Bellies, Silver . . . if you want to day trade, have a stop of about $500 but have an unlimited profit objective. So those days that Silver goes up limit you're there right until the close. The days when the S&P runs 3, 4, 5 hundred points, stay with it until the close. If you get out early, you might call the high every now and then, but over a long-term period, it's better to let the market flow with your position to the maximum profit, which is going to be getting out somewhere near the close.

The secret of day trading is big stops and big targets. Not little stops. Strangely enough, everyone has always thought the stops should be little, isn't that the way it works? How many of you fish? When you catch a big fish, do you pull him in and start to reel? No. You give him line, you play with him a little bit. You need to do that with day trading. You need to give it a little bit of room. If it runs against you for a little while, don't worry about it, you have your stop. Give it some room to fluctuate and oscillate around before it starts to take off again.

One final thing would be strategy. We've talked about money management. How about strategy? You can dance, if you will, from the Standard and Poor's to the Value Line and back from the Value Line to the Standard and Poor's. Have you ever gone to the circus? Go to the circus this fall and there's this little game there that kids play, called Gophers. There are round circles the gophers pop their heads out of and kids slam them with a big hammer. Have you seen those at the circus? All the kids just love it. The gopher comes up and boom! If you hit more than the kid next to you, you win a balloon. You pay 35¢ and you win a one cent balloon.

But that's what you have to think of in the marketplace. When the Standard and Poor's is weaker than the Value Line, boom! That's what you want to hit to sell. If you have a potential sell signal, we have an up close, look to see which market was up the least. That's where you want to take your sell signal.

If you have a buy signal because they're both down, look and see which one of those little gophers was down the least . . . boom! . . . that's the one you want to hit. It will usually be the Value Line, incidentally, but not always. So look between the two of them and go for the weakness. Since you've got these two sisters here, go for the weak one on sells. Then you can go for the strength for your buy signals.

You don't always have to trade the S&P's. You can move back and forth, you can do that with Treasury Bills, too, couldn't you? T-Bills, T-Bonds. Look at the family, where you have a family relationship. Take your buys on the ones that have been strong, which is hard to do. You want to buy the weak one, but that's wrong, don't do it. Buy the strength and sell the weakness. Use that as your strategy.

And the other point is: don't get carried away by thinking that because Bonds are up, the S&P must be up. That ain't necessarily so. They have in the past, and will in the future, move independently of one another.

DISPELLING MORE MYTHS

There are a host of market myths that simply aren't correct. One of them that I would like to dispel for short term traders, is the relationship of price change to volume participation. Most authors have advanced the concept that advancing prices on increasing volume is bullish, while declining prices on advancing volume is bearish.

We did a short study of this and the results are shown on the following computer print-outs:

Table #1 shows what happens if you had purchased the opening following a day when the volume was greater than yesterday and the close is greater than yesterday. In other words, you had advancing volume and advancing price.

Interestingly enough, in the case of the Standard and Poor's, you only advanced 47% of the time and had you made that purchase on the opening, you would have actually lost money. This indicates to me that increasing prices on increasing volume is not as bullish as most people have suggested.

The next way of looking at this relationship is to look at what happens if volume is less than yesterday, while prices are higher; this, according to the standard text books is exceedingly bearish. In fact, that is not the case in the Standard and Poor's, where prices closed higher 48% of the time. Had you purchased on the opening, you would have made a profit of $6,400 as Table #2 depicts.

The third relationship is an interesting one, and one that we can use as traders. Here we looked at what happens if volume is greater than yesterday while prices are down. In other words, volume picks up on a down market the following day. In the Standard & Poor's we closed higher 58% of the time, and if you had simply bought on the opening of that day, you would have made $43,875 as Table #3 depicts. Here is the data . . . the numbers are significant enough here that day traders should take note of what happens and watch the volume price relationship: if prices are down for the day and volume picks up for the day . . . expect a rally the following day.

The last relationship to look at is what happens when prices are down for the day and volume is also less than the previous day. In that case, if you had purchased on the opening the following day, you would have made a profit 52% of the time, as Table #4 shows, and would have profited by the amount of $2,225.

TABLE 1

IF VOLUME GREATER THAN YESTERDAY AND CLOSE GREATER THAN YES-
TERDAY, THEN BUY THE OPEN AND EXIT AT THE CLOSE
FROM 820421 TO 870310
$0 SLIPPAGE AND COMMISSIONS PER TRADE

TOTAL NUMBER OF CLOSED TRADES	350
TOTAL NUMBER OF WINNING TRADES	165
PERCENTAGE OF WINNING TRADES	47%
CUMULATIVE CLOSED PROFIT AND LOSS	-$13,300.00
OPEN EQUITY	$0.00
AVERAGE CLOSED TRADE	-$38.00
MAXIMUM NUMBER OF CONSECUTIVE LOSSES	9
MAXIMUM DRAWDOWN	-$26,999.99
AVERAGE WINNING TRADE	$625.00
AVERAGE LOSING TRADE	-$629.32
RATIO OF AVERAGE WIN TO AVERAGE LOSS	0.99
RISK/REWARD	0.89
MONEY MANAGEMENT	-12.53%
BIGGEST WINNING TRADE	$2,400.00
BIGGEST LOSING TRADE	-$4,000.00
NUMBER OF CLOSED TRADES ON LONG SIDE	350
PERCENTAGE OF LONG TRADES PROFITABLE	47%
AVERAGE WINNING TRADE LENGTH IN MARKET DAYS	1
AVERAGE LOSING TRADE LENGTH IN MARKET DAYS	1
TOTAL SLIPPAGE AND COMMISSIONS	$0.00
PROM FOR CLOSED TRADES	0.76
PROM FOR CLOSED AND OPEN TRADES	0.76
TOTAL MARKET DAYS IN STUDY	1236

TABLE 2

IF VOLUME LESS THAN YESTERDAY AND CLOSE GREATER THAN YESTER-
DAY, THEN BUY THE OPEN AND EXIT AT THE CLOSE
FROM 820421 TO 870310
$0 SLIPPAGE AND COMMISSIONS PER TRADE

TOTAL NUMBER OF CLOSED TRADES	282
TOTAL NUMBER OF WINNING TRADES	135
PERCENTAGE OF WINNING TRADES	48%
CUMULATIVE CLOSED PROFIT AND LOSS	$6,400.00
OPEN EQUITY	$0.00
AVERAGE CLOSED TRADE	$22.70
MAXIMUM NUMBER OF CONSECUTIVE LOSSES	8
MAXIMUM DRAWDOWN	-$20,850.01
AVERAGE WINNING TRADE	$767.22
AVERAGE LOSING TRADE	-$661.05
RATIO OF AVERAGE WIN TO AVERAGE LOSS	1.16
RISK/REWARD	1.07
MONEY MANAGEMENT	-1.03%
BIGGEST WINNING TRADE	$2,774.99
BIGGEST LOSING TRADE	-$3,625.00
NUMBER OF CLOSED TRADES ON LONG SIDE	282
PERCENTAGE OF LONG TRADES PROFITABLE	47%
AVERAGE WINNING TRADE LENGTH IN MARKET DAYS	1
AVERAGE LOSING TRADE LENGTH IN MARKET DAYS	1
TOTAL SLIPPAGE AND COMMISSIONS	$0.00
PROM FOR CLOSED TRADES	0.90
PROM FOR CLOSED AND OPEN TRADES	0.90
TOTAL MARKET DAYS IN STUDY	1236

TABLE 3

IF VOLUME GREATER THAN YESTERDAY AND CLOSE LESS THAN YESTER-
DAY, THEN BUY THE OPEN AND EXIT AT THE CLOSE
FROM 820421 TO 870310
$0 SLIPPAGE AND COMMISSIONS PER TRADE

TOTAL NUMBER OF CLOSED TRADES	250
TOTAL NUMBER OF WINNING TRADES	144
PERCENTAGE OF WINNING TRADES	58%
CUMULATIVE CLOSED PROFIT AND LOSS	$43,875.00
OPEN EQUITY	$0.00
AVERAGE CLOSED TRADE	$175.50
MAXIMUM NUMBER OF CONSECUTIVE LOSSES	8
MAXIMUM DRAWDOWN	-$8,500.00
AVERAGE WINNING TRADE	$730.03
AVERAGE LOSING TRADE	-$577.83
RATIO OF AVERAGE WIN TO AVERAGE LOSS	1.26
RISK/REWARD	1.72
MONEY MANAGEMENT	32.9%
BIGGEST WINNING TRADE	$2,899.99
BIGGEST LOSING TRADE	-$5,550.00
NUMBER OF CLOSED TRADES ON LONG SIDE	250
PERCENTAGE OF LONG TRADES PROFITABLE	57%
AVERAGE WINNING TRADE LENGTH IN MARKET DAYS	1
AVERAGE LOSING TRADE LENGTH IN MARKET DAYS	1
TOTAL SLIPPAGE AND COMMISSIONS	$0.00
PROM FOR CLOSED TRADES	1.43
PROM FOR CLOSED AND OPEN TRADES	1.43
TOTAL MARKET DAYS IN STUDY	1236

TABLE 4

IF VOLUME LESS THAN YESTERDAY AND CLOSE LESS THAN YESTERDAY,
THEN BUY THE OPEN AND EXIT AT THE CLOSE
FROM 820421 TO 870310
$0 SLIPPAGE AND COMMISSIONS PER TRADE

TOTAL NUMBER OF CLOSED TRADES	306
TOTAL NUMBER OF WINNING TRADES	159
PERCENTAGE OF WINNING TRADES	52%
CUMULATIVE CLOSED PROFIT AND LOSS	$20,225.00
OPEN EQUITY	$0.00
AVERAGE CLOSED TRADE	$66.09
MAXIMUM NUMBER OF CONSECUTIVE LOSSES	6
MAXIMUM DRAWDOWN	-$10,675.00
AVERAGE WINNING TRADE	$701.10
AVERAGE LOSING TRADE	-$620.75
RATIO OF AVERAGE WIN TO AVERAGE LOSS	1.13
RISK/REWARD	1.22
MONEY MANAGEMENT	12.64
BIGGEST WINNING TRADE	$3,750.00
BIGGEST LOSING TRADE	-$3,725.01
NUMBER OF CLOSED TRADES ON LONG SIDE	306
PERCENTAGE OF LONG TRADES PROFITABLE	51%
AVERAGE WINNING TRADE LENGTH IN MARKET DAYS	1
AVERAGE LOSING TRADE LENGTH IN MARKET DAYS	1
TOTAL SLIPPAGE AND COMMISSIONS	$0.00
PROM FOR CLOSED TRADES	1.04
PROM FOR CLOSED AND OPEN TRADES	1.04
TOTAL MARKET DAYS IN STUDY	1236

While I would never trade based on just these relationships, I hope I've been able to dispel for you some of the traditional thinking on volume price relationships. I've also helped pinpoint for you a high probability trade: down volume, down prices.

Norm Fosback, of Market Logic, has also done some interesting work on various indicators that predict the direction of tomorrow's market. Fosback's research uses the tick index, the measure of all stocks trading on an up-tick versus all stocks trading on a down-tick on the last sale, to predict tomorrow's market activity.

For those who don't know what the tick index means; if there were 500 stocks that last ticked up and 400 that last ticked down, you would have a positive tick index of +100.

This index is available on most quote facilities.

According to Fosback's research, the tick index is the most influential of the indicators he followed to forecast if tomorrow would be an up day or not.

Fosback says that, "If the final reading, at the end of the day, for the tick index on the New York Stock Exchange is positive, you have a 74% probability that tomorrow will also be an advancing day."

When it comes to forecasting down days, Fosback's research indicates that, when the trading index, (that is the ratio of advancing stocks to declining stocks versus the ratio of advancing volume to declining volume) is above 1.0, you then have a 64% probability that the following day will be a down day.

Fosback has put together a very interesting report on predicting tomorrow's market. You may want to write him at: The Institute for Econometric Research, 3471 North Federal Highway, Fort Lauderdale, FL 33306.

Finally, you may want to study <u>The Pattern</u> chart that shows what happens when the S&P trades and closes higher than yesterday's comparable figures. Note that prices open higher 59% of the time . . . but 37% of the time the open has been above the previous day's high! Luckily . . . almost 60% of the time the close of that gap day is lower than the opening. Here, day traders, is a great selling pattern. There are others — seek them out.

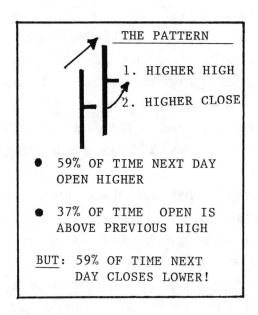

A DAY TRADING OSCILLATOR

Quite a few years ago, I developed the following day trade oscillator for a seminar. At this time, I wish to again share it with the public.

The oscillator is quite easy to construct, especially if you have Commodity Quote Graphics or any of the other quote machines. I use a 5 minute bar chart and take the difference between an average of the last two bars and the average of the last 10 bars on a closing basis. This particular oscillator is constructed by taking the average between the last 5 bars, high plus low plus close divided by 3; versus the last 20 bars; high plus low plus close divided by 3. Both of these oscillators tend to give extremely good signals, but are at their best during the first hour of trading.

The way I use the oscillator is as follows. If there is an opening gap to the upside, I then wait for the oscillator to cross to the downside. This would give me a sell signal.

By the same token, if there is a gap to the downside, I wait for the short term oscillator . . . the darker line on the charts in this book . . . to penetrate the longer term oscillator to the upside. This would give a buy signal. Once you're in, you can hold the position as long as you want. But I would definitely use a reverse crossing of the oscillator to give you your exit point, which is sometimes a sell short signal, but not always (vice versa for selling).

I'm showing numerous charts over a variety of time periods, going back several years so that you might see the volatility of the method.

It is simple to trade and quite mechanical. All you need to do is simply construct the oscillator, wait until there's a crossing to the upside, if there's been a down gap, then go long.

By the same token, to restate the rules for the sell signal, you first need to have a gap to the upside and then a penetration of the short term oscillator crossing the longer term oscillator. When that happens, you sell short and stay with that short until there is a penetration in the opposite direction.

The reason I believe the system works is that we are looking at two different time periods to construct our graphs. When the very quick time period of the market shows momentum has picked up, we identify that by the cross over. We know that the market is starting to rally. By the same token, we identify a trend reversal in the market when the short term oscillator has again peaked out . . . lost it's strength . . . and has turned back to the downside.

Note the chart in the Treasury Bond market of March 27, 1987. A sell signal was given at 97.24, following the up gap, and a cover signal was given at 97.16. That's not much, but it is 8 ticks or $259.00 per contract!

I do not use these oscillators for anything other than trading in the first hour or so time period. I am looking for a filling in of the gap, if you will, which is signified by the oscillator giving the penetration signals.

155

FACTS ABOUT "THE EVERY MORNING GAP"

Most every morning there is a gap in price from last night's close to this morning's opening range. The gap may be up or down, but it is almost always there. Seldom do we open a day's market at the exact same price that we closed the previous day.

There are some interesting statistics about such gaps. If yesterday closes up and today's open gaps higher, we will close above yesterday's close about 60% of the time. If we open down we will close below yesterday's close about 70% of the time. The reverse is equally true.

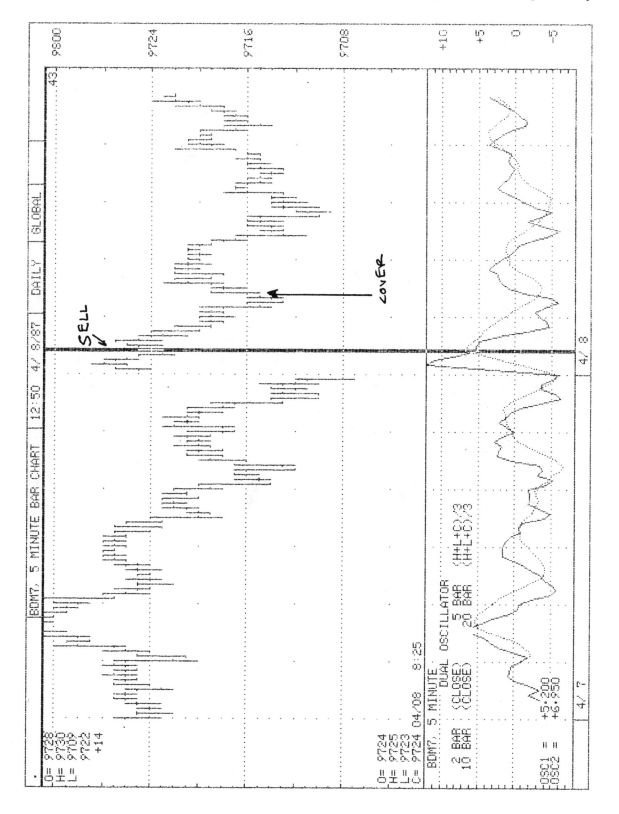

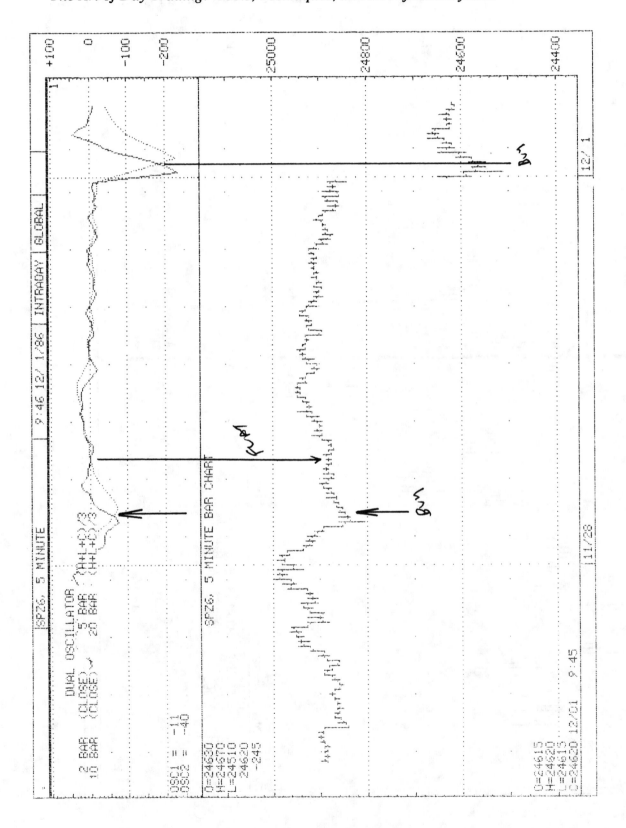

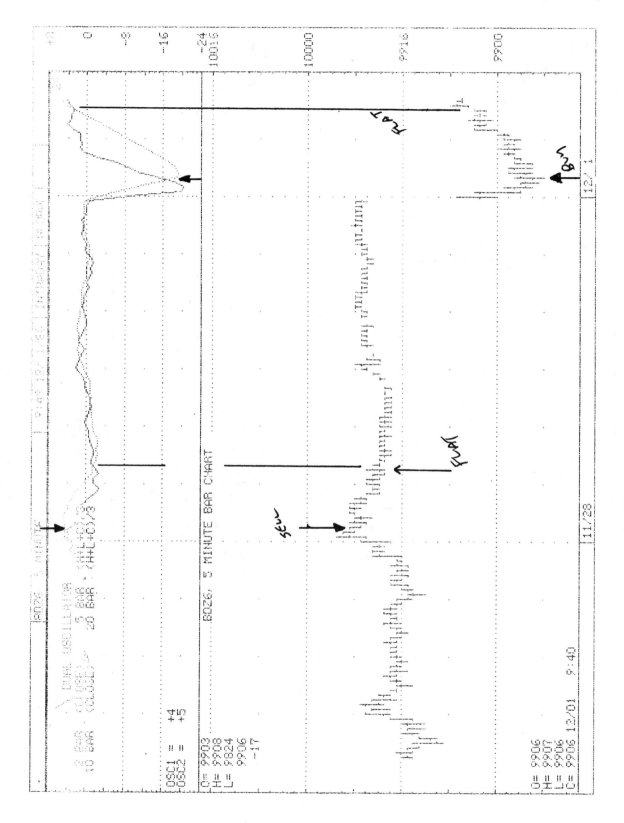

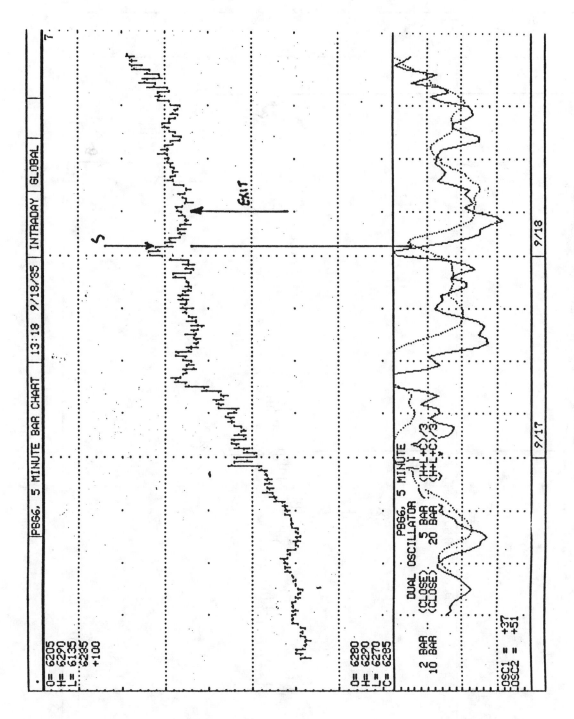

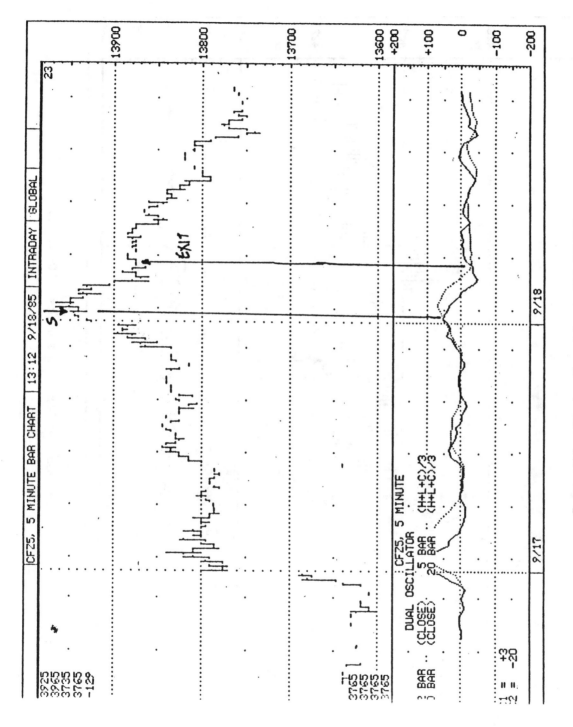

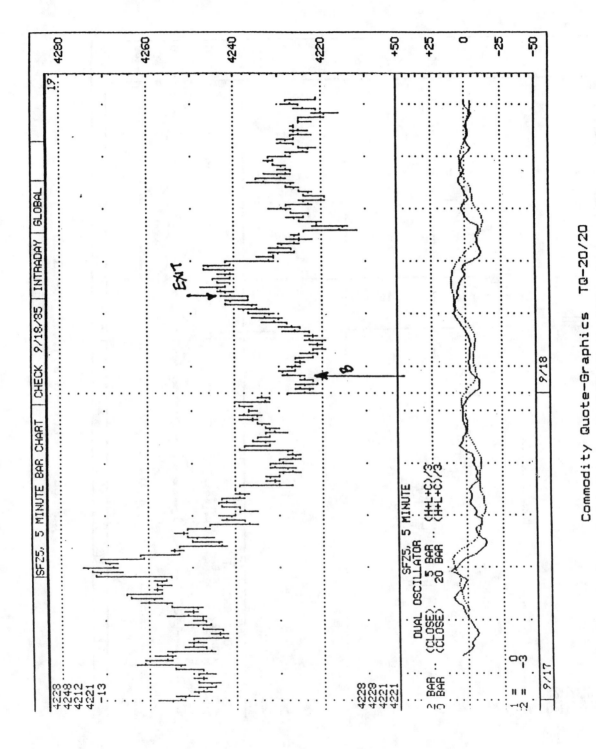

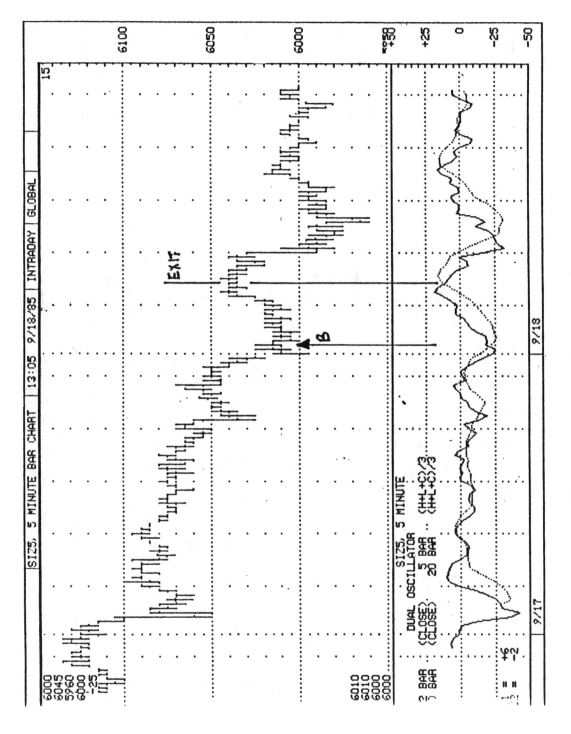

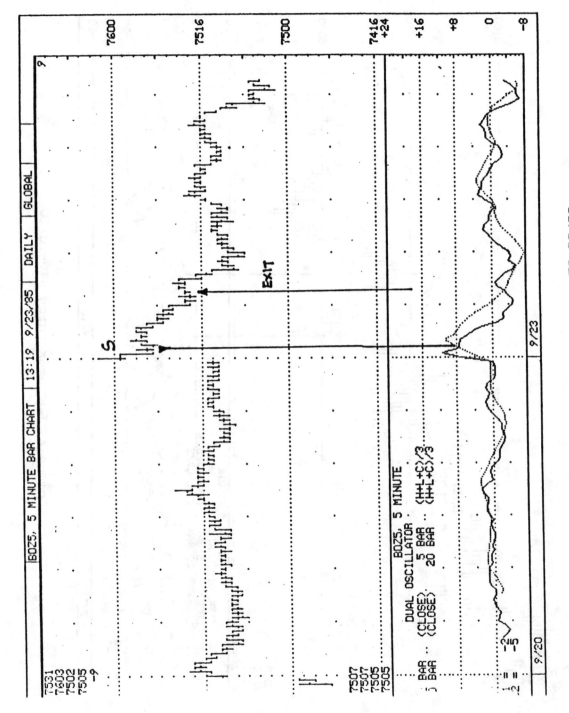

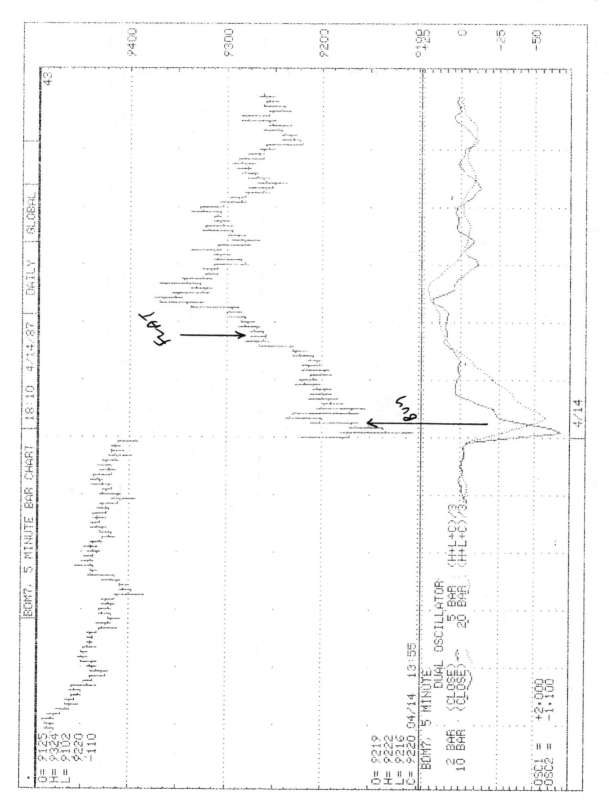

165

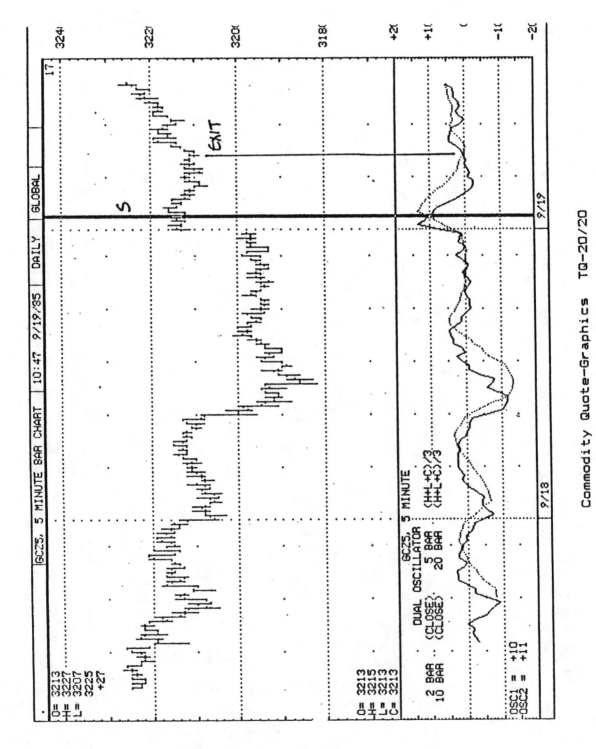

Chapter 9

Money Management
The Most Important Chapter In This Book

"Money Management is the most essential element to actually winning money from the casinos" . . . **Bobby Singer, the most successful blackjack player in history.**

It is the words of Bobby Singer, not Bernard Baruch, that should be handed out to all commodity traders.

The speculative challenge Singer chose to take up, gambling at blackjack, is a game where the odds are stacked against the player. Commodity traders are lucky, we may stack the odds in our favor. But consider for a moment the above words from a man who has made more money than anyone in the history of the world playing blackjack.

He did not say that his system is the most essential element to winning money from the casinos. No, he said his money management was what actually allows him to make money.

Imagine what successful money management can do in a game that is stacked in your favor!

Perhaps you don't believe gamblers. Then I suggest you read an interview done by J. F. Dalton with Stan Angrist, who since 1976 has written the widely followed commodities column in *Forbes* magazine. Angrist, who now writes for "The Wall Street Journal," became involved in futures in 1968 trading for his own account. In 1972 he wrote *Sensible Speculating in Commodities* published by Simon and Schuster. Among his other accomplishments, Angrist was a professor of mechanical engineering at Carnegie Mellon University for twenty years. In 1982 he resigned his professorship to devote full time to his column and other writings for *Forbes* and trading his own account. Angrist is as good as they come. It's worthwhile to listen to whatever he says.

J. F. DALTON: "Many of the traders we have interviewed feel that money management is an important aspect of trading. What are your thoughts?"

STAN ANGRIST: "Money management probably gets nowhere near the attention that trade selection does, and yet it could well be more important in the long run. All of us like to think that our trades will go well, but what most traders don't think about for more than an instant is what happens when the trade doesn't work, and we must face adversity. If we have taken on a position that is larger than is prudent for our account size, then we are faced with either a margin call or a cessation of trading or both. Why would we take on such a position? The answer is simple — greed. We have taken two or three good hits over the past week or so and with this one trade we will make ourselves whole and then some. So we do five contracts when we should be doing two and the next thing you know, we are facing a large-scale disaster. Skilled traders don't try to get even on one trade. The markets will be there tomorrow and the day after, so it makes sense to trade in lots that are appropriate to your account size.

Moreover, trading is always difficult under the best of circumstances, but when you add the stress of a margin call to normal trading tension, good judgement flies out the window like it was the bluebird of happiness. Save yourself a lot of grief — and money — trade in amounts consistent with your capital."

Despite how sophisticated one chooses to make proper money management, it will all boil down to this: you need a method that will maximize your winning streaks and minimize your losing streaks. That has been the goal of speculators since 1654, when Chevalier Sieve de Baussay visited a gambling den in Paris. He got so carried away with the calculations of games of chance that he ultimately worked with some of the world's most famous French mathematicians, Blaise Pascal and Pierre de Fermat. These gentlemen are the fathers of modern day probability theory.

The importance of this chapter, Money Management, simply cannot be understated. If it is true that the love of money is the root of all evil, then the lack of money management is the root of all evil when it comes to speculative gains, be it gambling, stock investing or trading commodities.

There is only one reason you need money management; it is to avoid losing your money . . . and in commodities about 90% of the players lose . . . need I say more?

Since commodity trading and stock market investing are not 100% sure things, the shrewd speculator will do everything within his power to develop a method of marshalling his cash assets in addition to timing his entries.

After all, commodity trading is a business. I cannot think of a business that does not have some form of cash management. Too often people forget that speculating is a business. They think it is a game or a challenge.

Well, it is both those things, but to win that game and challenge one must start from a business viewpoint. One must do everything possible to eliminate the probability of losing.

Wise money management prevents major market losses from occurring, which means you get to keep on playing the game. People who do not have an approach to money management end up not being able to play the game, as they are out of cash and do not have any money left to manage!

The history of financial panics is perhaps the best teacher we have of the importance of money management. Look, if you will, at the Knickerbocker trust panic of 1907. There had been early warnings of financial panic. Those of Jacob Schiff in 1906 were the best. He told bankers that "If the currency conditions of this country are not changed materially . . . you will have such a panic in this country that it will make all previous panics look like child's play."

Shortly thereafter, the Bank of England's gold account made new lows for the decade and the Bond market was hit with an absence of buyers. While this was taking place, none other than J. P. Morgan (who had recently taken up religion to the point of singing in Episcopal Church services) came into the central thrust of the panic. To stave off the panic with stock prices crashing, Morgan did two wise money management things. First of all, he began to

169

whip the trusts, stock companies, in shape to create financial stability. More importantly, Morgan provided cash to save the Knickerbocker trust. Depending on which story you listen to, Morgan personally put anywhere from 15 to 20 million dollars into the trust and various support systems for the marketplace and corporate economy. According to one account, Morgan agreed to purchase U.S. Steel Bonds to the tune of some 23 million dollars.

What saved a potential disaster for Morgan as well as the country was that he had enough capital to step in at the right time.

Morgan, and perhaps the country according to some historians, would have met a terminal margin call. Fortunately, for most parties concerned, this never came about because Morgan had enough capital to weather the storm.

This then is the first lesson of successful money management. You must have enough capital to weather more than the worst storm. I will write more about the formula for exactly how much capital "more than the worst storm" is. But for now I hope you have learned the lesson.

The crash of 1929 is an equally interesting case of money management. The reason people jumped out of office buildings, the reason corporation after corporation went bankrupt was not just because of a sense of fear throughout America, but the simple plain fact that we ran out of money. This happened for two reasons. The Federal Reserve System started tightening up money supply in late 1927, hence there were simply no dollars around. Additionally, corporations as well as individuals, had overextended themselves . . . bad money management . . . so when the storm came they didn't have cash to sit out the bad spell. The results were absolute disaster.

The best synopsis that I have heard (fortunately, or unfortunately, I was not old enough to have lived through the experience) was told to me when I was running for the U.S. Senate in Montana in 1978, a highly inflationary time period.

An elderly lady at a town meeting said the inflationary time period we were seeing then was very similar to what happened in the 30's. She said, "In the 20's we had no money so we could not buy anything. Now we have money but it doesn't buy anything." The conditions, she thought, were essentially the same.

Finally, I could never forget the story my wife's grandfather tells of having raised 300 lb. hogs that he couldn't sell for 25¢. Not 25¢ a pound, but 25¢ each! Since he couldn't sell them, and it cost too much for gas to take them to town, he had to take them to the back of his pasture and shoot them. So there you have it on a global scale; the effect of poor, or no, money management.

The bottom line of good money management is that you must always have enough capital. Just as the bottom line in sustaining a marriage is that you have to have enough love to last through the rocky times, so it is with trading commodities, stocks or any speculative endeavor. You must have enough of the basic energy, money in our case, to allow you to hang in.

It has been said, and documented throughout history, that some 80% of traders in stocks or commodities lose money. One study I was privileged to see showed that 85% of brokers at a major brokerage firm lost money trading in their own accounts!

The one reason we have such a high failure rate in speculation is because people like me have turned a small amount of money into a large amount of money. In the chapter on day trading, read how I turned $2,000 into over $30,000 in just a few months. Our success causes others to "go for broke"–and they usually do.

That makes for good interesting reading, but that is certainly not the way to success in commodity trading. Discipline and knowledge are the cornerstones to success. Not plunging for spectacular profits.

Whenever logical, rational, approaches appear to offer people little way out of their situation they try "luck" to elevate themselves psychologically or financially. But luck is not the answer. Wild forays, even though they could produce spectacular gains, are not the correct approach.

I believe a large part of the commodity trader's psychological makeup revolves around trying to prove something, not to better themselves financially. Thus, they do not have a rational approach to money management. Their motivation is not money, it's ego.

This is compounded by the fact that the greatest thrill in speculation is the thrill of winning. Some say this is the greatest thrill in life. At times I cannot argue with that.

Even with hindsight and years between me and what happened, I vividly recall my most exciting days in the marketplace would be the big losses. They are not necessarily enjoyable times, but they are highly exciting. Losing 50 to 100 thousand dollars in a day pumps more adrenaline into your brain than you can ever imagine...dumping over $1,000,000 is really exhilarating!

The heart of speculation, some psychologists say, is nothing more than excitement. Therefore, all commodity traders are in the game for excitement.

The best way of quickly achieving or compounding excitement is well known to professional gamblers.

One of the flashier professional gamblers said, "The only excitement of gambling is risking more than you can afford." A famous Hollywood screenwriter once said, "It is no fun gambling if I lose $2,000 and just write a check for it. What is thrilling is to make out a check for $15,000 knowing there is not a penny in the bank." I believe commodity speculators are grossly misunderstood, in that people think they tend to be greedy and are playing the game for financial rewards. We are not — we play for the thrill of it.

Even one of the world's most famous authors, Dostoevsky, was a plunger who openly admitted the main thing was the play itself. He swore greed for money had nothing to do with it. It was his passion for play that kept him in the game until he was totally ruined. Only then could he shake the devil from his back.

I hope by now you have had enough of the scenarios that develop to understand the importance of money management.

Money Management is the controlling or winning factor.

It is, if you will, the garlic or silver cross to hold in front of the Dracula or werewolf from the margin department. Commodity traders are always exposed to risk which can totally wipe us out. We need some type of barrier between us and risk. The barrier is not your system, intelligence, your billions, or good looks. That barrier can be only one thing: a correct form of money management.

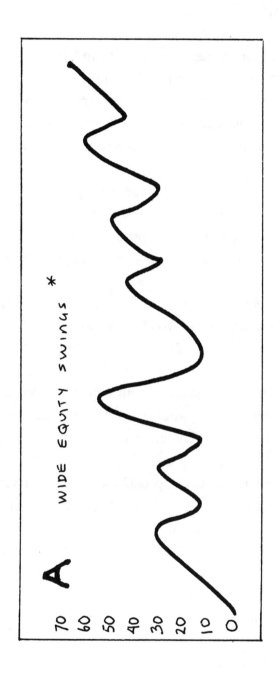

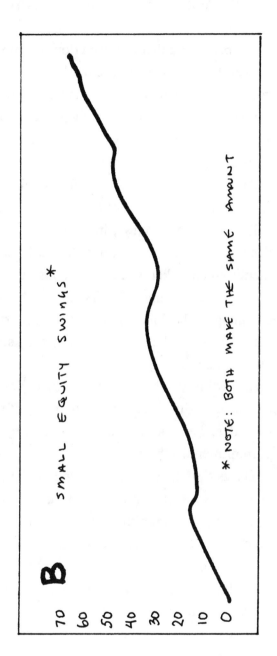

173

APPROACHES TO MONEY MANAGEMENT

The best thing that has been done on money management has come from Las Vegas and the gambling capitals of the world, not from Wall Street tycoons. Keeping in mind that the goal of effective money management is to increase your commitment to the market when you have the advantage in your favor and decrease your commitment to the market when the advantages are not in your favor, one can break this down into several basic money management approaches.

There are two basic philosophies running through all money management approaches. The first one is to increase your commitment to the market when you are winning.

The other approach is, ironically, exactly the opposite. This approach says you should decrease your commitment to the market when you are winning and increase your commitment to the market when you are losing.

The thinking behind the first approach is that when you are on a streak, push it to your full advantage. The thinking behind the second approach is that if you have a method that is right the majority of the time and the method starts having losing trades you are only that much closer to a winning trade.

Accordingly, when you have had a winning trade, or several winning trades, in a system and are out of balance with the numbers of winners that you would expect for a given number of trades, then you are that much closer to a losing trade. Therefore you want to reduce this commitment to the market.

Charts shown here depict when I think you can use the two approaches. Note that in Chart A you have a trading approach that has wide equity swings. Then it is advantageous to decrease your commitment to the market as you are meeting with success and increase your commitment to the market as you are meeting with failure. This should be self-explanatory from looking at the charts. As you can see, when you have huge run-ups in equity they only foretell a decrease or decline in equity prior to the next upsurge.

Chart B shows a different system. In this one there is very little equity dip. In this case the system is so reliable that as soon as you have made money from the system you want to pile it right back into the system because it is less erratic than its performance.

My own trading approach to the market shows that few, if in fact any, systematic approaches to trading commodities produce the type of portfolio results shown in Chart B.

So for my money, I think it is best to decrease your commitment to the market after strings of losses. Accordingly the various portfolio strategies I will suggest in the rest of this chapter are based on assumptions made from studying these charts.

First, though, let's learn all we can about risk, reward, probability and gaming theory before constructing a working approach.

THE ODDS OF DOUBLING YOUR MONEY

Few traders know it, but we can figure out, mathematically, the odds or chances of a commodity trader doubling his initial capital. The first criteria we need is the advantage you have over the game. In this case the game is commodity trading. The advantage, for our purposes, will be the odds that each trade you have will be a successful trade. If the odds are dead even it would be a 50-50 chance of making money on a given trade.

The second criteria will be the percent of capital needed for each individual trade.

On the following chart is shown the advantage you will have over the market, combined with the amount of capital at risk on each trade. The resulting number will be the chance you have of doubling your money. Finally, the fourth column shows the average number of trades you will have to make to double your money.

There are two significant facts to be gleaned from the chart. The first is that it is possible to have a riskless approach to trading commodities if one has a large enough advantage in the game and uses a small commitment of capital to trade in the markets.

Who would ever think it was possible to have a 99% probability of being successful in the market? Not many people.

If we have a system that is correct 60% of the time and if we commit 10% of our capital per trade we have an 88% probability of doubling our money, if we are willing to stick around for 75 trades. Interestingly enough, most of the short and intermediate term systems that I am aware of will require approximately 1 1/2 years for that number of trades to develop. Thus, a conservative approach to trading commodities could be said to double your money every 1 1/2 years — if you do in fact have a method that has a 60% advantage in the game and you're committing only 10% of your capital.

175

% of time System Wins	Size of "Wager" as % of Capital	Odds of Doubling Captial	Number of Trades to Double
55%	5%	87%	241
	10%	73%	80
	15%	60%	55
57.5%	5%	95%	220
	7%	90%	125
	10%	82%	75
	15%	76%	47
60%	5%	99%	170
	10%	88%	75
	15%	79%	40
65%	5%	99%	110
	10%	95%	60
	15%	88%	35
70%	10%	98%	50
	15%	94%	30
	20%	88%	20

Notice what happens if we have a system that is 70% correct and we commit 10% of our capital to each trade. Here we also have an 88% chance of doubling our money. Not much has changed there. The big change comes from the number of trades needed to double our money. We need only 50 trades to double our money instead of 75 trades.

The trick is to have a system that is highly accurate and to be willing to make a large commitment with your bankroll.

For practical purposes, a good trading system should give you a 60 to 70 percent win/loss ratio.

Accordingly, if your objective is to double your money with the highest degree of reliability, it appears you will want to commit approximately 5% of your capital on a per trade basis. That will give you an 87% chance of doubling your money but will take approximately 3 years to do so.

It will depend on your individual feelings as to what parameters you want to take — depending on how large a chance of doubling your money you want to have. You can use the table to help you determine how a system should be traded in terms of capital preservation. If you have a system that is just 50% correct you are obviously going to have to trade with less of your bankroll than with a system with 60% accuracy.

In summation, a commodity trader can indeed make money if he will do only two things; first, find a method or system that gives him an advantage over "the game." I would want a 55% advantage of wins to losses, with, of course losses less than wins. Second, the trader must make a commitment to each trade not on his whims or emotions but as a % of working capital. The more the % of commitment the less the chance of winning — but — the shorter the time period to win will be. The higher the percent of accuracy of the trading system the more capital you can commit to it, and additionally the shorter the time it will take for success to be attained.

% of
time
System
WINS

CONSECUTIVE LOSING TRADES

% of time System WINS	-2	-3	-4	-5	-6	-7
40	64.00	78.40	87.04	92.22	95.33	97.20
45	69.75	83.36	90.85	94.97	97.23	98.48
50	75.00	87.50	93.75	96.88	98.44	99.22
55	79.75	90.89	95.90	98.15	99.17	99.63
60	84.00	93.60	97.44	98.98	99.59	99.84
65	87.75	95.71	98.50	99.47	99.82	99.94
70	91.00	97.30	99.19	99.76	99.93	99.98

Probability Next Trade
will be a winner if last x# of Trades
have Lost.

The next table reflects the probabilities that any given trade in a system will be correct.

The left column shows the percent of accuracy of a given system. I have taken 5 possible systems: one with 45% accuracy, one with 50% accuracy, one with 55% accuracy, one with 60% accuracy and one with a 65% rate of accuracy. Then, reading across from left to right, I have devised a number that shows you what the probabilities are that the next trade will be successful if the last trade was not successful.

If you have a system that is 45% correct and that last trade was not successful you then have a 69.8% probability that the next trade will be successful. If you have two consecutive losing trades in a row you have an 83.4% probability that the next trade will be successful. If you had four losing trades in a row you have a 90.8% probability of the next trade being successful. If you have had 5 losing trades in a row you would have a 95% probability that the next trade will be successful. Then if you are unlucky enough to have 6 losers in a row, you would have a 97.2% probability that the next trade will be a winner.

This table yields fascinating and powerful numbers for money management.

Again, assuming you have an average system, one that is correct 50% of the time, you can quickly see that if you have had two consecutive losing trades you have an 85% probability that the following trade will be successful. Even more importantly, if you have had 3 losing trades in a row you have a 93.7% probability that the next table will be successful.

Let me separate the difference between odds and probability.

The odds of the system can never be changed. You will always have 50% odds that the next trade in the system will be correct.

But the probability of the next trade being correct is arrived at from different data. While the odds are constant and remain the same (the odds are always the percent of accuracy of the system), the probability of the next trade being correct is based on data of frequency of occurrences. Obviously with a 50/50 system about half of the trades should be correct, but when we have a string of consecutive losers the probabilities of the next trade being a winner are enhanced, as the above table depicts.

Do you doubt that? Then consider the following. I present you with a deck of cards, and your task is to select the ace of spades. Your chance of drawing it is 1 in 52. After you draw out 10 cards, your chances have improved to 1 in 42. Let's say all cards are drawn but 2, without the ace appearing. Now you have a 50/50 chance of drawing the card.

If we assume, as a trader must, that this system will continue working as well in the future as it has in the past, then after each loss (card taken out of the deck) the probability of getting the right card, a winning trade, has increased.

People trading with a limited number of dollars would want to wait until there have been enough consecutive losing trades that the probabilities are substantially in their favor of being successful.

Look what happens if you have a system that is correct 55% of the time: here if you wait for four consecutive losers you have an almost 96% probability that your following trade will be successful and a 98% probability that if that trade loses the next trade will be successful.

Now we are talking about some important data for money management! If you are to take only the trades in a 55% advantage system following 3 consecutive losers, your probabilities of each trade being a winner are 95%+.

Those are pretty good batting averages, especially for commodity traders. Let me point out that both of the above tables only depict figures and statistics ... anything is possible trading commodities. I have seen some 55% systems have as many as 7 to 10 consecutive losing trades. I also believe that the average trader has too many emotions rambling around in his head to consistently use the two tables presented here as his money management strategy.

Hopefully they will guide you if nothing else; also remember odds are stronger than probabilities.

Unfortunately, most commodity traders are more concerned with picking tops and bottoms and beating the market than making money.

But if your objective is to win money it can be done, despite what your broker, friends and neighbors, banker or minister tell you.

It is simply a question of having the intelligence to devise or purchase a method that has a good probability of winning and then having the discipline to correctly manage money in terms of the commitment you make based on trade selection criteria.

There is a critical difference between what money management can do for you in games of chance, Las Vegas style, and commodity trading.

Please let me explain: the way the market moves can be depicted as shown here. The market has bases of accumulation and distribution and then runups. Then another base of accumulation/distribution and a rundown, and on it goes. And always has. The market moves out of the trading range into an explosive move, into another trading range and then on to another explosive move.

The money is made, of course, in the explosive moves.

If you could simply isolate the explosive moves you would have the correct system.

There is a way we can help isolate these explosive moves. Keep in mind that the structure of the market calls for a time period of choppy market activity before substantial moves begin.

During most choppy market activity we will have a succession of losing trades as the market whips back and forth. If you are waiting for, say, three losing trades, the probabilities of a winning trade are in your favor (as we know from the above tables). We also know from the market structure chart that the odds the next trade will be a <u>big</u> winner are also increased because of the way the market moves. It goes from choppy periods to explosive periods, explosive periods to choppy periods. A study of any trading system shows that the average win following a number of consecutive losing trades is greater than the average win of the system in general. All bets in a 50/50 gambling game pay off 1 to 1. In commodity trading a 50/50 "bet" may pay off 1 to 1 or 10 to 1 because of market structure.

That bears out in real time application.

FROZEN PORK BELLIES	700105/800507
GROSS P/L	97688.34
TOTAL PROFIT	230756.91
AVE PROFIT	1053.68
TOTAL LOSS	-133068.56
AVE LOSS	-521.84
AVE PROF / AVE LOSS	2.02
% RETURN ON MARGIN	653.08
MAX UNREAL PROF	8289.09
MAX REAL PROF	7686.89
MAX UNREAL LOSS	-1610.27
MAX REAL LOSS	-1610.27
TOTAL # TRADES	474
# PROF TRADES	219
# LOSS TRADES	255
% OF TRADES PROF	46.20
TOT #DAYS IN POS	2493
# DAYS IN PROF POS	1841
# DAYS IN LOSS POS	652
AVE # DAYS IN POS	5
AVE # DAYS IN + POS	8
AVE # DAYS IN - POS	3
MAX # LOSSES IN A ROW	6
WRST RUN IN A +TRDE	-916.56
MIN EQTY IN SPAN	-2913.73
MAX EQTY LOSS IN SPAN	6804.41
STDEV OF LOSS TRADES	301.31
COMMISSION	54.00
MARGIN	1500.00
VALUE OF 1 UNIT MOVE	380.00

BELLIES FOLLOWING 3 LOSSES

Losing Trades ($)				Winning Trades ($)			
321	45	471	55	756	1809	311	458
	227	1459	19	2430	1834	829	1814
399	346		604	926	65	1075	1582
239	618		461	359	2845	329	223
	918		145	511	2003	3815	
286	857		312	723	1044	1422	
573	286		939	561	31	2407	
952	227		154	2728	899	1351	
						231	

NET + 38,060
NET - 8,324
69% Correct

Profit 4.5 times loss

181

Shown here is a system I devised for trading Pork Bellies. The data was run from 1970 to May 1980. As you can see from the table, the system is 46.2% correct with a gross profit of $97,688.00. More importantly though, the average profitable trade was $1,053.00. The next table shows what happens in the Belly trading system when we waited for 3 consecutive losing trades before we started trading. As you can see, there are 16 losing trades and 37 winning trades, giving this an accuracy of 69%.

Notice what happened. On balance the system itself was 46% correct. Yet when we waited for 3 consecutive losing trades our probabilities increased to almost 70%. That's staggering!

Most fascinating is that it is right in line with the probability table, which shows that after 2 consecutive losing trades we have a 60% probability the next trade will be a winner.

The wisdom of trading in such a fashion is further enhanced when we realize that it took 474 trades to produce that $97,688 profit.

That means that on balance we were trading for $206.00 profit on each trade, whether that was a winner or loser. Yet when we switched to waiting for 3 consecutive losing trades in a row, we then had a net profit of $29,736 divided by 53 trades, which shows our average trade was for $561.00. In short, we more than doubled the amount of money made per trade, while at the same time increasing our probability that the trades would be accurate! Again I want to dwell on the fact that most traders will not be able to exercise this amount of discipline. Even though this is the most reliable and most consistently profitable way to trade the market. Recent articles in "learned" journals claim that "higher expected returns cause the risk of ruin to increase faster . . . doubling the rate of return from 20% to 40% . . . almost quadruples the possibility of ruin."

This is not true if one uses correct money management. What I have shown here is that you can increase your return by using a three-tiered approach to managing money. The first tier is to have a system that gives you an advantage over the game. The second tier is to commit a correct amount of money based on the chances of winning. The third tier is to wait for a string of successive losses for entering the market. Once you have a winning series, move back to the sidelines and wait for another string of losses before stepping in.

Another interesting strategy comes from the one I use in games of chance where the odds are against me, and from studying clusters of losses. In my computer study of probabilities (containing 25,000 occurrences) at no time did three consecutive losses occur three times in a row. In other words, you will hardly . . . if ever . . . see the following pattern. Win, loss, loss, loss, win, loss, loss, loss, win, loss, loss (and finally) another loss.

182

A trader may seek out clusters of losses to develop his trading strategy. Incidentally, 25,000 "trades" would take an active system 480 years! These clusters of losses can help you in "cherry picking" trades.

CONSTRUCTING AN APPROACH TO MONEY MANAGEMENT

If the commodity speculator knew, for sure, when he had an advantage over the marketplace he could construct a more successful money management approach. If he knew when he was at a disadvantage with his trades he would know at that point to decrease his commitment.

There are three other elements one needs to look at to develop successful money management.

First, a person who has $10,000 must out of necessity have a different philosophy from the person with $100,000. They both need to develop a system to manage their capital. But it will be different. Second, you should study the overall system you will be trading to see how bad the system gets when it is at its worst. This shows you how much capital is needed to pull through the worst of times. Finally, one needs to know the odds of the next trade being successful. Certainly a system that produces 40% winners needs a different money management approach than one that produces 60% winners.

Keep in mind that the whole point of having money management is for risk avoidance. While human nature wants to maximize profits, money management is to avoid risk.

In a nutshell, risk avoidance simply means that regardless of what happens you will have enough capital to survive, recoup your losses, regroup your strength and continue playing the game.

THE OTHER SIDE OF THE COIN

Gambling literature is full of sage advice that says the key to casinos is to bet when the advantage is in your favor.

That is the whole function behind the approaches brilliant people such as Julian Braun have taken to the blackjack table and have been so highly successful with.

It is the same approach we need for the commodity market. Let's first establish the amount of capital that you will need to trade: the first step is to see what type of risk you need to avoid.

That means you must have data telling you what the worst possible drawdown or disaster has been for your system for the last 5 years. You need to determine what the worst equity dip has been. If the system made $100,000 trading Silver in the last five years you not only need to focus on that figure but also have to check to see the maximum amount of money needed for the worst drawdown. Perhaps the system lost $50,000 at one point before it comes back to the win side. Therefore, you would have needed at least $50,000 in capital plus enough margin for one contract.

MY OPERATING RULE

My operating rule for successful money management is that you first determine the maximum risk exposure you have seen in the past. Multiply that by 150% to tell you the amount of cushion you will need, to make certain that no matter what happens (in fact if things get worse by 50% than we have ever seen before) you will still be able to trade.

Let's take a look at an actual example using the Pork Belly system mentioned earlier. Maximum equity drawdown using the system was $6,804. This means you would have had to have $6,804, plus enough margin to trade one contract, to weather that worst possible storm. We would take $6,804 and multiply that by 150%, meaning that to successfully trade the system you would have to have $10,206 plus enough margin for 1 contract. This is the base from which you can start trading. What we have done here is protect ourselves from the risk of ruin. We next want to turn our attention to figuring out a way to maximize money management to increase the profitable results from a system while further limiting our exposure.

184

The best way to make certain that you are a successful trader is to understand the difference between speculating versus gambling. You can tell the difference by simply going to Las Vegas where the system is stacked against you.

In fact we can figure, mathematically, what the odds are of a commodity trader doubling his initial capital.

As an example of the difference between theoretical and actual performance I am next showing results that a leading advisor sent out to his followers. As you can see, his theoretical results were quite good. Theoretically he should have been making money, but in actuality his accounts were losing money.

THE SIMULATED TRACK RECORDS
OF CSCRPM, INC.'S
$35,000 19-COMMODITY "MWT3 W" NET PERFORMANCE
REACHES A 14 WEEK HIGH!

THE ACTUAL TRACK RECORD
OF CSCRPM, INC.'S
$35,000 19-COMMODITY
"MWT3 W" NET PERFORMANCE
MAKES A 14 WEEK LOW . . .

TWO MONEY MANAGEMENT APPROACHES

Now I want to share with you what I think are the best money management approaches. If you recall from earlier in the chapter, I said that you must first determine the amount of money you have to trade a system and that you should have enough for one contract plus 150% of the maximum equity dip seen. If your maximum equity dip was $10,000, you are going to have to have $15,000 plus margin for one commodity. If you then start trading that commodity on a one contract basis you may be successful.

You can begin adding to your commitment to the market in one of two ways. The first, and most conservative approach, is to simply wait until you have made enough money (150% of the maximum drawdown) . . . to trade one more unit. In the case of the system cited above, you would have to earn $15,000, at which point you could then start trading 2 contracts. Once you made another $15,000 you could increase and take 3 contracts on every trade, and you would probably be trading 6 to 10 contracts.

Notice you have correctly managed your money at all times. You always had enough for the worst possible equity dip seen and are playing the game the way it should be played.

In any game where you have the advantage, the most successful approach will be to have small commitments over a long time period. In a game where the odds are against you the only way you can come close to beating the game is to have large commitments on a small number of wagers. The person who tries to beat the gambling casinos with small bets is literally chicken feed for the casinos because the odds, which are against the player, will catch up with him. The only way you can ever hope to overcome the odds in a casino is to have large commitments over a short time period, hoping you can catch times when lady luck runs in the favor of the player not the house. If you stay around long enough, lady luck leaves the tables and probabilities take over.

Probabilities are much more powerful than lady luck. That is why we want to have smaller commitments to the market with a lot of capital behind us. We have probabilities, not lady luck, on our side when we are following a successful system . . . if we can but keep the doors open long enough we will prosper.

THE SECOND APPROACH TO MONEY MANAGEMENT

Over the years I have tried many ways of increasing the profits from a system. My first attempts were mostly rudimentary versions of the old Martingale philosophy that after one losing trade I would take two contracts. On my next losing trade I take four contracts, and on my next losing trade I double up again. It went one, then two contracts, then four, then eight, then sixteen, then thirty two contracts, etc. After a string of 6 losses I was trading 64 contracts. That's hard. It takes a tremendous amount of money, let alone guts.

What I have devised over the years, since that basic approach, are two methods that allow you to take advantage of increasing your earnings in a system through correct money management.

The first system is a very easy one to follow: The system says that once the actual results of the system are out-of-whack with the expectations of the system, you can then start increasing your commitment.

As an example, if you have a commodity trading system that is 60% correct, which is what most of the trading systems that I currently use are, you should wait until the results are out-of-whack with the expectations. When 6 of the last 10 trades (60%) have been unsuccessful, you should then start increasing your commitment to the market by stepping up one unit. In other words, after 6 losses you would take 2 units on the next trade. Whether that trade is a winner or a loser you would trade 2 units on the next trade, and continue trading on a 2 unit basis until you have had 6 out of the last 10 (60%) winners.

This is the most conservative approach to money management that increases your commitment. It is for people who don't need a tremendous amount of excitement but do want to enhance a system's performance.

ONE UP, BACK ONE

This next approach to money management is for those who are more speculatively inclined. It also has the unique advantage of carrying you through systems that are right only 30% to 40% of the time, still allowing you to make money without the exposure of doubling after each loss.

The way this system works is that following every losing trade you will increase your unit commitment on the next trade by 1 unit.

For the sake of discussion, say that each unit is one contract and you lose on the first trade. You would then have two contracts on the next trade. If that trade is a loser you would have three contracts. If that trade is a winner you would then revert back to two contracts for the next trade. If that trade is a winner you would step back to 1 contract. By adding one contract after every loss and deducting one contract, reducing your commitment, after every profit you will quickly find that you are able to come out on top of the situation.

The approach I have just presented to you is a successful money management approach.

I have tried a wide variety of other management approaches, such as the Martingale approach, or approaches that increase by more than one contract after every loss. Or

187

approaches that try to get two winning trades in a row with an additional commitment on both of those trades. In a system that is highly accurate, say 60%, that might be successful. But in actual trading experience, and with systems that are under 60% accuracy, I think you are going to find out the average trader simply does not have enough of a bankroll for that type of speculative activity.

As one who has studied literally thousands of gambling systems and money management approaches, I hope you believe my assessment of what works. I don't consider myself a gambler, in any way whatsoever. After all, there is a difference between gambling, which is taking chances, and speculation. Speculation comes from the Latin word specular, which means to observe. I think that is what a successful commodity trader does. He observes facts, events, and data and makes judgements as to what all of that information means and trades accordingly. A gambler simply hopes lady luck is riding with him.

There are, then, four main money management factors for you to consider. Let's assume that you have $10,000 worth of risk capital to make money with in the marketplace.

Note that this is not the approach that most traders take. They essentially see themselves as having unlimited resources, because after they lose all their money they start over again.

This is the wrong approach. You simply must say OK, I have $10,000 to risk trading commodities. Once that's gone that's it.

You also need to know why you are risking that money. You are certainly not risking the money for the fun of commodity trading or for the thrill of generating commissions for your broker. There is only one reason you are risking money; to make money.

Making money, however, is too general. You need to have a goal. Once the goal is known you can see if the amount you are risking is worth the amount of return you hope to get, your goal.

I think it is logical to assume that if you are risking $10,000 you would want to be rewarded or have a gain of at least an equal amount. In short, your goal would also be $10,000.

The remaining two factors would be the advantage you have over the game of commodity trading. If you have a good system it should, on balance, have essentially the same percentage of losses in the future as it has had in the past. The last controlling factor, and it is a factor you do have control over, is the amount of contracts you will take on any given trade. In other words, how much of your stake are you willing to risk on each trade?

These and only these are the four key elements of money management. It is the disciplined ability to monitor these four elements that will enable you to make money. You have control of risk capital, the system you choose, your goals and your trade size. There is only one uncontrollable element left in this approach . . . actual trading.

Even Pascal proved, way back in 1654, that your chances of winning a gambling game even when the odds are against you can exceed 50% just on the way you manage your money and controlling the size of your bet. You now know that if you place very small wagers in a game that is stacked against you, you will ultimately lose your bankroll.

The other side of that coin is that when you place small bets on a game where the odds are in your favor you ultimately will come out a winner.

The first rule of good money management must be that your bet size must be a small enough percentage of your capital to insure that when things get bad and luck and everything else run against you, there is still enough money to weather the storm. That one or two, or even five or six, or even ten or twelve, losing trades will not send you to the poorhouse.

It is for this reason that your commitments need to be held at a constant value. In other words, the vast majority of the time you should be trading the same number of contracts on each and every trade. On occasion we can tell that the advantage is more in our favor. Only then will you want to gingerly increase your commitment to the market. When the advantage is against you, you will want to decrease your commitment to the market.

In my own trading style I have a variety of indicators and tools that I use to trade the market. When I see that these are preponderously Bullish I will take a large position on a buy signal. But unless these criteria are there, I simply revert back to my base unit, whatever it happens to be, for the commodity or system that I am trading.

I do a good deal of day trading. I usually day trade 25 Standard and Poor's contracts every market day. If, however, my indicators are extremely Bullish I may step that up to 50 contracts. That is the exception rather than the rule. The rule is to stick by my fixed units. Losers always overtrade, winners always undertrade. A sign I saw in Paul Tudor Jones' office says it best, "Big Positions Cause Big Problems."

Hopefully, some of the tools in this book will give you an insight into when the market is more ready to respond to buy or sell signals that will develop.

We can also use statistics to tell us when the market should respond more favorably to our signals. The best way of doing this is to simply see if the system has been clicking or not. So the second source of knowledge about our advantage comes from the system's current performance.

189

ACTUAL MONEY MANAGEMENT APPROACHES

Now let's look at how we can apply this great general theoretical discussion to actual application.

CHANCE CONTROL

What I want to now focus on is controlling the chance, or probability, that our next trade in the commodity market will be a winner.

First, let me say that I need to break down the various commodity systems. There are those that usually have winning trades 40% of the time or more. The 40% winning systems can make money because the profits are so much larger than the losses. Generally, systems will break down into one of these two categories. I will talk about both categories.

If you have a system that is correct 40% of the time or less, then I would suggest that you try the following approach to improve your system's performance: Await three consecutive losing trades. If you have had three losing trades, and have been trading one contract on each trade, following the third losing trade, go to two contracts on the next trade. If that trade is a loser, stop the process and again wait until you have three losing trades. Following three more losing trades, go to three contracts on the next trade. If that trade is a winner, fine, start back at one. If that trade is a loser, wait until you have three more consecutive losing trades. Take four contracts on the next signal, etc.

If you have a system that is correct 50% of the time or more, wait for two losing trades and then begin the method I have just taught you.

In summation, a commodity trader can indeed make money if he will do only two things: First find a method or system that gives him an advantage over "the game." I would want a 55% advantage of wins to losses, with, of course, losses less than wins. Second, the trader must make a commitment to each trade based not on his whims or emotions but as a % of working capital. The smaller the % of commitment the greater the chances of winning. The larger the % of commitment the less the chance of winning — but the shorter the time period to win will be.

DEVIATION FROM THE NORM

Here is another interesting approach to money management. Let's say you have a system that should be right 60% of the time. When it suddenly is wrong 60% of the time, then start increasing your commitment to the market, taking one additional contract on every trade until the system swings back into being correct 60% of the time.

Any system will have highs and lows. I have seen systems that are 60% correct be right 15 trades in a row. By the same token, I have seen those 60% correct systems drop to the point of being correct only 30% of the time. What I want to see is a 60% system suddenly go into the area of being correct only 40% of the time. Then I take an additional unit on every signal until the system is back to being correct 60% of the time. This is a very profitable way of increasing your total dollars of profit without substantially increasing your risk because you are only adding one unit on each signal. You are essentially waiting until the pendulum has swung one way . . . and then riding the pendulum back to the positive area . . . then decreasing your exposure just before it may swing back to the other direction.

Finally, I would like to reveal to you what I think may be the best strategy for a well capitalized, grind-it-out approach.

We are playing a game where the advantages are in our favor. Despite what your broker, friends, bankers, neighbors and every one else will tell you, this means that we need to have as much of a "grind-it-out" approach as possible.

After all, we have already learned that a sure way to lose money in a gambling casino, where the advantage is against you, is to make small bets over a long period. Casino's love that. What we have to remember is that we are the opposite of players in the casino. We are the casino. The odds are in our favor. Accordingly, we need to have a system that grinds it out.

What can the best grind system be?

The best grind approach I have been able to come up with that works even on systems that are correct only 40% of the time works as follows: Wait for three losing trades in a row. Following these three losing trades, on the next trade take two units or contracts. If that trade is a losing trade, we would then increase to have three units on the next trade. If that trade is a losing trade, four units. And on you would continue. After each losing trade you would add one additional unit. By the same token, when you get a winning trade you would step back and trade one less unit on the next trade. As an example, if you had three successive losing trades in a row on your fourth trade you would have three contracts. If that is a winner, you would then revert to two contracts on the next trade.

You do not want this string of numbers to continue running out forever. It is important to realize that once you have recouped the losses from 3 losing trades, and all other losses between them and your winning trade, you would stop and go back to your one unit basis.

Here is just one example in actual practice with a system that I followed:

		With Money Management	Without
- 795	1 contract	- 795	-795
- 681	1 contract	- 681	-681
- 410	1 contract	- 410	- 410
- 227	2 contracts	- 454	- 227
+ 458	3 contracts	+ 1374	+ 458
- 754	2 contracts	- 1508	- 754
- 700	3 contracts	- 2100	- 700
+ 1527	4 contracts	+ 6108	+ 1527
		+ 1534	- 1582

This is an interesting situation. Notice that we had a very bad run in the market. Two out of eight trades were winners. Without money management we would have lost $1,582. Yet with the money management technique that I have taught, we went from being behind to being ahead $1,534. I have used this approach on many, many commodity systems and have found it to be the best slow grind method for trading. Especially for systems that have approximately 40% accuracy.

SOME COMMON ERRORS

The most common error I have seen traders incorporate into their speculative action would be the following: The Martingale Strategy.

Here is one that is most intriguing and that I have played around with myself. It says that after every losing trade you double the number of contracts that you were trading on the last trade. If you have one contract on a trade and lost, on the next trade you would have two. If that lost, you step up to four. If that lost you would have eight. If that lost you would have sixteen, if that lost you would have 32, if that lost you would have 64.

Between you and I, dear reader, I have played this game and it is the most precarious, the most thrilling, challenging . . . and sickening way to trade the market.

First of all, most of us don't have the capital to play in that fashion. And even if we did the problem is the one winning trade you finally get with your 64 contracts may only be for a couple of cents, not enough to recoup all of your previous losses. Most of us simply cannot handle the tremendous trauma and psychological pressure that go with this approach. Additionally, it requires a great and vast amount of money or a very liberal banker to push you through this type of trading.

The next most common error I have seen is for traders to greatly increase their commitment to the market following their winnings.

I am a great believer in contrary opinion, a great believer to be contrary to anything. Whenever things have been going real well for you, that is when you have to be on guard and be careful.

Prosperity is a disaster.

Disaster is the most prosperous starting point. I question money management systems that say that once your equity has increased by some amount you will instantly start trading more contracts. Remember, the mere fact that your equity is increasing says your system has been extremely successful and success, from my experience with it, is a fleeting thing. As soon as you get it, it starts to slip away. By the same token, what I have found to be extremely profitable is failure. As soon as my systems are out of whack and I am not making money is the time to pounce upon the market, because that is the time when the pendulum will swing back to the form.

IN SUMMATION—
HOW YOU CAN NEVER LOSE TRADING COMMODITIES

For the sake of argument, I am going to assume you have a system that is right 50% of the time. There are quite a few of those on the market now. I will also make the basic assumption that the system will continue being correct 50% of the time in the future, just as it has in the past, and that the profits are larger than the losses.

If you have such a system (there are many with even better results) then it is impossible for you to lose trading commodities. How?

To begin with, I suggest you determine the largest equity drawdown that particular commodity trading system had. Let's say that the largest drawdown . . . the worst performance it ever had before it turned around and made new highs in equity, was that the system lost $12,000. I would multiply that by 150%, which means that you would have to have $18,000 worth of equity plus enough to trade the commodity. Let's say the margin for the commodity was $5,000. You would require a total of $23,000 to trade one contract of the commodity using that system.

I would continue trading on just the one contract basis until you had $18,000 profit. At that point you could double your commitment to the market and start trading with two contracts. Once you have made another $18,000 profit you could then start trading three contracts. By doing this you only increase your commitment to the market when you have increased the amount of capital you have to weather the storm. Notice that only after you have won do you increase, proportionately, the amount of capital you are willing to commit to the game when the game gets tough.

I believe this is the only way you can successfully increase your base commitment to the market. There are many systems that say you should increase your base to the market as soon as you have made 10-15-20 or 30% on your money. Perhaps even 100% on your money. I think that is a totally irrelevant and useless figure. The only relevant figure is to increase your commitment to the market when you have made enough capital to sit through the worst storm. Then you're playing with the house's money and if that storm comes along it is a little easier to see their money leave through your hands than your money.

In fact it is all your money. You earned it. Trading commodities is a most difficult way of making a living. But nonetheless, your cushion to sit through the storm is in a sense "their"

194

money. I suggest you do not start increasing your commitment to the market until they have given you plenty of a cushion. I have deliberately chosen the figure of 150% times the worst equity dip ever seen. The system may get into an even worse equity dip, but I cannot imagine a decent system having an equity dip of 50% greater than the worst one seen so far.

HOW LONG IT WILL TAKE
TO DOUBLE YOUR MONEY WITH YOUR SYSTEM

You may be interested in knowing how long it will take for you to double your money. Here is another formula to give you the answer.

What you need to do is divide the total number of profits your system has made over a long time period by the number of trades. I would suggest you use five years, without any atypical markets in there, such as the runaway Silver Bull Market of 1980.

You will then have a figure that represents the average dollars made per trade, whether it is a winning trade or a losing trade. Remember, you divide total trades into total net profits.

If, as an example, the average win per trade is $175.00 and you need a $23,000 account because you know your worst equity dip was $18,000 and margin is $5,000, you would then divide $175.00 into $23,000, which tells you that after approximately 130 trades you will double your $23,000. You should then determine how frequently your system trades. If it trades 60 times a year you are going to double your money with this system in approximately two years.

That may not sound like the most sensational thing in the world. But if you play the game in the fashion I have outlined you are literally trading commodities on a risk-free basis. You will have a 98%, or perhaps 99%, chance of coming out of the market not only a winner but a winner who has doubled his money, something precious few commodity traders ever do! Sure they dream about it, but do it? Nope, they don't!

A final error commodity traders make, and especially portfolio managers, is based on the assumption that the more commodities you have in your portfolio or stable of trading vehicles, the less erratic your performance, and hopefully, the better your performance will be.

I can think of no one better to quote to substantiate this point than Fred Gehm, who in turn cites a study done at Cornell which shows that, unfortunately, the amount each additional commodity lowers the risk of the portfolio diminishes quite quickly.

In fact, Fred says, "The total avoidable risk can never be lowered below the portfolio's correlation coefficient . . . no matter how large your portfolio is." Basically Fred says that since the coefficient should be about the same for each commodity, the risk of the total portfolio can never exceed the risk of one single commodity.

To Fred's way of thinking there is, "little reason to diversify beyond two or three commodities."

Fred can prove this with all sorts of statistical tables and mathematical formulas, that are, quite frankly, way over my head.

My proof comes from actual trading in the marketplace. At one point I was under the impression that if you had a wide basket of commodities, say 10 or more, it would be just about impossible to lose money trading commodities because when some are losing, others would be making money.

But alack and alas, my *actual* experience in the marketplace shows it is possible for all of them to lose money at the same time! That happened. It was painful, believe me. Although I may not be smart enough to figure out all of Fred Gehm's formulas I do know pain. It tells me the bottom line is that he is correct. My results show that simply increasing the number of commodities in your portfolio is not a sure fire way to success.

Wise portfolio diversification consists of adding non-related commodities. For example, a Belly, Beans and Silver make more sense than a Silver, a Gold, a Bond and a T-Bill.

My best year of trading so far was 1987 — where $10,000 went to over $1,000,000 in less than 12 months. During that time I traded primarily two commodities and used a money management approach similar to what I've taught here. I hope you will duplicate my success.

Chapter 10

The Odds of Doubling Your Money

(Editor's note: This chapter contains some of the material from the previous chapter. It is, however, expanded with greater detail and some further ideas and applications. The duplicate material has been left in for completeness).

We can figure out mathematically what the odds, or chances, are of a commodity trader doubling his initial capital given two independent criteria. The first significant criteria is the advantage that you have over the game. In this case, the game is commodity trading. The advantage, for our purposes, will be the odds that each trade will be a successful one. If the odds were dead even, it would be a 50-50 chance of making money on any given trade.

The second criteria will be the percent of capital used on each individual trade.

On the following chart is depicted the advantage you have over the market combined with the amount of capital at risk on each trade. The resulting number will be the chance you have of doubling your money. Finally, the 4th column shows the average number of trades you will have to make to double your money.

There are two significant readings to be gleaned from this chart. The first is that it is possible to have a riskless approach to trading commodities if one has a large enough advantage in the game and uses a small commitment of total capital to trade the markets.

Who would ever think it was possible to have a 99% probability of being successful in the market? Not many people.

197

The Odds of Doubling Your Money

TABLE IX

BET SIZE SELECTION TABLE

YOUR ADVANTAGE OVER THE GAME	TRADE SIZE AS PERCENTAGE OF MARGIN	CHANCE OF WINNING DOUBLE YOUR MONEY*	AVERAGE NUMBER OF TRADES TO DOUBLE MONEY
5%	3%	97%	620
	4%	92%	320
	5%	88%	240
	6%	84%	190
	10%	73%	80
7.5%	5%	95%	220
	7%	90%	125
	10%	82%	75
	12%	78%	50
10%	5%	99%	170
	9%	92%	95
	10%	88%	75
	15%	79%	40
15%	5%	99%	110
	10%	95%	60
	15%	88%	35
	20%	82%	20
20%	10%	98%	50
	15%	94%	30
	20%	88%	20

If we have a system that is correct 60% (10% advantage) of the time and commit only 5% of our capital per trade, we do in fact have a 99% probability of doubling our money, if we are willing to stick around for 170 trades. Interestingly enough, most of the short and intermediate term systems that I am aware of will require approximately 1 1/2 years for that number of trades to develop. Thus, a conservative approach to trading commodities could be said to double your money every 1 1/2 years (if you do in fact have a method that has a 60% advantage in the game and are committing only 5% of your capital).

Notice what happens if we have a system that is 60% correct and we commit 10% of our capital to each trade. Here we drop down from a 99% chance of doubling our money to an 88% chance of doubling our money. Not much has changed here. The big change, however, comes in the number of trades needed to double our money. Now we only have to have 75 trades to double our money versus having 170 trades.

Accordingly, using the same average trade per system it will take approximately half a year to double your money.

The trick, of course, is to have a system that is highly accurate and be willing to make a large commitment of your bankroll.

For practical purposes, most of the good trading systems should give you somewhere in the area of a 50 to 55 percent win/loss ratio.

Accordingly, if your objective is to double your money with a high degree of reliability, you will want to commit approximately 4% of your capital on a per trade basis. It will give you a 92% chance of doubling your money and will take approximately three years to do so.

It will vary from trader to trader as to what parameters to take, depending on how large a chance of doubling your money you desire. You can also use the table to determine how a system should be traded in terms of capital preservation in money management. If you have a system that is just 50% correct, you are obviously going to have to trade with only 2 or 3% of your bankroll on any given trade.

The higher the percent of accuracy of the trading system, the more capital you can commit to it. Additionally, you know how long it should take for success to be attained.

The next table I want to call to your attention is one that can be put to greater advantage by people who have only a small number of dollars for trading commodities.

199

% of time System WINS	CONSECUTIVE LOSING TRADES					
	-2	-3	-4	-5	-6	-7
40	64.00	78.40	87.04	92.22	95.33	97.20
45	69.75	83.36	90.85	94.97	97.23	98.48
50	75.00	87.50	93.75	96.88	98.44	99.22
55	79.75	90.89	95.90	98.15	99.17	99.63
60	84.00	93.60	97.44	98.98	99.59	99.84
65	87.75	95.71	98.50	99.47	99.82	99.94
70	91.00	97.30	99.19	99.76	99.93	99.98

Probability Next Trade
will be a winner if last x# of Trades
have Lost.

This table reflects two sets of data. One is the odds that any given trade in a system will be correct.

The left hand column shows the percent of accuracy of a given system. I have taken five possible systems: one with 45% accuracy, one with 50% accuracy, one with 55% accuracy, one with 60% accuracy, and one with 65% accuracy. Then, reading across from left to right, we have determined the probability that the next trade will be successful if the last trade was not successful.

If you have a system that is 45% correct, and the last trade was not successful and is the first unsuccessful trade, you then have a 59% probability that the next trade will be successful. If

200

you have two consecutive losing trades in a row, you have an 83% chance that the next trade will be successful. If you have four losing trades in a row, you have a 90% chance that the next trade will be successful. If you have had five losing trades in a row, you would have a 95% probability the next trade will be successful, and then if you are unlucky enough to have six losers in a row, you would have a 97% probability that the next trade will be a winner!

This table yields fascinating and powerful numbers for money management.

Again, assuming you have an average system (one that is correct 50% of the time) you can quickly see that if you have had two consecutive losing trades you have an 85% probability that the following trade will be successful. Even more importantly, if you have had three losing trades in a row, you have a 93.7% probability that the next next trade will be successful.

Let me separate the difference between odds and probability.

The odds of the system can never be changed. You will always have 50% odds that the next trade (in a system that is right 50% of the time) will be correct.

But the probabilities of the next trade being correct are arrived at differently. While the odds are constant and remain the same . . . the odds always being the percent of accuracy of the system . . . the probability the next trade will be correct is based on data of frequency of occurrences. Obviously, with a 50-50 system about half of the trades should be correct. But when we have a string of consecutive losers the probabilities of the next trade being a winner are enhanced, as the above table depicts.

This is great for people trading with a limited number of dollars who are trading a system that does not have a high degree of accuracy. Wait until you have enough consecutive losing trades that the probability of being successful is substantially in your favor.

Look what happens if you have a system that is correct 55% of the time: If you wait for four consecutive losers you have an almost 95% probability that your following trade will be successful, and a 98% probability that if that trade loses the next trade will be successful.

Those are pretty good batting averages, especially for commodity traders. Let me point out that both of the above tables only depict figures and statistics. Anything is possible trading commodities. I have seen some systems have as many as 7 to 10 consecutive losing trades. Of course, those are systems that have a low percent of accuracy. I also believe that the average trader has too many emotions rambling around in his head to consistently use the two tables presented here as his money management strategy.

Unfortunately, most commodity traders are more concerned about picking tops and bottoms and beating the market than making money.

But if your objective is to win money, it can be done despite what your broker, friends, neighbors, banker or minister tell you.

It is simply a question of having the intelligence to devise or purchase a method that has a good probability of winning, and then having the emotions and discipline to correctly manage money in terms of the commitment you make per trade and the trade selection criteria.

WHY LOSSES ARE SO PROFITABLE

The most significant thing I can tell you about waiting for a consecutive number of losing trades in any method is that a unique factor also develops. After you have had three or four losing trades in a row, the probability of the next trade being not only a winner but a substantial winner is way in your favor.

Let me explain this to you. The way the market moves can be depicted by bases of accumulation and distribution and then run-ups. Then another base accumulation and distribution, then a run-down. And on it goes, as it always has. The market moves into a trading range, out of the trading range, into an explosive move, into another trading range, and then into another explosive move.

The money is made, of course, in the explosive moves.

If you could simply isolate the explosive moves, you would have the perfect system.

There is a way we can help isolate these explosive moves. The structure of the market calls for a time period of choppy market activity before substantial moves begin.

During most choppy market activity we will have a succession of losing trades as the market whips back and forth. If you are waiting for, say, three losing trades the probability of a winning trade is in your favor, as we know from the above tables. We also know from the structure of the market the odds the next winning trade will be a big winning trade are also increased because of the way the market moves. It goes from choppy periods to explosive periods, explosive periods to choppy periods. Correct money management then will show the average win following a number of consecutive losing trades will be greater than the average win of the system in general.

That bears out in real time application.

In 1980 I wrote about a method of trading for Pork Bellies from 1970 to 1980. The method was 46.2% accurate, the average profit per trade was $206. The following reprint from the system manual tells the story.

TRADE SELECTION – HOW TO INCREASE THE BELLY PROFITS $57,166, THE COPPER PROFITS $21,017.

I have studied so many forms of money management that even I can't believe it; from the gambler's specials like Martingale to the computer boys % of portfolio increase. Most are very complicated. What I am about to show you is not complicated at all and requires little extra margin money to participate in. Most money management systems suppose you have unlimited dollars. You and I know that is not true.

Even worse yet, one "hot" money management method I saw had you buying 600+ contracts of bellies on a signal to achieve their "good" results. Come on, who's kidding who? It's hard enough to get 60 bellies filled, let alone 600. Needless to say it was written by a college professor!

The system of money management I have developed for the Belly program is based on what I call chance control. At no time does it involve pyramiding or chasing a losing streak with more positions or money.

The idea came to me while fly fishing in Montana. I noticed that the last few times I'd gone fishing my "luck" was very bad. That was unusual as I normally limit out (if I want to) yet on this particular trip I again "hit my stride" and had a dandy day of fishing.

That set me to thinking, maybe the markets are like fishing in that after several bad sessions a good one is coming very, very soon. If so we might be able to isolate the big winners.

THE THREE LOSS RULE

I looked at my methods and quickly realized that indeed the theory is correct, given any method that usually works 50% of the time. If it falls apart and has THREE CONSECUTIVE LOSING TRADES then you can start "betting" that a good one is due. This is a trade selection.

If you apply this concept to Bellies, some amazing things start happening . . . you start catching the big winners and increase the % of accuracy from the standard system's 50% to over 60%!

THE RULE

All one needs do is wait for three consecutive losing trades, then take two contracts on each trade thereafter **until** you have a winning trade. Had you done that in Bellies the net profit would have been increased by $29,736. I'm listing here the trades one would have taken following the three trade rule. You will note they are marked on the computer printouts that follow as well.

BELLIES THREE LOSS RULE RESULTS

Losing Trades				Winning Trades				
321	45	571	55	756	1809	311	458
	227	1459	19	2430	1834	829	1814
399	346		604	926	65	1075	1582
239	618		461	359	2845	329	223
	918		145	511	2003	3815	
286	857		312	723	1044	1422	
573	286		939	561	31	2407	
952	227		154	2728	899	1351	
						231	

NET + 38,060

NET - 8,324

69% Correct

Profit 4.5 times loss

Notice what happened. On balance the system itself was 46% correct. Since we waited for three consecutive losing trades, our probabilities increased to almost 70%. That's staggering!

Most fascinating is that it is right in line with the trade probability, which showed that after two consecutive trades we have a 60% probability the next trade would be a winner.

The wisdom of trading in such a fashion is further enhanced when we realize that it took 474 trades to produce that $97,688 profit.

That means that, on balance, we were trading for $206.00 profit on each trade, whether that was a winning or losing trade. Yet, when we switched to waiting for three consecutive losing trades in a row we then had a net profit of $29,736.00. Divided by 53 trades, this showed that our average trade was for $561.00. In short, we more than doubled the amount of money made per trade, while at the same time increased our probabilities that the trades would be accurate. Again, I want to emphasize the fact that most traders will not be able to exercise enough discipline to trade the market in this fashion. Still, this is the most reliable and consistently profitable way to trade the market.

The Odds of Doubling Your Money

I have shown here that you can increase your return by using a three-tiered approach to managing money. The first tier is to have a system that gives you an advantage over the game. Second, commit a correct amount of money based on the chances of winning. The third tier is to wait for a string of successive loses before entering the market. Once you have a winning trade then move back to the sidelines and wait for another ruin situation to hit other traders with losses before stepping in.

Next, let me show you a chart that depicts how you should "wager" given that you have, or do not have, an advantage over the "game." Note that when you do not have an advantage you have a 0% chance of winning if your bet size is small and can only "make" money if you bet large (and infrequently) hitting a lucky bet. When the advantage is with you it all reverses. Here your highest probability of winning will come with small "bets," as over the long run the system will remind you. But if you "have a hunch and bet a bunch" on any one trade in a winning system it decreases your odds of winning. That strategy works best in a negative chance game.

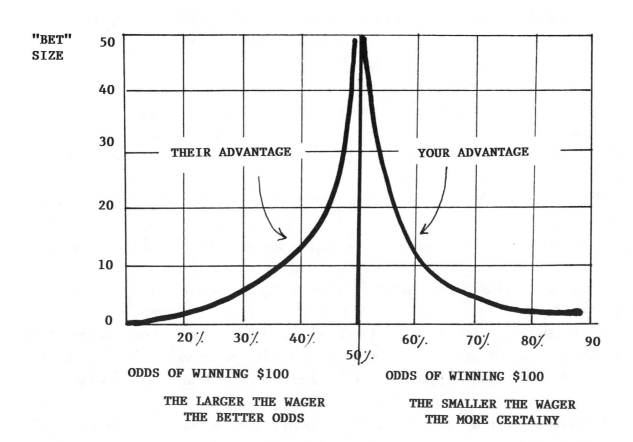

"BET" SIZE

THEIR ADVANTAGE

YOUR ADVANTAGE

50%

ODDS OF WINNING $100

ODDS OF WINNING $100

THE LARGER THE WAGER
THE BETTER ODDS

THE SMALLER THE WAGER
THE MORE CERTAINY

TRADING SYSTEM EVALUATION

In the old days a commodity system would be sold on what I call the hope, faith and charity method. The system seller would hope that a great number of people would show up, he or she would express faith in his method, and hope the students had the charity to pay him a decent price for the system.

He would show them charts of examples of what the system did in the past. We evolved to the next stage, which was showing computer printouts to verify that this did take place in all instances in the past. One had a better sense of how the system did because of all the research.

However, most of these methods were curve fit and what worked in the past may not work in the future.

Finally, in 1984, to the best of my knowledge, a system was introduced not based on what the chart book showed, but what actually happened in real time trading.

In the fall of 1984, Ed Walter and I offered a commodity system that was first traded in real-time trading for approximately 12 months prior to announcing it to the public.

The last system I offered was sold to the public on a 30% down and 70% to come from the real trading profits basis. I suppose that is the fairest way to sell a system, but so far no one else has followed my lead. A good system should have either a real-time track record or have its costs come from actual future time profits.

I believe, and hope, that in the future all commodity systems will be proven with real time dollars and real-time accounts prior to being offered to the public.

Believe me, there is a world of difference between what a system shows should happen and what actually happens, after slippage, emotional factors, and brokerage commissions are figured in. If you are going to buy a system, please use the caveats and criteria from this chapter to evaluate the system.

## Chapter 11

How To Place Your Orders

Figuring out how to manage your money, when to buy, when to sell, what commodities to buy and sell is just part of the overall game. You still have to give the actual orders to your broker for execution in the markets of your choice.

Most commodity books totally overlook this area of trading, but I think it is an important one to be commented on, especially for people who are new to trading commodities.

Sure, you can just call your broker, whomever he or she might be, place your order and walk away from the market. This is a way to trade, but it is one that I certainly don't recommend, nor do other experienced traders. To optimize your profits in the market, you can and should pay close attention to the fills you are getting on your orders. Once you start doing any trading at all . . . serious trading . . . you will find that you are very concerned about where you are filled. That is, did you buy at 58.65 as requested, or did you get filled at 58.85, which is higher than you wanted to pay?

The pursuit of profits dictates that we must not only be frugal, but we must watch each and every penny to make certain we are not being ripped off by bad fills.

I give seminars throughout the country and at virtually every seminar someone will ask me about fills. They seem to think there is a game that is played by people on the floor which is called, "Give the public bad fills."

This may or may not be true. Frankly, I don't think it is entirely true though I have certainly complained about my share of bad fills. I have been able to reduce the number of bad fills with the strategy I'm sharing with you in this chapter.

Let me first show you the importance of getting good fills.

One of the systems I use (to trade the Standard and Poor's 500 and Stock Futures Index) averages a trade about every week and a half. This means in a typical year it will trade 30 times.

On 30 occasions my broker will go into the marketplace to buy one contract of Standard and Poor's and liquidate it later on.

The commissions that I am being charged may not amount to nearly as much as slippage if I do not place my orders correctly.

If I lose one tick going in to the market and one tick going out of the market, I will lose $50. I need to multiply this $50 by the total number of trades, 30, and suddenly you see why I want to focus your attention on getting good fills. We are now talking about losing $1,500 because of the slippage factor. $1,500 may not sound like much to you, but as a professional trader, trading 50 to 100 contracts at a time, you can see how this adds up to more than pocket change. I want to get as much of the money I rightfully deserve as is humanly possible.

Oddly enough, there are a wide number of highly touted commodity trading systems that will produce an average profit of $95 to $120 a trade before slippage. Thus, once you deduct slippage from these commodity trading systems your average trade is for about $40.00.

I would just as soon put my money on black or red than see all of my supposed profits eaten up in commissions and slippage.

The importance of slippage is relevant to the type of commodity system or approach you are trading. If you are doing a long term trading program, one that has only one or two trades a year, slippage is not an important part of your business. So what if you give back $150 during the year, that really does not amount to much out of the overall commodity profits that your long term system should produce. But the shorter your visibility of the market, the quicker you are in and out of the market . . . the more times you trade, the more important slippage and commissions will become.

210

More than a handful of commodity traders have moved from where they live throughout the world to Chicago so they can go down to the Chicago Board of Trade or the Merc and trade on the floor, thus reducing the commissions even more. Commissions and slippage are an important consideration in the game. If they are important enough for some of the world's greatest traders to move from London or Australia to live in Chicago, they are important enough for you to monitor. Another reason for paying particularly close attention to slippage is to eliminate additional frustrations.

Believe me, trading the markets is frustrating enough — trying to make money in this most challenging of all intellectual games. When you see profits that are rightfully yours disappear because of slippage, it becomes even more so. One of the nice things about the advent of the discount brokerage firms is that they immediately report back to you where your fills are, much quicker than the old wire houses ever did.

You still may not get the fill that you want, but at least there is no doubt in your mind. You know, almost instantly, at what price you were filled.

Fills can cause frustration in two areas. The first that I touched on is that you don't get the price that you want. Or even worse, you don't get a fill at all. It is really frustrating to see the market start turning away without you when you know you should be in the market place. Is there something you can do about this? Yes there is.

WHAT TO DO IF YOU GET A BAD FILL

If you do any active trading you will, regardless of how close you watch your fills, from time to time receive fills that you feel are unjust.

As an example, not too long ago I had an order to buy 40,000 bushels of March Soybeans at 450 3/4. Prices opened at 450 1/2 and I was filled at . . . are you ready for this . . . 453!

That was, in my opinion, an absolutely horrible fill. But what could I do about it?

Well, there are several things you can do about bad fills. The first one is to ask for time and sales. The time and sales report will show you each trade that took place, at what time it took place, and with some exchanges, how many contracts traded. By asking for time and sales you are shown an absolute record of what traded at what prices, so you can see if you are justified in getting the fill that was given to you.

211

Not always, but at least 85% of the time, the time and sales reports will show that the price you are given is the price that you are relatively entitled to.

You can only get an estimate of your fill. If the people on the floor can show that your fill is in that basic logical price sequence, that is good enough for them, their work is through and that is your fill.

I have had fills reported back to me that were not good fills and I asked for time and sales, and it has vindicated my viewpoint. To really drive the point home, if I think I have an absolutely miserable fill, I will ask for time and sales from not just the brokerage firm that I am dealing with, but from one or two other brokerage firms. I have found that there is some discrepancy in time and sales. There is nothing more embarrassing to a brokerage firm than to have them give you one time and sales report, then you come back to them with another report form another brokerage firm showing different transactions which show you should have been filled at the better price you were looking for. The first step is to ask for time and sales. If the time and sales shows little justification for your fill there is not much you can do about it at this point.

However, I do keep a running report of the fills that I have at several different brokerage firms and have been known to show the brokerage firms the confirmation slips from their competitors so they can see the type of fills I am getting at the other firm.

What if there is a difference between fills at one firm and another firm? You have a choice; First complain about the bad fills and let them know you are going to move your account unless you get better fills. If you still see no better fills, vote with your feet.

Move your account.

It may be that you don't have the capital or that you are not trading at more than one brokerage firm. Then what do you do? If you are following an advisory service, I would suggest you contact the advisor after the trades have been made to see what type of fills his other subscribers are reporting from various brokerage firms. You can then compare to see if your fills are comparable to those that the rest of his subscribers are getting.

Most of the time, at least 90%, the brokerage firms will rule in favor of who filled your order, not you when it comes to complaining about bad fills. Nonetheless, I think it is important that we keep pressure on brokerage firms and people on the floor to make sure we are filled at decent prices. And there is that other 10%!

I am appalled that an exchange as large and historic as the Chicago Board of Trade does not allow traders to use stop limit orders. A stop limit order, as you will learn, is one that limits the price that you will be filled. Thus prices cannot skid through your price. You are filled at that price or not filled. Never have I seen or heard of a logical explanation why this historic exchange does not allow stop orders. I am totally perplexed. Since it trades all of the grains in the country and now the all-important Treasury Bond contract, hopefully pressures will be applied and they will see the light and allow stop limit orders to be placed by traders. That would do a great deal and go a long way in stopping trader's claims of getting ripped off on the floor.

Let's take a look now at the various ways you can place an order on the exchange. Once you learn the type of orders that are available to you, I will show you the way I use these to give me the best possible fills. Let me assure you, I don't always get the fills I want, but over many years of trading I have developed a reasonable approach to getting the market orders that are to my advantage, not to the advantage of traders on the floor. To know which order to place, you need to understand how orders work when it comes to commodity trading.

There are different kinds of orders that you will select from in your trading. A contingent order, an offer order, a time order, and an order to cancel a previous order.

The market order is the simplest order to understand. It is simply as described, a market order. The instant the broker gets the order from you, he goes into the market to fill the number of contracts you have decided to buy or sell at whatever the current price is.

This is the type of order traders use when they want to get an immediate execution. They, for one reason or another, feel the market is about to move for, or against, them and want to be immediately in or out of the position. That's why they use a market order. The order they give their broker will read as follows: "Buy one Feb Pork Belly at the market." The broker receives that order and gives it to his floor broker, who then steps into the pit and buys it at whatever the prevailing price is. There is no way of knowing what your price will be.

You don't really care what your fill will be, because the urgency of the situation is forcing you to use a market order. You are basically saying, "I want in," or "I want out." "I am not too concerned what price I pay, just get me into or out of this position." It must be executed when it reaches the floor at the best possible price. Of course, the best possible price is something that is subject to negotiation and depending upon which firm is filling, you may get filled at one price or then again at another. This is the type of order you use when you want to immediately get in or out of a position.

The next orders you should know about are called contingent orders. In other words, you will not be filled unless some other thing takes place, your order is contingent on something else happening. One example of this would be a limit order. You would call your broker and say "Buy one contract of February Pork Bellies at 65.65 or better." This means that once prices are at or below the figure you have given your broker, the order then becomes a market order and will be subject to the best possible fill your brokerage firm can get to you at that time.

When you place your order to buy at 65.65, bellies are trading above that price so you will not be filled because this an "or better" order. Prices must do something . . . the contingency. They must go to your price of 65.65. Then your order becomes a market order, and you will be filled at the market price.

The next order is known as the limit order. Here you give your broker the order to buy the Bellies at 65.65 on a stop limit. He can fill you only at 65.65, or better. He cannot fill you at a higher price. As an example, let's say your order is above the market, to buy on a stop limit at 65.65. Prices are currently trading at 65.00. Because some major news comes out, Bellies immediately gap up to 65.67. Since there is no trade between 65.65 and 65.67 you will not be filled on the order, nor will you be filled on the next several ticks, unless prices retrace back down to 65.65. This order dictates you will be filled only at your price. Or a better price. It does not become a market order once your price is touched. It becomes an order to fill at exactly your price or a better price after your price is reached.

Literature provided by the exchanges and study material to prepare for the Series 3 Commodity Examinations indicates that this is the most rarely used order. Yet in my view it is the best order for an active trader. We'll go more into detail on this order later on.

A stop order becomes a market order when price reaches your price. Here the contingency again is that prices must reach your level and, the instant they do that, your order becomes a market order. A Stop Limit order has a contingency that prices must first go to your price, then you will be filled at your price or better. If price structure crashes right through your price and continues trading at a higher price, in the case of a buy, you will not be filled, prices will continue to zing along their way. Whereas a stop order would have been filled at a higher price (at the market) and have you in for the ride. The stop limit order does not afford you that luxury. By the same token you will never get a fill worse than the price you wanted to buy.

In the case of a stop order, you may get a fill higher than your price whereas in a stop limit order you can be filled only at your price or better.

A MIT order is short for "market if touched." This is similar to the limit order but there is a slight difference in that if price trades to your buy at 65.65 on a limit, there are no contracts filled for you at that price. If the next quote were 65.50, you would not be filled at 65.65. A market order, or MIT, would be filled because the contingency becomes a market order once the contingency is triggered. With an MIT the instant that prices touch your order the broker will execute your order, regardless of whether the price is higher or lower. Your order immediately becomes a market order. It is not a bad order for day traders to use if they are not overly concerned about slippage of one tick. You frequently will get a one tick slip on an MIT order. That is about the most I recall seeing in a normal or orderly market.

You can also have an OCO order. The OCO means one order cancels the other. As an example, you may have an order to buy a Belly at 65.65 selling a Belly at 64.65 OCO, One Cancels the Other. If you are filled at 65.65, the sell at 64.65 is cancelled and you are long, it is a convenient order for us to have in the marketplace if we think prices will break out of the congestion zone. You may place a buy order at one level and a sell at another. Whichever way the market moves that order will be executed, and the other will be terminated.

The time of order is also important. Unless you specify otherwise, the order you give your broker will expire at the end of the day. If you tell your broker to buy the Bellies at 65.65, he will place that order in the marketplace and if there is no fill he will not replace that order the next day. You will have to tell it to him again unless you say the order is "good until cancelled;" GTC. A GTC order will stay in the marketplace until you specifically cancel the order. This is the type of order you would use if you were waiting for prices to pull back into a buy zone, and just weren't certain which day it would happen. You would then place a good til cancelled order, hoping prices would drift back into your zone.

Just make certain that if you give GTC orders and the situation changes later on, you will remember to pull your order when you decide you no longer want to buy the commodity. You may also have an order to buy at the opening or to buy on the close. This is called market on opening (MOO), or market on close (MOC). I refer to these orders as murder on close, because there tends to be a great deal of slippage on the closing ranges. You may lose anywhere from one to eight ticks on an MOC order. Your fill on a market on close order may not represent the actual closing or settlement price for the day. Remember, the settlement price is established by the clearing house, not by the exchange. You will get a price that is at or within the settling range at the end of the day. At the end of the day there is a high and low of the last few moments of trading. Usually, if you are getting out of a long position you will get the low end of that trading range. If you were getting out of a sell position you will get out at the high end of that trading range. Funny, huh?

It shouldn't happen that way, don't ask me why it does, but in my trading I have noticed time and time again it does. This is why it is extremely important to use a brokerage firm that has their own people on the floor, or works closely with a clearing member who will work their heart out to give you the best possible fills.

Slippage is dangerous in this business. There is also an order known as a "Fill or Kill" order. I think in my 20+ years of trading I have only used it twice. I suspect you will not be using it. The order though, for informational purposes, must be done at once or the order is cancelled. If you want to buy your Bellies at 65.65 right now, but don't want to be jacked around by the bid/ask on the floor, you say "Buy one Feb Belly 65.65 FOK" (Fill or Kill). If a broker cannot immediately execute the order for you it is cancelled. The few times I have used this order are when I felt that people on the floor were playing a game between the bid spread and were not filling me on either side, so I placed a fill or kill order to see if I couldn't break that log jam between the bid and ask. That is what I think the purpose of the order is for. There are more esoteric orders for placing spreads, but since I am not a large spread trader, I don't understand those myself. I suggest you talk to your brokerage firm if you want to learn these.

You've learned what an OCO order is, one cancels the other. You need to know you can also have a straight cancel order. If you have given your broker an order to buy Feb. Bellies at 65.65, and decide for whatever reason you no longer wish to own Bellies at that price, you simply call them up and say, "This is a straight cancel buying 1 Feb Belly at 65.65." You may also give an order known as a CFO or cancel former order. I have never used this myself, but it is in the textbooks so I suppose it is something you should be aware of. It's used similarly to the straight cancel order. Now comes the hard part — using these orders to our advantage. Ninety-eight percent of the time I use one of two orders, either a stop or a stop limit order.

In the particular approach I have to the marketplace 98% of the time I will be a buyer only if prices rally to my price level. In other words, I want the trend moving in my direction, so I will then have a buy at my trend reversal point, when buying, on a stop above the market.

If I am afraid I will get a bad fill I will use a stop limit order to make certain prices don't gun through and lose a tick or two slippage. A stop limit order guarantees me of getting my price, though it does not guarantee me of getting into the market, whereas a stop order guarantees me of getting into the market but does not guarantee me getting my price.

THE SECRET OF USING STOP LIMIT ORDERS

The secret of using stop limit orders is that you have to be relatively close to the market. Let's say your system gives you a price to buy, and you place an order at that price. Instead of getting filled there, prices, for whatever reason, move so quickly that you are not filled. Now you are sitting on the sidelines or short and wishing you were long. What do you do?

I will tell you the way I handle this . . . once the price of the commodity advances to my entry point and I am told I am not filled on a stop limit order I maintain my stop limit order for 45 minutes and sometimes up to 1 hour. If I am not filled after one hour I then go into the marketplace and try to pick a point (you will next read about how to pick a point) and buy at that price.

My experience is that about 95 out of 100 trades I take will be filled on my stop limit order.

On the remaining 5 orders, I will be filled slightly higher or lower than my original entry price, depending on which way I am trying to trade, but it will pay to use the stop limit orders over a long period of time. I have not missed a serious or major move in the marketplace by using stop limit orders.

To wrap it up for you again then, if I am not filled on my stop limit order I give the market at least one hour to move back and fill at my price. If I'm still not filled I then go in and get what I consider the best possible price fill at that time. I am more than willing to give the market time to move back and forth into my price zone. This is for system trading. I would not necessarily use the same type of orders when day trading.

217

DAY TRADE ORDERS

When it comes to day trading, of course, it is a different ball game. Here, because you usually only have one shot at it during the day, you have got to get into that market. This means I usually have at least one half of my position on a stop order. If I get filled worse on my stop, that's fine, I will then let the market get back to my original entry price or a more advantageous price and put on the other 1/2 of my position. That way I usually have an average cost better than what the system dictated. In the event I don't get the better cost because the market just blasts right through, I do get the initial order, and am not left at the waiting gate.

HOW TO PLACE AN ORDER WHEN YOU PICK A POINT

It is common for traders, particularly day traders, to pick a price level at which they think the market should top or bottom, then try to trade around that point. If this is your trading style, you will notice how the market has traded during the day. Based on some rule, if you think it is currently a good sell, you then need to use what I call the Pick-a-Point approach to placing your order.

Picking a point is a little bit different from other trades. It is not important how you pick the point, but more important how you get executed. Most traders who pick a point simply use a market order once they feel the market has reached a significant trading point. I think this is wrong, and here is why; in close analysis of my own short term trading records as well as watching numerous other short term traders, I have seen that unless you are superman when it comes to being a trader, you are not going to, very often, pick the absolute high of the move . . . nor will you even come close. Unless you are an extremely brilliant or lucky person, I doubt if you will very often get an absolute high for a sell point or the absolute low for a buy point. Accordingly, why use a market order? A market order is usually going to give you a worse price than an or-better basis. When I pick a price to sell, I want it to be slightly above the market and I place an order to sell on an or-better basis at that point. If prices collapse with the trade, so be it. I miss the trade. But I have found there are not too many people who have enough foresight to pick those absolute reversal points in the market on a consistent or frequent basis. Since we don't have that ability to consistently pick the absolute highs in the market, then let's place our price slightly above the market, so if it starts to rally it runs up into our price. We do our selling there, hopefully on some additional last burst of strength. In any event, we are selling at a better price than if we simply went into the market immediately with the butterflies kicking around in our stomach and our minds screaming to sell.

Of course, if you happen to be a better trader than I am and can call the absolute turns in the marketplace you would use a market, or an MIT order, but until I develop the ability to magically predict these turning points long in advance and right to the absolute last tick, I am going to continue using orders that are on an or-better basis above for a sell, below my point for a buy. Hopefully, I am doing my selling into the last run in the market or doing my buying in the last push down of prices (as others are selling when in fact they should be buying).

If you do not have your own quote facilities I suggest you contact your broker a couple of times each day to see what prices are doing. In the event you are filled, your broker should call you immediately with what your fill price is. Hopefully, you will develop into a good and profitable trader and be able to afford your own quote facilities and move into commodity trading on a full or part time basis without much delay.

## Chapter 12

Larry Williams On Fear And Greed

It's been said the best speeches are given by the people most qualified to give them, that giving a good speech is simply a matter of having earned the right to give that speech.

Hopefully, it's the same when it comes to writing articles because I feel qualified for this article on fear and greed . . . more qualified than I've ever been in life.

Currently on any given day I will be long or short somewhere over 2,000 Bonds and who knows how many S&P's.

That means every tick in the Bond market will make . . . or lose me . . . $62,500. Believe me, if you want to get in touch with fear and greed there's no better way of doing it than to have each tick in the Bond market represent $62,500!

While trading commodities does create an unreal sense of value and economic worth, nonetheless I can appreciate $62,500 . . . I can appreciate it leaving me and I can appreciate it coming to me.

My experience is that trading in large amounts gets you more immediately in contact with the emotions of fear and greed. It really does not matter how much you are winning or losing, it's all in relationship to how much you have to win or lose. I know. I started trading, at one point of my life, with simply what I could charge on all of my credit cards. The pressures of fear and greed then were almost as great, though not quite, as now.

The question is, how do traders go about handling fear and greed? What can you do to compensate or cut back on the impact of these emotions?

Certainly, if you don't learn to get these two wild horses under control, you will experience financial difficulties trading commodities.

That's because fear will force you in a strange fashion to either hold on to losing positions too long or to get out of positions too early, that would have turned profitable.

The problem with greed is just the opposite. Here, pure greed will force you to hold on to positions you should be getting out of because you always think there's another tick . . . or two . . . or several hundred . . . left in the market for you. Hope may spring eternal, but uncontrolled greed will be the demise of commodity traders.

You cannot escape these two emotions of fear and greed. They are just like yin and yang, they go hand and hand, they are like success and failure, salt and sugar, night and day; they separate making or losing money.

There are several practical ways I have developed to eliminate fear and greed; the first is to have a System.

WHY A SYSTEM IS IMPORTANT

Don't think this a novel or a new idea. In Homer's Iliad, he tells us, "Let us put our trust rather in the council of great Zeus, King of mortals and immortals."

That's really what we system followers do. We are putting our trust in the system, our God; the system thus can eradicate the emotions of fear and greed. These emotions should have no impact on a system trader.

However, there is a world of difference between "should" and "won't." Fear and greed will still impact the system trader and I'll talk, in a few minutes, about how I attempt to handle fear and greed in my system trading.

Those of you who are not system traders have a greater problem. You don't have a Zeus to whom you can shift responsibility; thus, you must be in a constant state of alert, battling fear and greed.

So how can you do it . . . how can you go after these two dragons, putting them to rest?

First, let's look at what we are dealing with here — emotions. Now I am no psychologist, but I have had enough winning trades and losing trades to have a sense of how one can go about desensitizing the impact of emotions.

In fact, the word desensitization is perhaps the most significant psychological tool I could share with any commodity trader.

Remember the movie The Exorcist?

If you don't, try to call up any other spooky movie. It's almost certain that the first time you saw the movie it had its frightening moments. In the case of the Exorcist some people were scared flat out silly.

However, if those people had seen The Exorcist 30, 40 or 50 times, can you imagine them being scared on the 39th or 40th screening?

Of course not. Regardless of how scary anything is, if you see it over and over and over it starts to lose impact and your mind can act rationally, without emotions running amok.

Thus, one approach to sublimating fear and greed is to desensitize yourself by having a physical action, involving money, that has thousands of decisions all having fear and greed at stake.

Even an active commodity trader may only feel the tugs of fear and greed on four or five trades a day.

However, there are other activities involving money that may have you exposed to literally hundreds of ultimate decisions with money.

To desensitize myself from fear and greed many years ago I wagered small amounts at gambling casinos, not really caring if I won or lost money. The idea was to repeat the process over and over and over, literally thousands of times, to desensitize myself from being pulled into having any emotions about what happens to money. After you win or lose several thousand decisions you start to gain some control of your emotions . . . . you start to realize that you can be in charge of them, rather than having them in charge of you. This type of desensitization for commodity traders will take a long time and is something not everyone can do. But if you've got the time and patience, it's one of the best physical ways I know to go after desensitizing emotions.

Another approach might be to simply come into contact with the reality that simply nothing matters.

While this may be too much Zen for some, I think it is of great value. Alan Watts said "Nothing is more important than something, because there is no way of seeing something without having the background or context of nothing." If Watts were still living, I'm certain he would go beyond that statement, telling us that the only real problem in our life is our mind. So once one learns to escape your mind, which really for the most part is your ego speaking, you will have escaped the impact of fear and greed.

We commodity traders experience that too. It is the Satori concept, which is truly a warrior's state of being. But it appears it cannot occur until your mind is totally free of thought. Once you get all your thoughts and considerations about the world out of your head, then you become pure awareness. Your body will be active, yet sensitive and relaxed. In the state of Satori, the commodity trader will also find that prices seem to be not only in his control, but also moving much slower than usual. There is still a certain cadence or beat, but now you are in communication with this pulsation.

In this state of Satori, which I have experienced on occasions, there is no concept of fear and greed. There is simply nothing to pull at you because fear and greed are not considerations or thoughts.

From this I have deducted that if one can get to the point that fear and greed are not considerations . . . that fear and greed don't matter, one is less impacted by them.

So, how do we pull this off? The way of getting to that point goes back to the original Zen comment that nothing has value to it. This may be hard for some readers to grasp or intellectually accept, but it is a truism. This is an intellectual thought, but needs to be experienced at an emotional level before it will be of value to the commodity trader.

We all express it in one form or another, even in our own humor regarding the market, when we say, after winning or losing days, it's only money . . . it's only more zeros past the base number; thus, we attempt to give a sense of nothingness to money.

When you get to the point that in fact there's a total sense of nothingness to money or market success or failures, you will then reach that state of nirvana, or Satori; you have a realization or transformation that allows you to view what goes on in the market as simply having no value.

If it has no value, then of course there cannot be fear. You cannot be fearful of losing nothing nor can you be greedy about gaining something that is nothing. It's like the line in Kris Kristofferson's song, Bobby McGee, "Freedom's just another word for nothing left to lose."

Indeed, this is a strange attitude or approach to have, especially towards something that people covet as much as money. But this is the attitude that will free you of the charge and emotional trauma that will come from these emotions.

In St. Paul's epistle to the Philippians, he admonishes "Let this mind be in you, which is also in Christ Jesus, who being in the form of God did not think identity with God as a thing to be clung to, but humbled himself and made himself of no reputation."

Here you have expressed the exact thing that Watts and the Zen Roshi are trying to say. When we attach importance to something, you become so screwed up about it that you cannot function correctly around it; so it is with our money. When we attach importance to it, in come our viscous dragons of fear and greed.

We system traders have it a little bit better, because we can intellectualize without going to the emotional/intellectual level. We need not surgically remove these emotions.

Consider this . . . if you are a system trader, you have selected a system to follow. You are following that system for numerous reasons, some of which may be: it's easy to follow; it works well in the markets you like to follow. The truth of the matter is you are following a system for two reasons: 1) it has shown the ability to eliminate losses and 2) the mirror image of that is it has been profitable for you.

Isn't this really another way of talking about fear and greed? Aren't systems really created to get us away from these two emotions?

You see, once you start following a system, what you actually have said to yourself is, I am happy with the profits the system generates, I am pleased with the profits this system generated; therefore, I will follow the system.

If that's true, I then ask you, "If you are happy with these profits, why in the name of the commodity god or goddess would one want to try to get more profits from the markets? Isn't that foolish?" Yes, of course it is.

If you are satisfied with the system, it means you are satisfied with the profits that system makes; thus, that satisfaction tells you there is no need for you to be greedy . . . there is no need for you to try to hold on to positions when the system says you shouldn't. Nor is there a need to try to take trades the system says you shouldn't or add additional contracts, etc.

If you're a system follower, you have already admitted to yourself, at an intellectual level, that you are satisfied with your profits.

The profit satiation the system provides you is your assurance that you do not have to do anything but follow the system, that you are content with the system's performance.

225

Therefore, there is no reason for you to try to stretch out the system's performance . . . to cheat trying to eek out an extra buck or two. Be content with the system and you will have eliminated totally the impact of greed.

Let's next turn our attention to fear. As I said, systems are constructed for two reasons, one to handle greed and the other to handle fear.

Let me explain this. The reason I have developed systems, and I'm certain everyone else has developed systems, is to make certain we don't lose money.

After all, the practical reason we develop systems is to make money. But of even more importance, to not lose money — we know some 90% of all commodity traders do. The key point to having a system is to enable us to not lose money.

What you're really saying . . . if you're a system follower . . . is that you have developed a set of concise rules that have managed the commodity markets and your money in such a fashion that you are able to accept what losses occur in the system, knowing that losses are a part of the process and also knowing that the system controls these.

Ah, hah! There it is . . . the kernel of truth. The system controls losses far better than you can control losses. Once you grasp that, you will realize there is no need to not follow your systems. There is absolutely no way your emotions, your consideration, your friends or whatever, will be able to do a better job of managing losses and money management decisions than a well thought out system.

Hence, the system becomes your shield, to protect you from the emotion of fear. You can walk through the valley of evil and fear no death when you have your system. Your system has clearly told you, yes, there will be losses but I, the system, will manage and control losses for you.

Once you throw away the shield, you are on your own big boy, and who knows what's going to happen. You certainly don't! But we do know that you and other people most always make the wrong decisions when the emotion of fear comes sneaking in.

Yes, if you have a system you don't have to have fear. You can approach the market from that Satori viewpoint, because there is no need for fear; you have already turned it over to your Zeus. Your trust is in the system, that it will handle losses . . . the origination of fear . . . greater than you can.

Thus, a system becomes almost a father confessor for its follower. The problem is system followers have not intellectualized or rationalized to the level I hope I have brought you, so

226

they buck the system. When the system says buy, they sell. When the system says take profits, they hold on. When the system has a loss, instead of following the system, they continue holding the losing trade.

There is no need for system followers to do this once they realize they chose the system because it has made profits and those profits are satisfactory for them.

Hopefully, this section will help you stab an ice pick into the heart of the emotions of fear and greed and stop these emotions from shilling you.

I assure you that the elimination of all removable risk is the most plausible way of staying alive. When there is nothing at risk because you have a sense of nothingness, your life will be vital and well. If you cannot get to that point, then have a system. It will control and protect you from risk better than any other alternative.

## Chapter 13

Trin Test . . . . .
Standard & Poor's
From 3/22/83 To 3/10/87

Shown here are what would occur if you (a) bought on the close of or (b) bought on the following open, and exited your position the following close if the daily closing trin value were between what is shown in column (A) and .05 above that. Sells are just the inverse of these numbers. For instance, if yesterday's Trin reading were between .35 and .4, then there would be an 85% chance today would be an up day, with an average amount of $440, versus last night's close. By the same token, there would be a 15% chance, historically, that tonight would close up from last night, and the average day would still be a $440 up day.

The Trin number was developed several years ago by Richard Arms and is now available on many quote services. The Trin (short for Trading Index) number is calculated by the following formula:

$$\left(\frac{\text{\# Advancing Stocks}}{\text{\# Declining Stocks}} \right) \bigg/ \left(\frac{\text{Advancing Volume}}{\text{Declining Volume}} \right)$$

Put another way, it is an advance/decline ratio, comparing number of stocks versus total volume.

(A)	(B) TOTAL TDES	(C) WIN %	(D) AVG WIN /LOSS	(E) RISK/ REWARD	(F) DRAWDOWN	(G) TOTAL EQUITY	(H) AVG TRADE
Close to Close							
.35	13	85%	.51	2.83	-$3,050	$5,725	$440
.4	15	47%	.4	.35	-$5,200	-$5,200	-$347
.45	24	58%	.47	.66	-$3,550	-$2,725	-$114
.5	35	54%	1.11	1.32	-$3,875	$2,250	$64
.55	56	57%	.87	1.15	-$6,200	$2,875	$51
.6	54	59%	1.31	1.9	-$2.525	$10,975	$203
.65	67	46%	1.16	.99	-$5,450	-$25	-$0
.7	65	51%	1.11	1.14	-$5,575	$3,200	$49
.75	63	43%	.78	.58	-$12,600	-$10,100	-$160
.8	77	44%	1	.78	-$12,900	-$6,350	-$82
.85	72	47%	1.12	1	-$11,000	$100	$1
.9	61	44%	.75	.59	-$15,275	-$12,025	-$197
.95	47	45%	1.18	.95	-$6,125	-$725	-$15
1	59	47%	1.1	.99	-$6,075	-$150	-$3
1.05	50	42%	.62	44	-$13,300	-$10,675	-$214
1.1	60	37%	.85	.49	-$16,550	-$13,100	-$218
1.15	44	34%	1.46	.75	-$7,100	-$3,700	-$84
1.2	28	46%	1.2	1.03	-$4,550	$300	$11
1.25	24	33%	.48	.24	-$9,100	-$8,675	-$361
1.3	11	18%	.28	.06	-$7,475	-7,475	-$680
1.35	13	46%	1.23	1.05	-$3,250	$300	$23
1.4	14	57%	1.53	2.03	-$1,825	$2,625	$188
1.45	13	31%	1.17	.51	-$2,275	-$2,025	-$156

1.5	11	55%	5.08	6.09	-$675	$4,200	$382
1.55	14	50%	1.01	1	-$2,350	$25	$2
1.6	5	60%	2.87	4.3	-$925	$3,300	$660
1.65	7	29%	1.55	.61	-$1,950	-925	-$132
1.7	4	50%	.35	.35	-$1,775	-$1,150	-$288
1.75	6	17%	1.11	.22	-$2,200	-$2,200	-$367
1.8	5	20%	1.43	.35	-$1,125	-$1,125	-$225
1.85	1	100%	0	.35	$0	$250	$250
1.9	1	0%	0	0	-$150	-$150	-$150
1.95	1	0%	0	0	-$25	-$25	-$25
2	3	100%	0	0	$0	$2,375	$792
2.05	3	100%	0	0	$0	$975	$325
2.1	0	0%	0	0	$0	$0	
2.2	0	0%	0	.42	$0	$0	$0
2.25	0	0%	0	.42	$0	$0	$0
2.3	1	0%	0	0	-$75	-$75	-$75
2.35	0	0%	0	0	$0	$0	$0
2.4	0	0%	0	0	$0	$0	$0
2.45	0	0%	0	0	$0	$0	40
2.5	1	0%	0	0	-$475	-$475	-$475

Open to Close

.35	13	77%	1	3.33	-$2,625	$6,425	$494
.4	15	40%	.68	.45	-$3,500	-$3,500	-$233
.45	24	58%	.61	.85	-$2,600	-$1,050	-$44
.5	35	43%	1.52	1.13	-$5,150	$1,100	$31
.55	56	55%	.88	1.09	-$7,875	$1,775	$32
.6	54	54%	1.41	1.63	-$4,650	$8,900	$165
.65	67	51%	.94	.96	-$6,850	-$825	-$12
.70	65	57%	1.03	1.36	-$5,175	$7,075	$109
.75	63	44%	.7	.56	-$11,050	-$9,925	-$158

.80	77	44%	.95	.74	-$11,600	-$6,775	-$88
.85	72	50%	1.11	1.11	-$9,575	$2,500	$35
.90	61	46%	.64	.54	-$18,900	-$14,150	-$232
.95	47	49%	.93	.89	-$6,375	-$1,800	-$38
1.0	59	47%	1.22	1.1	-$5,100	$1,650	$28
1.05	50	42%	.67	.48	-$12,500	-$9,925	-$199
1.1	60	42%	.85	.6	-$14,475	-$9,375	-$156
1.15	44	41%	1.28	.88	-$5,650	-$1,550	-$35
1.2	28	46%	1.03	.89	-$5,025	-$850	-$30
1.25	24	37%	.51	.3	-$8,400	-$7,675	-$320
1.3	11	27%	.23	.08	-$7,200	-$7,200	-$655
1.35	13	38%	1.63	1.02	-$2,950	$125	$10
1.4	14	64%	.98	1.76	-$1,450	$1,750	$125
1.45	13	38%	.81	.5	-$2,400	-$1,975	-$152
1.5	11	73%	4.07	10.85	-$450	$5,175	$470
1.55	14	57%	1.04	1.38	-$1,850	$1,100	$79
1.6	5	60%	3.98	5.96	-$575	$3,475	$695
1.65	7	29%	2.34	.93	-$1,700	-$125	-$18
1.7	4	50%	.81	.8	-$1,950	-$375	-$94
1.75	3	0%	0	0	-$2,100	-$2,100	-$700
1.8	5	0%	0	0	-$2,000	-$2,000	-$400
1.85	1	100%	0	0	$0	$300	$300
1.9	1	0%	0	0	$-25	-$25	-$25
1.95	1	100%	0	0	$0	$200	$200
2.0	3	100%	0	0	$0	$1,950	$650
2.05	3	67%	2.29	4.57	-$175	$625	$208
2.1	0	0%	0	4.57	$0	$0	$0
2.15	3	67%	.87	1.75	-$300	$225	$75
2.2	0	0%	0	1.75	$0	$0	$0
2.25	0	0%	0	1.75	$0	$0	$0
2.3	1	100%	0	1.75	$0	$50	$50
2.35	0	0%	0	1.75	$0	$0	$0

2.4	0	0%	0	1.75	$0	$0	$0
2.45	0	0%	0	1.75	$0	$0	$0
2.5	1	0%	0	0	-$775	-$775	-$775

## Chapter 14

Some Closing Thoughts

In this chapter I'm going to try to condense what I have told you in the previous chapters as well as give you more insights into how I personally trade the market. Perhaps you can gather some of the essence of how I go about making my living in the marketplace.

First let me re-emphasize that people like myself and other experts are not where you should turn to make your fortune in the marketplace.

You are the source of your success, happiness, joys and sorrows. It's certain you can always find whoever called the last big market move, but equally certain is that you can't tell in advance who's going to call the next big market move.

It's amusing to turn through the pages of Investor's Daily or other market-related media, and read all the ads of the chest thumpers who have recently made tons of money, so they claim. But not one of them will guarantee they're going to catch the next move or the next hot stock or hot commodity.

If you try to play the game of "latch on to the good expert," you're simply going to be going from one hot hand to the next hot hand. As long ago as biblical days we've been told, "the first one now, shall later be last." Don't take my word for it. Let's take the word from a few of the experts. Even such astute market prognosticators as Doug Casey, who's had some brilliant forecasts, have also had some equally embarrassing ones. While he correctly predicted, in 1985, a soaring stock market, he went on to predict a rise in interest rates, which simply didn't happen. In fact, the Bond market rallied substantially as interest rates declined. Casey went on to predict that in 1985 there would be a squeeze in Oil stocks and an acute shortage in Crude Oil; another forecast that didn't come true. Casey, along with other analysts, predicted a bull market in commodities in the 1985 time period, which is another one of those recommendations that I'm certain they would just as soon forget.

My friend, Bob Prechter, who has had one of the best forecasting records of any of us, especially when it comes to the stock market, astonishingly maintained that we would see higher interest rates . . . somewhere in the area of 18% . . . in the 1986-87 time period when interest rates were 10 to 11% below this forecast. For years people such as C. B. Meyers have been forecasting that not only would our banking system collapse, but so would the entire country. Obviously, none of those things have come to pass. Jerome Smith, our most futuristic thinker, forecast in December 1985 that "things would be back to double digits on the Consumer Price Index by late 1986."

John Pugsley, another famous forecaster, told people to "start looking away from the stock market and towards commodities, precious metals and the shorting of interest rate futures." All this in December 1985, which was 180 degrees opposite of what one wanted to do as reality unfolded in 1986-87. It's amazing what things people will grab in an attempt to forecast the market. Jimmy Rogers, who is a finance professor at Columbia University Graduate School of Business and an astute market trader, told a group of us, in the summer of 1986, that the stock market was about to enter a 1929 phase (this was just prior to one of the largest up moves in the history of the stock market) because "there are too many 29-year-old millionaires" and that the graduating class of Harvard, which the previous year had favored working for one of the toy companies that went bankrupt, had this year chose to work in the brokerage firms.

Jimmy Rogers may yet get his depression, but his timing could not have been worse. Had you sold short at that time, or anytime in the next 12 months for that matter, you would have had your head handed to you.

Always among the forecasters are those who try to scare the pants off of you. Try this one on for size: Jim Grant, in his February 1987, Grants' Interest Rate Observer said, "If at the end of this crash you have $15,000 and no one else does, you will be incredibly well off and will be able to consider yourself an amazing financial figure."

Where do people come up with things like this? Fifteen thousand dollars is all you're going to have left because of a crash. Notice that he hedges his words in that he says, "If no one else has $15,000, you'll consider yourself well off." But can you imagine people who currently have assets of hundreds of thousands of dollars, and there are millions of those people in America, ending up with $10,000 or $15,000? I doubt it, don't you? Seriously, think about it.

Please don't think that it's just market letter writers that have been known to make such erroneous forecasts. Such dignitaries as John Kenneth Galbraith and Milton Friedman, in 1985, were forecasting higher inflation rates. One of those authorities was looking for substantially higher interest rates. But perhaps because of liberal political readings, the media has never jumped on the forecast of either one of these gentleman who have been about as wrong as everyone else. Inflation did not pick up during 1985-86, or even in early 1987, to any substantial degree. So whether you listen to college professors or market letter writers or forecasters like the Aden sisters, who have repeatedly forecast that Gold would go to the $2,000 area, or even the erudite Kiplinger Letter, none of their forecasts have shown a consistency of success that one requires to trade.

Please, please, do not think that I am deliberately picking on these people, because I too have made forecasts and while some of them have been brilliant, many have been equally un-brilliant. We are all human — you require that we forecast so we do . . . our forecasts should be used as guidelines, not absolutes.

The point I want to make, the point that I hope you absorb and totally absorb, is not to listen to what other people say. Your forecasting abilities are just as good as mine, Bob Prechter's or anyone else's. While we may give you some insight and understanding in the marketplace, don't rest your hat or your bank account on our predictions; instead, learn yourself about how the markets operate.

In today's mail came this forecast, "Emergency Bulletin . . . dangerous economic developments imminent . . . nine global developments are threatening your nest egg . . . " Really now — the only threat to your nest egg is following this emotional economic gibberish.

The mere fact you have read this book this far indicates to me that you are the type of person who is interested in learning and knowing how things work, as opposed to just blindly following people. I assure you that if you do blindly follow even the best of the experts, the time you put all your money on their one forecast you know will be right . . . it will be wrong, and you — dear reader — will be out in the cold.

Don't expect too much from the experts. Instead turn to the reality of the marketplace. There's lots of hard data you can research to find out for yourself how the markets move and operate. You can learn from studying the experts, but rely on your own strengths.

Let me interject a simple trading technique that you may want to look at. The following section shows the relationship of volume to closing price patterns:

VOLUME, CLOSE, OPEN PATTERNS

S&P from 820421 through 870310 (1236 market days - 2 days buildup)
Volume is the cash volume on the NYSE as published at the bottom of column 2 of the front page of The Journal. Patterns represent, respectively, volume vs. previous day's volume, close vs. previous day's close, and finally today's open vs. yesterday's close. All numbers assume a long trade, therefore a short trade would have the exact opposite numbers.

Test 1 — Enter today's close, exit tomorrow's close

PATTERN (V, C, O)	TOTAL TRADES	WINNING TRADES	TOTAL DOLLARS	WINNING PERCENT	AVERAGE TRADE
- - -	148	73	($9,825)	49%	($66)
- - +	143	81	$22,675	57%	$159
- + -	121	41	($25,000)	34%	($207)
- + +	145	85	$40,400	59%	$279
+ - -	98	53	($1,650)	54%	($17)
+ - +	137	96	$54,575	70%	$398
+ + -	156	66	($28,525)	42%	($183)
+ + +	148	73	($9,825)	49%	($66)

Test 2 — Enter tomorrow's open, exit tomorrow's close

- - -	148	84	$22,500	57%	$152
- - +	143	66	($7,775)	46%	($54)
- + -	121	55	$3,850	45%	$32
- + +	145	72	$2,575	50%	$18
+ - -	98	61	$23,500	62%	$240
+ - +	137	77	$26,950	56%	$197
+ + -	156	81	$6,900	52%	$44
+ + +	170	74	($15,575)	44%	($92)

People have said many things about how price works in relationship to volume. Here we can see on a conclusive basis which relationships do exist. What I'm showing here is the matrix that examines what happens if volume is down for the day, closing is down for the day and the following morning's opening is + or - from the previous night's close. If you have that type of a pattern, what should develop the following day? As you can see, the most bullish of these patterns would be: Down volume on an advancing day with a higher opening the following morning. In that instance, the most bullish of these patterns would be an advancing volume on a day that the market closes down, with the market opening higher the following day. 70% of the time, in the Standard & Poor's 500 futures, prices rallied the next day. Had you simply bought on that opening, you would have made $54,575. The next most impressive pattern would be a day that has lower volume, yet closes higher and opens higher the following morning. That type of activity produced $40,400 in profit and 59% of those trades were correct. The next column is self-explanatory, and shows what happens if you buy on the opening the following day; what percent of time the prices close higher than the opening.

This is the type of work and research you can perform yourself to see the relationships that exist in these markets. Another short term indicator I've talked about earlier in the book is the Tick Index. My closing thoughts on this particular tool are:

239

CLOSING IN ON THE TICK

As mentioned in the chapter on day trading, some authorities think the tick index is one of the better indicators of tomorrow's market activity.

We decided to find out for ourselves, so we put tick data into the computer covering December 29, 1986, through April 16, 1987. For those of you who don't follow this particular indicator, the Tick Index is the net difference between stocks who traded up on the last tick or trade versus those that traded down on the last tick or trade.

As an example, if there were 856 stocks that traded up on their last trade and 335 stocks that traded down on their last trade, the net Tick Index would be positive and the value would be +521.

There are three separate Tick Indexes. One is the Tick Index covering the New York Stock Exchange, one for just the Dow Jones Thirty Stocks, and finally one for the American Stock Exchange Index.

In the following data, the Tick Index is not nearly as good a predictor of tomorrow's market action (at least in this time period) as I think it should be.

To test the indicator, we simply bought on the close if the Tick Index was positive and exited the next close. If the Tick Index was negative, we would sell on the close, exiting the next close. Had one actually done that you would have lost money. Only 48.5% of the trades using the New York Stock Exchange Tick Index were profitable. You would have lost, after commissions, $3,075 on March 1987's S&P 500 Index. We can also see the performance following the Dow Tick Index or the Amex tick; neither of those were profitable either.

There may be a way of using the Tick Index successfully. If you notice, when you have extremely negative readings the market tends to rally the next day. For an example, look at January 21, 1987, with a -599 Tick Index and a substantial rally the following day in the market. The next time we saw this type of occurrence was on March 19, 1987, with a -690 Tick Index and again a nice rally the following day. The same thing was true about April 7, where we had a -630 Tick Index and a large rally the next day. Of course, to simply look at the Tick Index as having forecasting significance for tomorrow's close should not be done.

Frankly I think a new service, Futures Settlement Guide, 2905 Newton Drive, Lago Vista, Texas 78645, offers more short term forecasting than the old indicators. This service polls 50-100 traders after the close each day as to their bullishness, then publishes these results on

240

a telephone hotline. Clearly, when the majority are bullish the market is about to go down. When the camp becomes infested with bears, prices rally. Their charts, shown here, present a convincing case for trading the public.

Some Closing Thoughts

CLOSING TICK
This looks at last night's tick value at the close. If positive, it assumes
going long at the close and exiting at tomorrow's close. Tick is broken out
three different ways in this test. Data is from Barrons (which reports tick
tick as N.A. for some days when they could not obtain it).

CONTRACT	DATE	OPEN	HIGH	LOW	CLOSE	NYSE TICK	P&L	DJIA TICK	P&L	AMEX TICK	P&L
MAR 87	861229	246.75	247.30	243.35	243.65	-257		-6		-201	
	861230	243.70	244.80	243.05	243.45	-330	0.2	8	0.2	-120	0.2
	861231	243.45	244.20	240.60	242.15	N.A.	1.3	N.A.	-1.3	N.A.	1.3
	870102	243.50	247.75	243.40	246.75	941		-16		353	
	870105	248.50	254.15	248.30	253.25	687	6.5	0	-6.5	248	6.5
	870106	252.90	254.85	252.50	253.55	830	0.3	4	0	770	0.3
	870107	253.45	257.20	253.10	256.25	310	2.7	N.A.	2.7	N.A.	2.7
	870108	255.95	257.55	255.45	257.30	624	1.05	14		196	
	870109	256.55	260.60	256.15	259.50	295	2.2	2	2.2	185	2.2
	870112	258.95	262.60	258.55	260.75	313	1.25	14	1.25	186	1.25
	870113	259.80	261.50	259.30	261.35	211	0.6	-2	0.6	58	0.6
	870114	261.50	264.20	259.60	263.30	418	1.95	-2	-1.95	64	1.95
	870115	264.10	268.40	263.40	266.95	376	3.65	22	-3.65	24	3.65
	870116	268.50	268.80	265.45	266.70	-286	-0.25	8	-0.25	-35	-0.25
	870119	265.00	271.50	264.80	271.40	412	-4.7	20	4.7	47	-4.7
	870120	271.00	272.75	268.60	269.40	171	-2	18	-2	-107	-2
	870121	269.00	272.10	268.35	268.90	-599	-0.5	-8	-0.5	-134	0.5
	870122	268.90	276.90	268.50	276.40	N.A.	-7.5	N.A.	-7.5	N.A.	-7.5
	870123	276.65	282.60	266.00	269.30	-366		-22		-100	
	870126	271.00	271.85	268.40	271.35	-74	-2.05	-4	-2.05	-23	-2.05
	870127	272.50	275.80	271.85	274.45	244	-3.1	22	-3.1	37	-3.1
	870128	276.00	277.80	273.45	277.55	462	3.1	16	3.1	29	3.1
	870129	278.80	278.80	272.60	275.15	265	-2.4	16	-2.4	16	-2.4
	870130	274.40	275.50	271.90	274.15	472	-1	14	-1	60	-1
	870202	273.00	278.60	273.00	277.35	83	3.2	-10	3.2	97	3.2
	870203	278.10	279.05	275.70	276.35	-206	-1	-12	1	72	-1
	870204	276.70	281.00	275.50	280.70	418	-4.35	20	-4.35	137	4.35
	870205	281.20	283.40	278.50	282.35	343	1.65	18	1.65	69	1.65
	870206	282.50	283.20	280.35	281.20	34	-1.15	14	-1.15	8	-1.15
	870209	281.10	281.35	277.70	279.35	34	-1.85	14	-1.85	8	-1.85
	870210	279.10	279.50	273.70	275.85	196	-3.5	8	-3.5	-13	-3.5
	870211	276.20	278.25	275.00	277.65	163	1.8	-14	1.8	101	-1.8
	870212	278.00	278.40	274.10	276.75	3	-0.9	10	0.9	-32	-0.9
	870213	276.25	282.30	275.70	282.05	79	5.3	-10	5.3	21	-5.3
	870217	281.50	287.25	281.15	287.05	374	5	24	-5	34	5
	870218	288.75	289.00	283.45	286.70	2	-0.35	20	-0.35	-39	-0.35
	870219	286.50	287.50	284.40	286.20	N.A.	-0.5	N.A.	-0.5	N.A.	0.5
	870220	286.35	287.10	284.50	285.65	264		-2		8	

870223 286.10 287.00 279.00 282.85 !	-198	-2.8 !	-20	2.8 !	-27	-2.8
870224 283.35 284.20 281.60 282.45 !	62	0.4 !	2	0.4 !	37	0.4
870225 282.00 286.50 281.75 283.90 !	151	1.45 !	4	1.45 !	3	1.45
870226 282.90 285.60 280.50 283.55 !	13	-0.35 !	8	-0.35 !	0	-0.35
870227 284.25 285.05 282.80 283.55 !	33	0 !	16	0 !	68	0
870302 284.60 285.80 282.40 283.60 !	-179	0.05 !	-12	0.05 !	38	0.05
870303 283.30 284.70 282.80 284.10 !	69	-0.5 !	0	-0.5 !	-11	0.5
870304 284.50 289.20 284.40 289.00 !	457	4.9 !	8	0 !	89	-4.9
870305 289.40 291.90 289.40 290.20 !	122	1.2 !	10	1.2 !	26	1.2
870306 289.75 291.30 288.50 291.20 !	255	1 !	20	1 !	40	1
870309 289.90 289.90 286.80 288.40 !	-132	-2.8 !	12	-2.8 !	-74	-2.8
870310 288.70 291.40 287.40 290.90 !	N.A.	-2.5 !	N.A.	2.5 !	N.A.	-2.5

Contract Rollover - - - - - - - - - - - -

870310 290.30 293.15 289.10 292.65 !	N.A.	!	N.A.	!	N.A.	
870311 293.50 294.20 290.50 291.65 !	-60	!	0	!	-30	
870312 292.20 293.95 290.85 292.65 !	-97	-1 !	-10	0 !	95	-1
870313 292.65 293.55 291.05 291.20 !	-168	1.45 !	2	1.45 !	-12	-1.45
870316 289.80 289.85 287.80 289.65 !	.N.A	1.55 !	.N.A	-1.55 !	.N.A	1.55
870317 290.00 295.35 289.55 295.25 !	389	!	18	!	•68	
870318 295.80 296.75 292.00 294.55 !	262	-0.7 !	24	-0.7 !	6	-0.7
870319 294.40 296.80 293.70 296.00 !	-690	1.45 !	2	1.45 !	-12	1.45
870320 296.30 300.00 296.15 299.80 !	821	-3.8 !	26	3.8 !	-35	-3.8
870323 301.20 304.25 299.60 304.15 !	173	4.35 !	20	4.35 !	-33	-4.35
870324 303.30 304.75 302.55 304.20 !	145	0.05 !	8	0.05 !	2	-0.05
870325 303.70 304.50 301.90 303.60 !	51	-0.6 !	2	-0.6 !	-28	-0.6
870326 305.50 305.70 302.65 303.40 !	170	-0.2 !	7	-0.2 !	51	0.2
870327 303.40 303.40 297.20 297.35 !	-328	-6.05 !	16	-6.05 !	-31	-6.05
870330 292.50 292.50 286.70 290.45 !	-185	6.9 !	2	-6.9 !	-141	6.9
870331 291.70 293.35 290.30 291.25 !	N.A	-0.8 !	N.A	0.8 !	N.A	-0.8
870401 288.90 294.70 288.20 294.55 !	397	!	10	!	4	
870402 295.30 295.95 293.05 293.60 !	-61	-0.95 !	-10	-0.95 !	47	-0.95
870403 293.40 303.90 293.20 303.45 !	235	-9.85 !	0	-9.85 !	117	9.85
870406 305.00 305.40 302.70 304.05 !	255	0.6 !	16	0 !	6	0.6
870407 303.20 306.10 295.50 296.40 !	-630	-7.65 !	-14	-7.65 !	-93	-7.65
870408 300.00 301.60 296.00 300.30 !	169	-3.9 !	20	-3.9 !	-120	-3.9
870409 300.00 300.05 291.80 295.05 !	-162	-5.25 !	4	-5.25 !	-123	5.25
870410 293.50 296.00 291.30 293.40 !	-79	1.65 !	16	-1.65 !	-57	1.65
870413 293.80 295.30 284.40 284.55 !	-474	8.85 !	-20	-8.85 !	-264	8.85
870414 280.00 284.25 275.90 280.00 !	-60	4.55 !	18	4.55 !	-258	4.55
870415 283.00 286.75 280.35 285.20 !	55	-5.2 !	-6	5.2 !	-11	-5.2
870416 286.50 291.00 286.50 288.90 !	-66	3.7 !	-18	-3.7 !	41	-3.7

TOTAL TRADES	70	69	69
WINNING TRADES	34	28	33
PERCENT WINNERS	48.57%	40.58%	47.83%
CUMUALTIVE P&L	($3,075)	($25,350)	($4,000)
AVERAGE TRADE	($43.93)	($367.39)	($57.97)

243

FutureSource Screen Printout

9/30/88 15:08

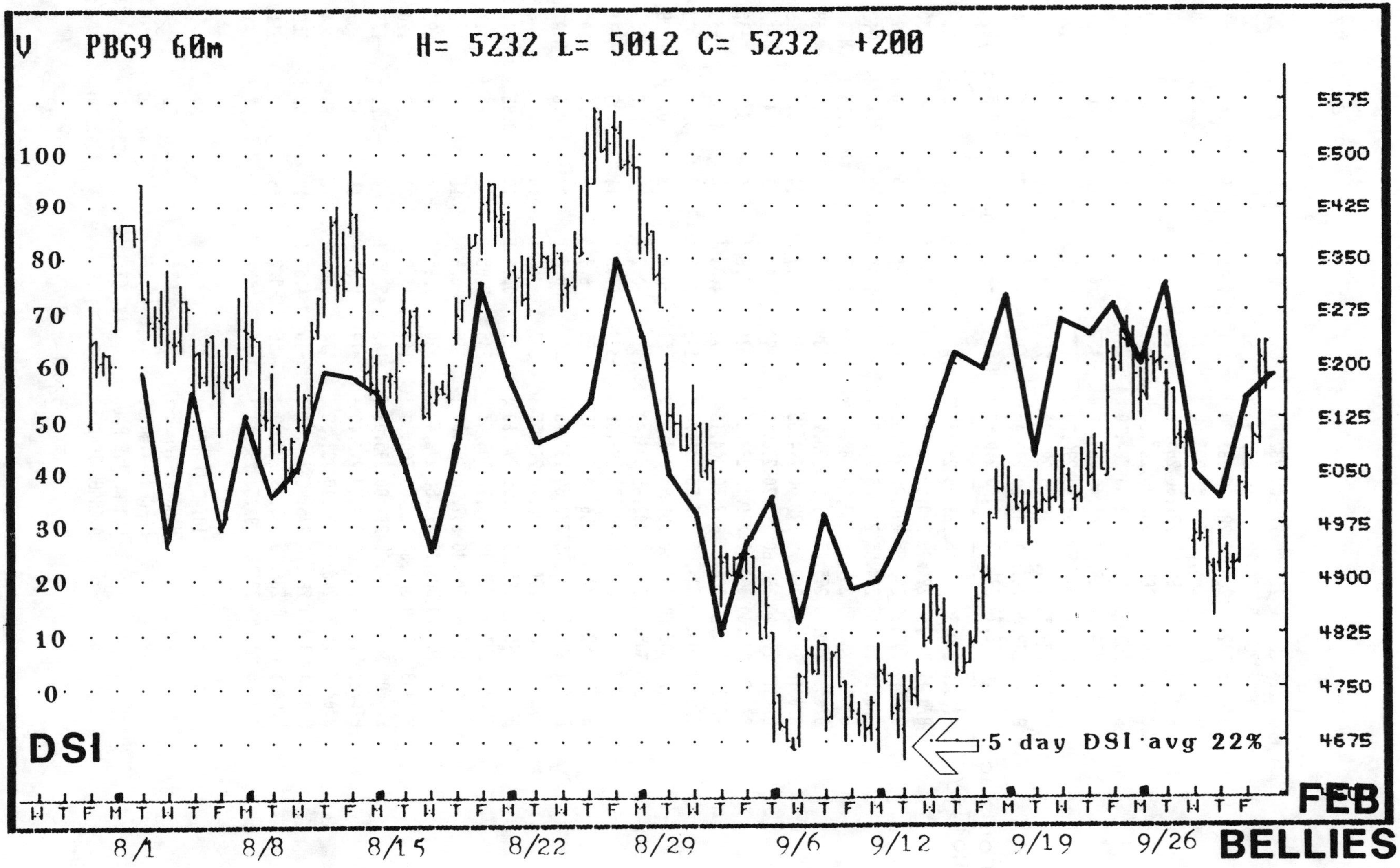

v PBG9 60m   H= 5232 L= 5012 C= 5232 +200

DSI   BELLIES FEB

244

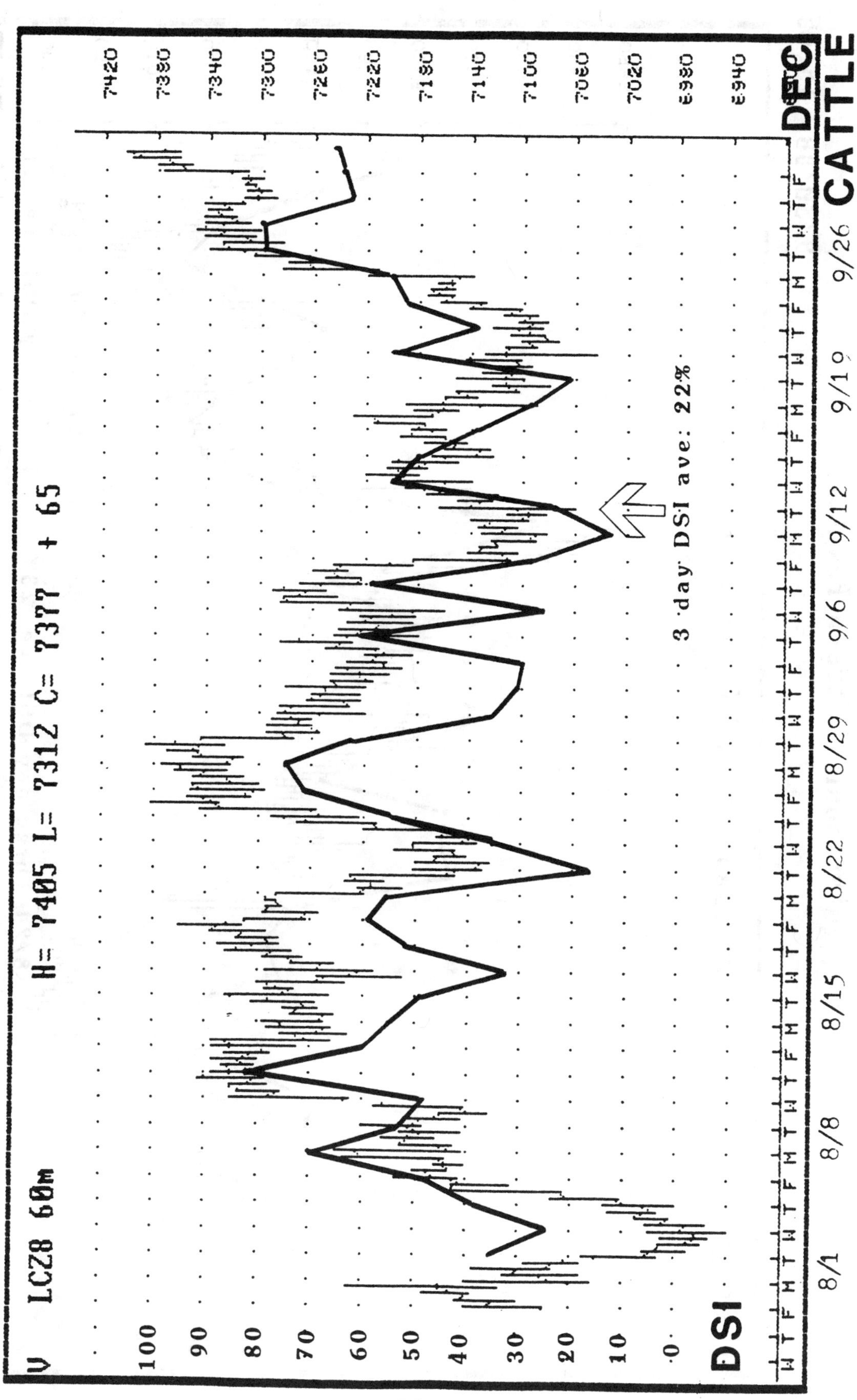

FutureSource Screen Printout
9/30/88 14:50
LCZ8 60m
H= 7405 L= 7312 C= 7377 + 65
3 day DSI ave: 22%
DSI
DEC CATTLE
8/1
8/8
8/15
8/22
8/29
9/6
9/12
9/19
9/26
7420
7380
7340
7300
7260
7220
7180
7140
7100
7060
7020
6980
6940
100
90
80
70
60
50
40
30
20
10
0

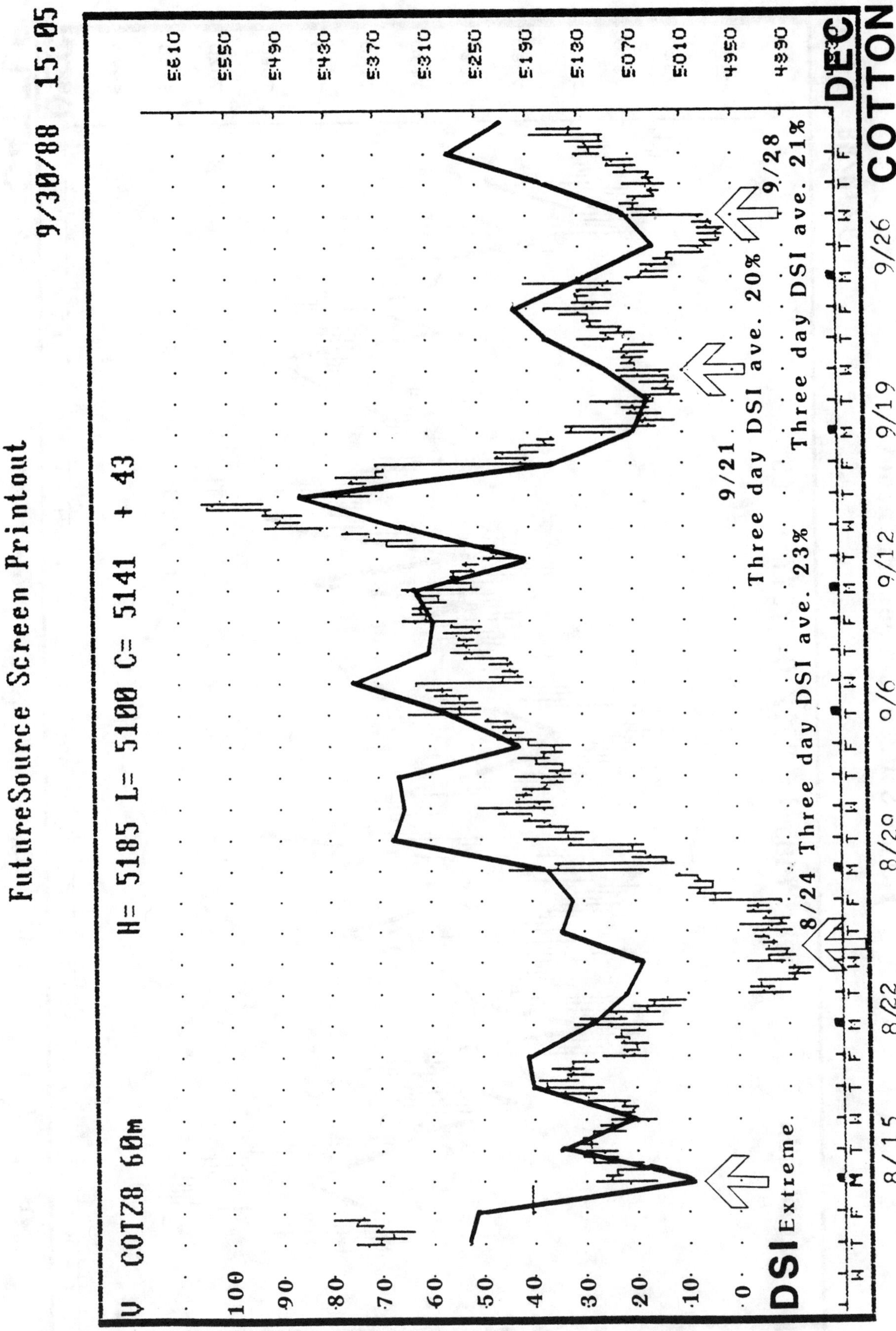

FutureSource Screen Printout
H= 5185 L= 5100 C= 5141 + 43
9/30/88 15:05
COTZ8 60m
DEC COTTON
DSI Extreme
8/24 Three day DSI ave. 23%
9/21 Three day DSI ave. 20%
9/28 Three day DSI ave. 21%
8/15
8/22
8/29
9/6
9/12
9/19
9/26
5610
5550
5490
5430
5370
5310
5250
5190
5130
5070
5010
4950
4890
100
90
80
70
60
50
40
30
20
10
0

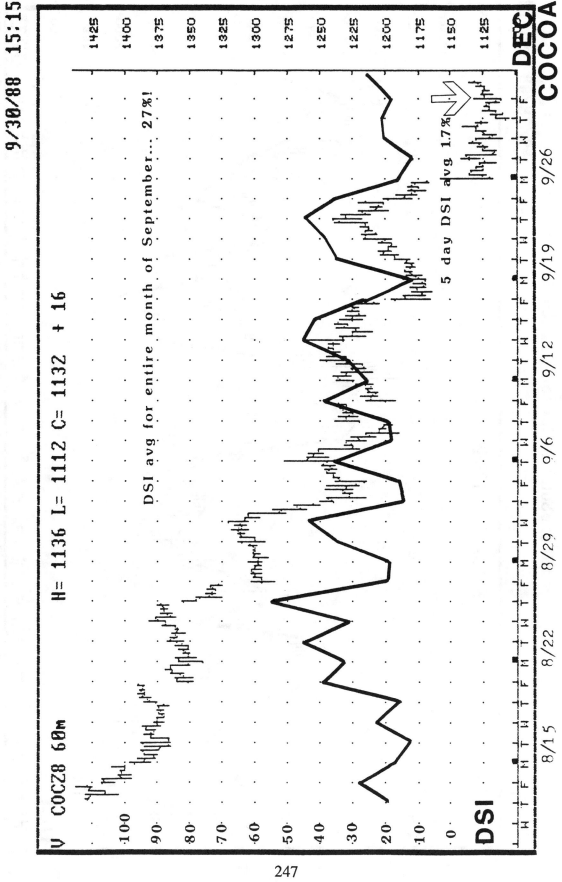

FutureSource Screen Printout

9/30/88   15:15

V COCZ8 60m   H= 1136 L= 1112 C= 1132 + 16

DSI avg for entire month of September... 27%!

5 day DSI avg 17%

DEC
COCOA

DSI

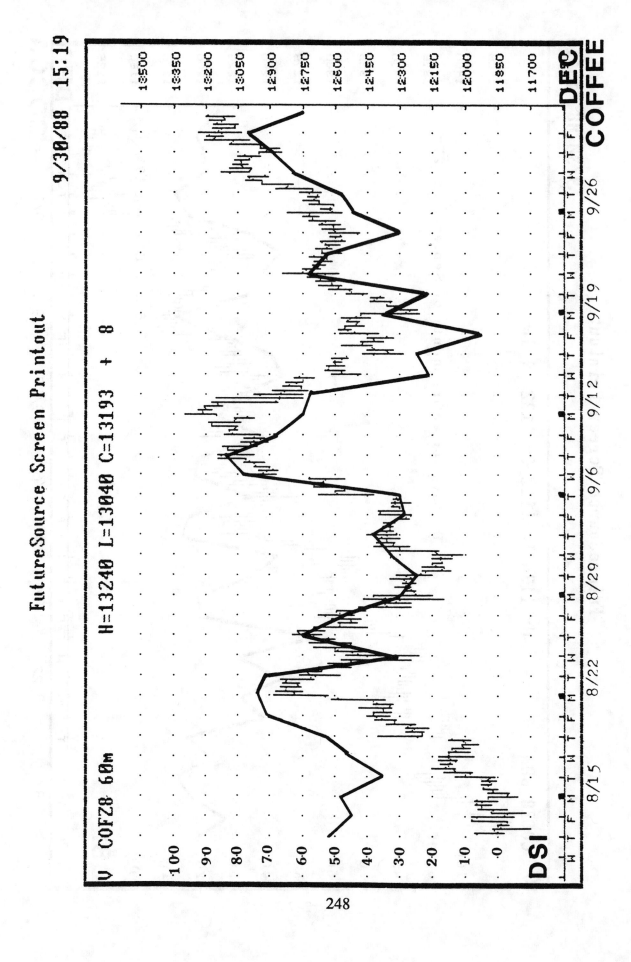

FutureSource Screen Printout   9/30/88 15:19

v COFZ8 60m   H=13240 L=13040 C=13193 + 8

248

DSI   COFFEE DEC

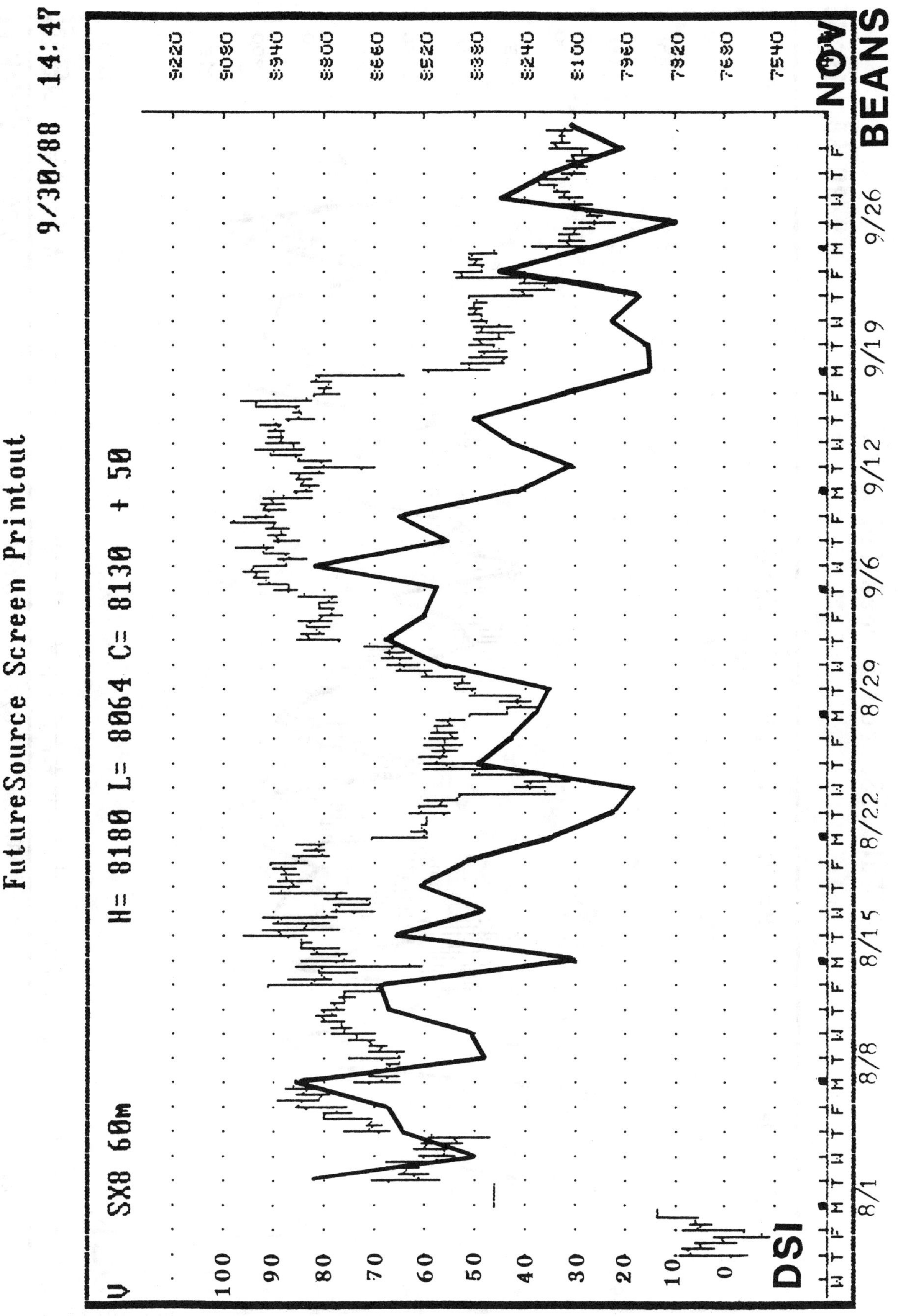

FutureSource Screen Printout   9/30/88 14:47

V   SX8 60m   H= 8180 L= 8064 C= 8130 + 50

BEANS   NOV

DSI

249

FutureSource Screen Printout

9/30/88 14:46

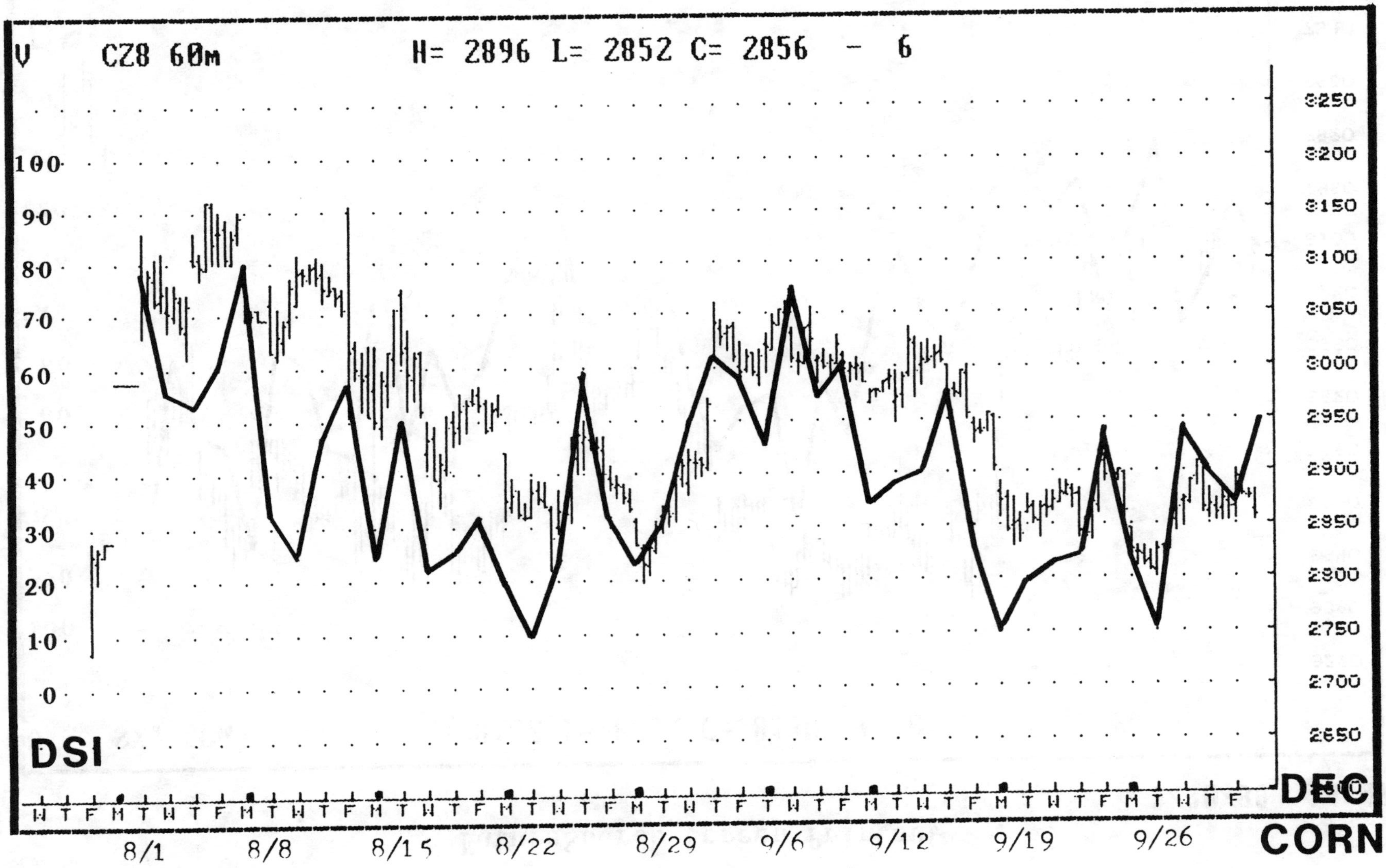

H= 2896 L= 2852 C= 2856 - 6

CORN

DEC

DSI

250

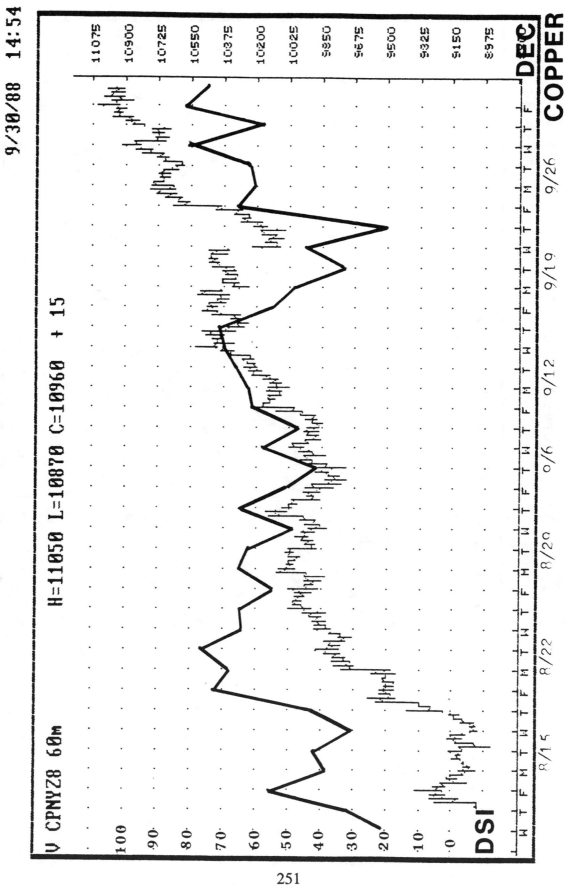

FutureSource Screen Printout   9/30/88 14:54

V CPNYZ8 60m   H=11050 L=10870 C=10960 + 15

COPPER

DSI

251

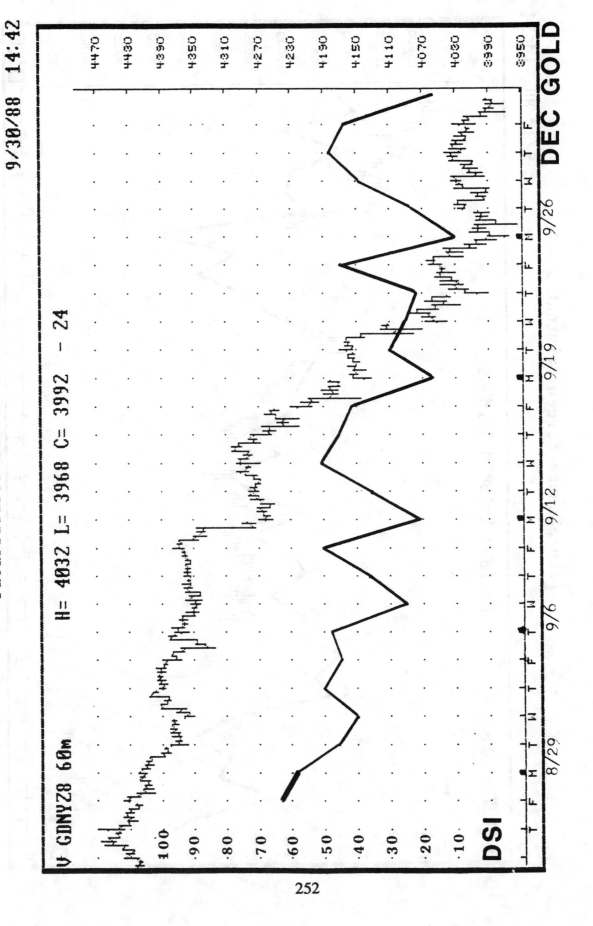

FutureSource Screen Printout   H= 4032 L= 3968 C= 3992 - 24   9/30/88 14:42

DEC GOLD

252

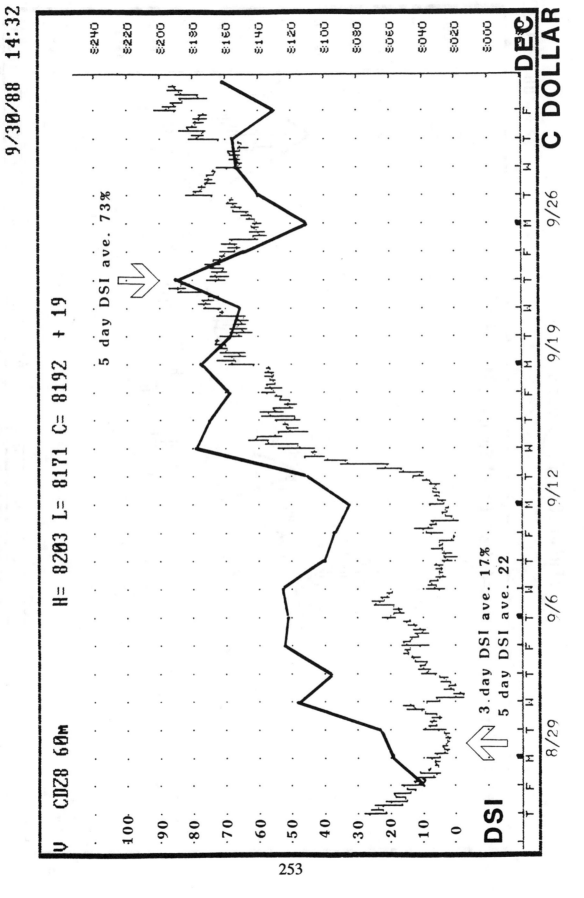

FutureSource Screen Printout   9/30/88 14:32

H= 8203 L= 8171 C= 8192 + 19

CDZ8 60M

C DOLLAR

DEC

5 day DSI ave. 73%

3 day DSI ave. 17%
5 day DSI ave. 22

DSI

253

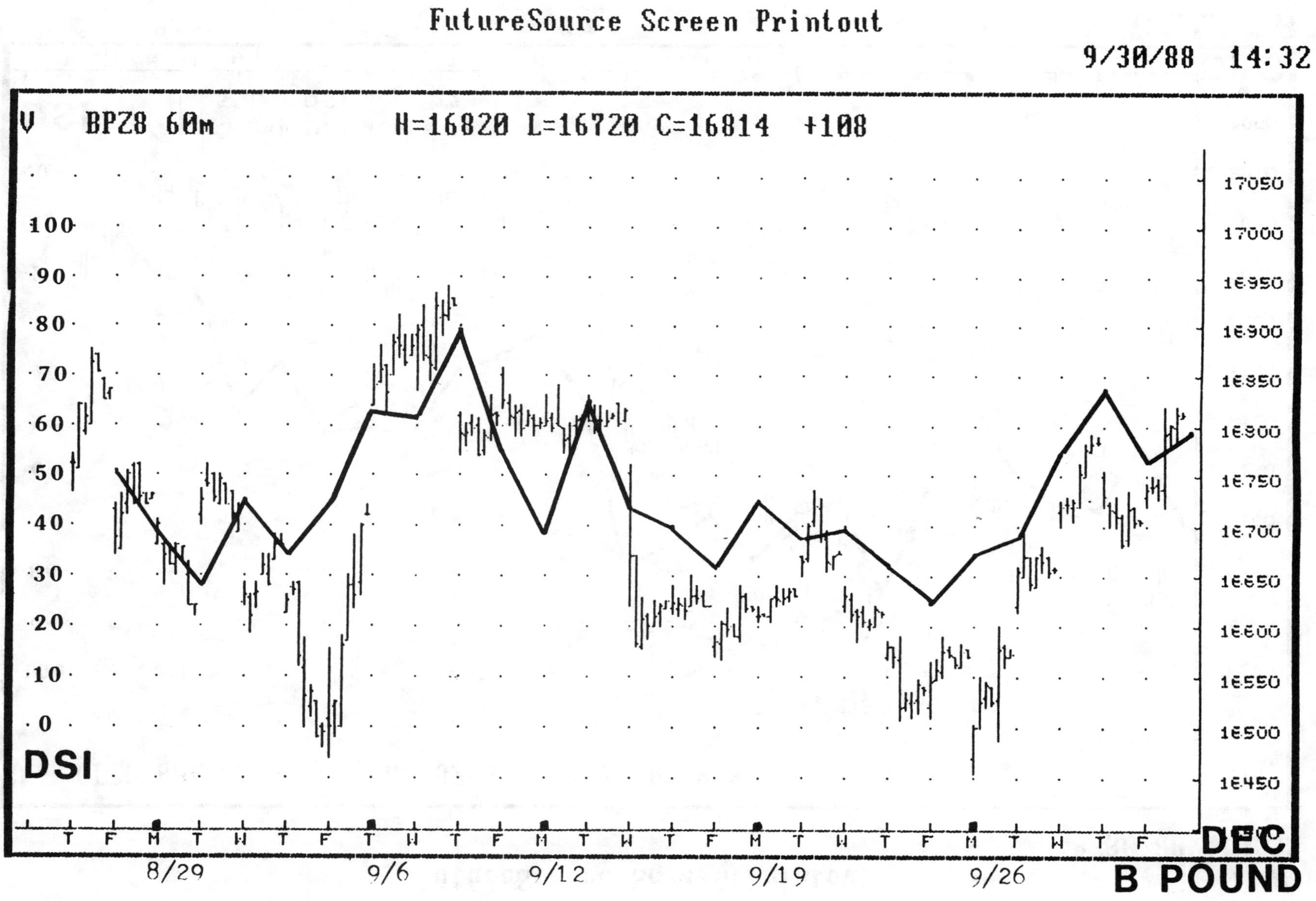

FutureSource Screen Printout
9/30/88 14:32
V BPZ8 60m
H=16820 L=16720 C=16814 +108
100
90
80
70
60
50
40
30
20
10
0
DSI
17050
17000
16950
16900
16850
16800
16750
16700
16650
16600
16550
16500
16450
T F M T W T F T W T F M T W T F M T W T F M T W T F
8/29
9/6
9/12
9/19
9/26
DEC
B POUND

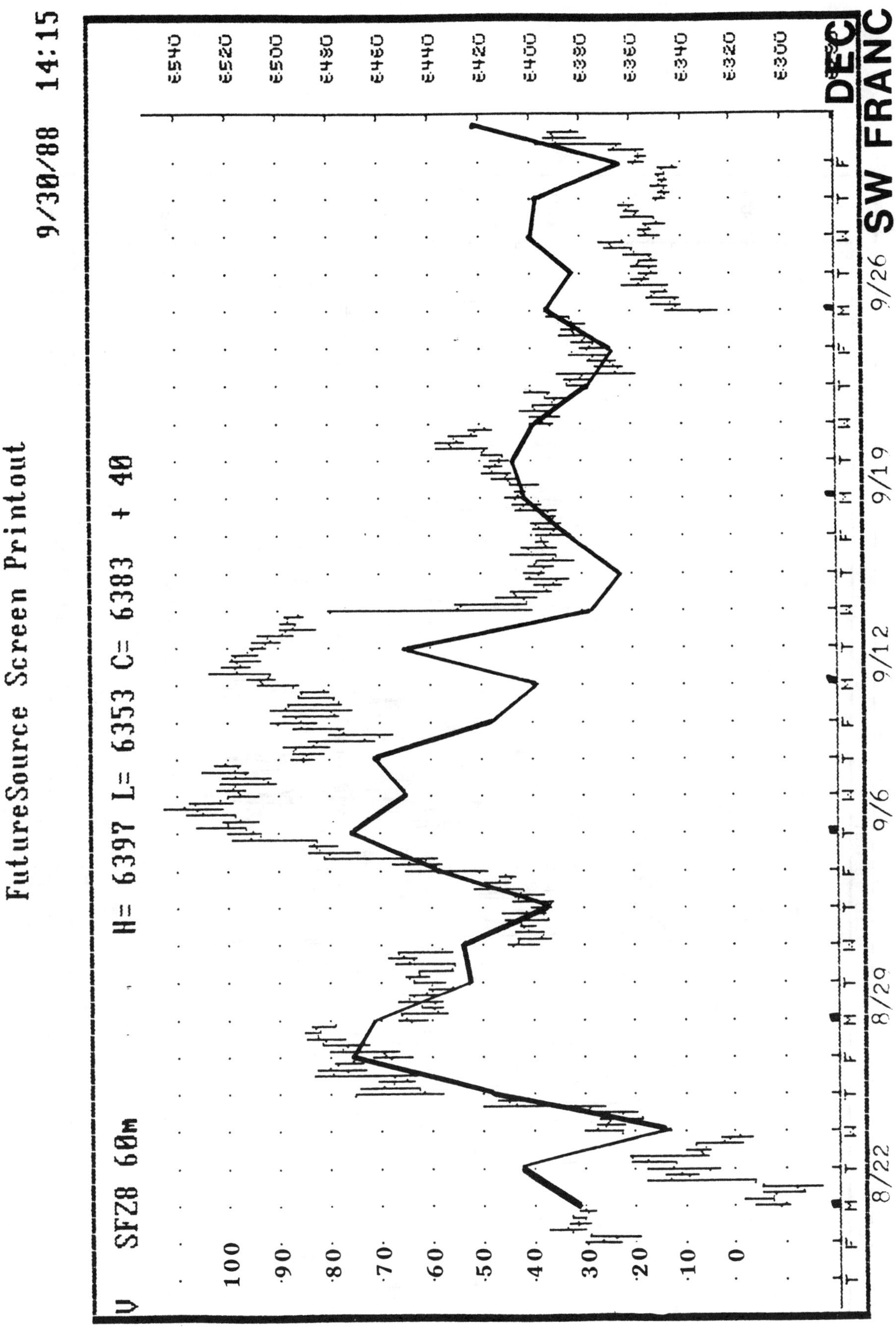

FutureSource Screen Printout
9/30/88 14:15
V SFZ8 60m
H= 6397 L= 6353 C= 6383 + 40
DEC
SW FRANC
6540
6520
6500
6480
6460
6440
6420
6400
6380
6360
6340
6320
6300
100
90
80
70
60
50
40
30
20
10
0
8/22
8/29
9/6
9/12
9/19
9/26

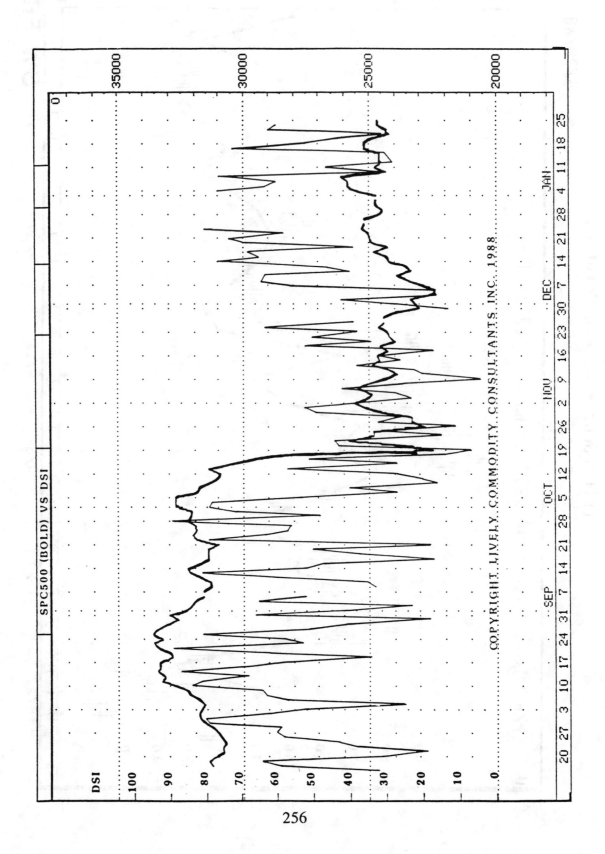

COPYRIGHT LIVELY COMMODITY CONSULTANTS INC. 1988

256

Finally, for you very short term traders, I am showing a simple day trade technique called SLI, which stands for Simple Little Indicator, with its performance in various markets.

SLI DAY TRADE SYSTEM

Here's a Simple Little Indicator for day trading that can give you a 60% plus advantage when day trading.

There are many formations and/or patterns that day traders can profit from. This pattern, discovered by Ralph Vince, has many uses, but ideally suits the day trader.

The system first demands, for a buy signal, a strong market. This is identified by establishing a higher high than all previous 13 day's highs.

We then require a short term oversold condition. Our requirements here are: 1) a down close immediately following the 13 day high, 2) an equal or lower opening the next morning.

Finally, we need a show of strength to trigger a buy. This is identified by trading at last night's close (the down close), where we buy long.

A sell signal is just the reverse; that is, a low below the previous 13 daily lows, then an up close followed by a higher open, then trading down to the down close where a sell is triggered.

For this record we used no stops. As you can see, the pattern is operative in virtually all markets.

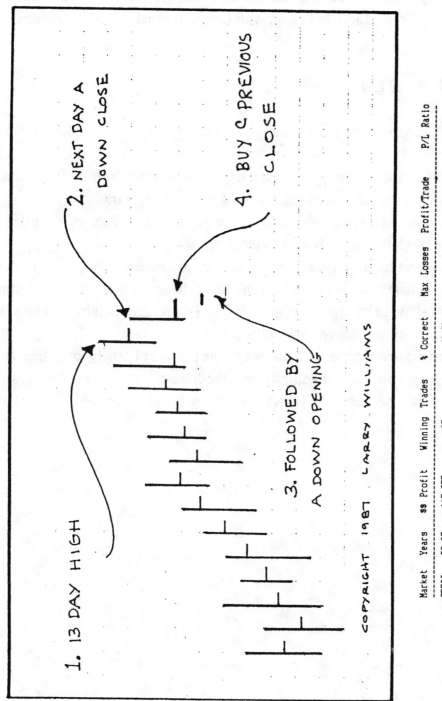

1. 13 DAY HIGH

2. NEXT DAY A DOWN CLOSE

3. FOLLOWED BY A DOWN OPENING

4. BUY @ PREVIOUS CLOSE

COPYRIGHT 1987 LARRY WILLIAMS

Market	Years	$$ Profit	Winning Trades	% Correct	Max Losses	Profit/Trade	P/L Ratio
SP500	82-87	$15,975	85	63.5%	4	$190.00	2.04/1
TBOND	79-87	$21,750	110	63.6%	4	$200.00	2.61/1
SILVER	81-86	$ 880	25	56.0%	3	$ 35.00	1.48/1
SFRANC	80-86	$ 5,312	81	60.5%	5	$ 62.50	1.70/1
EDOLLAR	82-86	$10,400	207	64.7%	7	$ 50.00	1.95/1
BELLIES	78-86	$18,810	339	59.0%	5	$ 57.00	1.40/1
SBEANS	80-86	$ 1,125	97	53.6%	6	$ 11.50	2.38/1

258

As you can see, this tool (which is something we have just recently developed during the writing of this chapter) has a very good record of calling short term market moves.

One of the things that I have tried to do throughout my life is to look at all things in all ways. In one of my books I was ridiculed because I mentioned that there appears to be a relationship between the full moon, new moon cycle and commodity prices.

Since then, a whole host of evidence has come forth on a rather academic basis which, to me, indicates that in fact there are relationships.

While I don't know anything about astrology, I do think there is some type of relationship between what happens in the celestial bodies and commodity prices. If you are interested in this, you may want to contact: R. R. Handler, Box 924, Neenah, WI 54956. They publish an interesting report on the Lunar Cycle in the Stock Market of 1986. The conclusions are somewhat awesome, if one believes them.

The point the author makes is that the new moon and full moon phases, at least in 1986, showed substantial gains, while the first and last quarters showed substantial losses. The largest gain for the year came during a new moon phase, with the largest loss for the year coming during the first quarter phase. The full moon phase showed a gain of some 270 points, which accounted for more gains in the stock market than any other phase in the moon cycle. The last quarter accounted for the largest loss in terms of the full moon cycle.

This is not included to convince you one way or the other about astrology. It is simply to present evidence to you; to get your mind to look at all things, in all ways.

GETTING YOURSELF TOGETHER

Once you have accumulated all of the data and the skills it takes to become a commodity trader, you will still have the ever constant problem of overcoming your own physiological motivations, your own inability to deal with fear and greed.

I believe trading commodities is the easiest way to make money if one has a system and follows it. What complicates the game is A) getting a system that works and B) being able to follow it.

Ninety-five percent of this book focuses on teaching you and giving you tools and systematic approaches to the market. Precious little of it is based on how to handle yourself psychologically. So here goes my two bits worth on how you go about handling the emotional pressures of this thrilling game.

To begin with, I think it may help you to realize that I am not a commodity trader.

I do not view myself as a commodity trader, far from it. I view myself as a system follower, and I have chosen to follow a system that trades commodities.

I could have chosen any other system for my occupation, such as being a lawyer, a doctor, a bricklayer or bank teller, it wouldn't matter. Whatever profession one chooses, there is a systematic way to go about doing it. The more you deviate from that system, the more problems you'll encounter. So don't view yourself as a commodity trader, view yourself as a system follower . . . that is once you get a system worth following.

Even then you will find there are tremendous emotional and psychological pulls that get you to do one thing or another in the marketplace.

I've recently begun doing research with subliminal tapes that direct the conscious, and perhaps subconscious, mind to be able to respond as a system follower, as opposed to responding as a trader.

Frankly, I don't know what's going to develop of this, but Jake Bernstein (who as you may know is a psychologist by trade) and I have begun working on this problem. We want to see if there isn't a way of getting through the mind to make certain the mind becomes an active part of the system, as opposed to a reactor doing whatever it chooses to do in the commodity market.

If you have any interest in this, please write me at: Box 8162, Rancho Santa Fe, CA 92067, and I will gladly send you information on what success we are able to have testing a large number of traders who will be given subliminal tapes that they will listen to repeatedly . . . over and over and over . . . .and see if that does make a difference in their ability to cope with the market.

Speaking from my own personal experience, I can tell you that it has made a difference for me to listen to tapes that I had made. It will be interesting to find out, once we have tested this on a group of traders, to what extend it may change, hopefully for the better, their own trading styles.

Certainly, though, if one can lose weight, develop willpower, overcome anxieties, etc. through subliminal tapes (which has been widely advertised), then one should be able to improve his commodity trading and/or system following abilities. Time will tell on this, but it is certainly one of the most exciting things I've played with in the market for some years.

After you have developed your system, you should ask yourself, how would a computer which has been used to test your system . . . whether it's an adding machine or a fancy IBM . . . react to today's market? Where would the computer be buying or selling? That is what you should be doing.

The nice thing about having a system is that once you have developed a system, you always have an answer as to what you should do when the market's moving against you. I don't know, but your system knows, so simply refer to the system, the computer or whatever it is and do what the system says you should do.

In reality, you should not try to make money in the market, you should simply try to duplicate the performance of your system. I suspect that the closer you duplicate the performance of our system, the more profitable your overall trading will be.

OFFENSE AND DEFENSE

The vast majority of the tools shared with you in this book, as well as tools you would learn in other books, seminars, etc. are basically what I would call offensive tools; they give you the ability to strike forth in the marketplace; to go out and try to make money. But with any game, you not only need an offense, you also need a defense. So let's talk briefly about defense.

A lot of traders would do well to take to heart what Chuck Noll, head coach of the Pittsburgh Steelers, had to tell his team when he said, "Before you win it, you must first not lose it."

It's funny, while America seems enthralled with football, especially in love with quarterbacks and the offensive moves, we do have some fans who love to chant, "Defense, Defense, Defense." Those who do realize the integrity of Noll's statement. Without defense, you're not going to win. The same is true in the commodity market. While I've given you swords and bows and arrows, I must also give you a shield. If you think about it, the shield I've given you is your money management techniques.

The importance of that shield, defense, perhaps can best be visualized when you think that the last football team to win the Super Bowl back to back was the Steelers. During that time period they had the second best defense of all teams, allowing about 10 points per game. In the following years the top defensive team has almost always won its division, and most of them have gone on to win the Super Bowl. Hopefully, the lesson from football will be learned by commodity traders. Defense is important.

If you hope to win in the wacky world of trading commodities, you need more than sticks and stones. You need the shield to protect you. So I reiterate that you read everything possible on money management. It is the most important thing I give you in this book . . . forget the systems, forget the techniques I've taught you. You need a shield, you need a defense and money management is your defense. You will live and die by your ability to practice good defensive strategies in trading commodities. Let me give you an idea of why money management is so important. What follows is a table that shows the difference between a buy and hold strategy, a trading strategy without money management and finally, a trading strategy with money management.

BUY & SELL VS TRADING WITH MONEY MANAGEMENT
STARTING EQUITY $10,000

STARTING PRICE $1,000

TRADE	1 CONTRACT	BASE EQUITY	EQUITY WITH MONEY MANAGEMENT AT 30%		EQUITY
1.	-100	9,900	x 3	-300	9,700
2.	+300	10,200	x 3	+900	10,600
3.	-100	10,100	x 3	-300	10,300
4.	-200	9,900	x 3	-600	9,700
5.	+500	10,400	x 3	+1, 500	11,200
6.	+200	10,600	x 3	+600	11,800
7.	+200	10,800	x 4	+800	12,600
8.	-200	10,600	x 4	-800	11,800
9.	+100	10,700	x 4	+400	12,200
10.	+300	11,000	x 4	+1,200	13,400

ENDING PRICE $2,000

+1,000	+1,000		+3,400

BUY HELD +1,000   TRADE 1 UNIT + 1,000   WITH MONEY MANAGEMENT +3,400

MORAL: TRADING BEATS BUY & HOLD
IF ACCOUNT IS "RECAPITALIZED"

Notice that if you buy a commodity at $1,000 and sell it at $2,000, you made $1,000; that's the buy and hold approach. Assuming that $1,000 was the absolute low and $2,000 was the absolute high, you could not have done better, so I'll credit you with the full $1,000. If you're very successful along the way, you may be able to trade and get the same number of points, which again equals $1,000. However, with money management, notice what takes place using 30% of your account, which is about right, per each commodity you trade.

In the reality of most commodity systems, you're going to end up making $3,400. In other words, you have a higher rate of return, actually a staggeringly higher rate of return (340% higher during the same time period) because you used money management.

Now if you're sharp, you may notice that we used 30% of the equity; hence, we had three times the profits or losses on each trade. If you had done that with the buy and hold strategy, you would have made $3,000 with the trading strategy. But again, you netted $400 more with the trading strategy <u>and</u> the money management.

As long as you recapitalize your account, you will make more money trading than you will buying and holding if you use money management.

The point here is that you must pay as much attention to money management as you pay to picking your buys and sells in the marketplace. Again, read everything you can on money management. The two things I have done during the years that helped me the most, in terms of money management and the psychology of trading, is to read everything on money management from university publications and to read virtually every system that's been offered on gambling, because, as I've pointed out, in gambling the only element the gambler has to control is money management; hence, gamblers have written a lot about this subject.

Another thing I used to do would be to go to any of the gambling dens and play their silly games with large or small stakes. It really doesn't matter. Whether you're losing money or winning money it's all the same rush. Whether you're long 100 Bonds or losing $10.00 in roulette, you still feel the same basic emotional rushes, especially if it is a comparable percent of your bankroll!

But by sitting at the tables, you start to develop a sense of how losers . . . the people around you . . . operate. And get in touch with your own personal emotions when you start losing or winning. It's very cheap to get in touch with these emotions in gambling casinos because they don't deal with the gargantuan sums that we do as commodity traders. Additionally, you can go through two or three hundred decision processes in an aggressive evening at the tables; whereas, it may take you as much as two years to have the same number of decisions interacting with your emotions in stock or commodity trading. This is the best way I know to desensitize the emotions of winning and losing.

A PERSONAL STORY

Let me close this chapter of the book with a personal story about 1987 and my own trading style. I am doing this for two reasons, one to show you what can be done in the marketplace . . . to give you some hope and inspiration . . . but also to make it well known that Larry Williams is more than an author, more than a lecturer; Larry Williams is also a superb commodity system follower.

In January of this year I began trading in the World Cup Trading Championship, sponsored by Robbins Trading Company: 222 S. Riverside Place., Suite #351, Chicago, Il 60606. A large group of commodity traders entered this contest with a more or less winner take all approach; whereas, a person who turns his $10,000 into the most money at the end of the time period would collect not only the title of World Champion Commodity Trader, but also most of the money that had been pooled by the various traders.

For a moment, let me ask how much money do you think one can make trading commodities from January to June 1st, starting with a $10,000 account. What would satisfy you . . . $20,000, $30,000, $100,000?

Or do you have extremely high goals, do you think it would be possible to turn the $10,000 into $400,000?

Most people would tell you, if you told them you turned $10,000 into $250,000 in five months trading commodities, either you were extremely lucky (there had been a major move that you had participated in) or . . . you're lying to them.

Well, as it happens, in 1987 most all of the trades in my championship account were day trades. I did not take advantage of any major trend moves in the market. Yet the $10,000 grew to a high of $920,000 before an equity dip in late May bringing the account back into the $600,000 area.

Yes, that's right — $10,000 went just shy of $1,000,000, backed off to $600,000 and now, as this book comes to an end, we'll see if I can't get things back on schedule and get the $600,000 to well over $1,000,000 (it did).

I would think that by the end of 1987 the account should be somewhere over one million dollars. All starting with a meager $10,000 investment. Don't think I'm the only one to do this. One of my good New York City friends, known more for his panache and medical skills, turned $500,000 into over $5,000,000 in less than a year!

Some Closing Thoughts

Editor's note: Larry Williams closing balance on Dec. 31 was $1,147,607. So he did, indeed reach his goal.

There are many things that allowed this to take place. First of all, I have been trading the commodity market for some 20 years, and I should know by now what I'm doing. I have a superb form of money management which has been given to you in this book. And I have some pretty good tools for trading the market, which, for the most part, have been shared with you.

But what I have done is certainly not unusual. In fact, looking back at the trades that I made, I can think of many of the trades where I didn't follow the rules, where I didn't do the right thing, where I could have done better. So what can one do when he maximizes his trading ability? Well, the sky's the limit.

I thank you for laboring through my writings. Sometimes they're not as clear as I wish them to be. It's difficult when writing about a technical and complicated subject such as the commodity markets, to make your comments concise and easy to learn. Especially for people who have just heard about commodities. But, I hope you have been able to learn from this book. The commodity markets . . . and for that matter life in general . . . have been very good to me. I think it is an obligation upon all of us to give back some of what we get. I have gotten a lot out of life, a lot out of the markets. I hope you will take what I have done here and get out even more for yourselves.

Thank you for coming on this journey. I hope that at sometime our paths cross in the future.

## Chapter 15

Advice From The Experts

I personally culled through my library and lists of reference sources to show you a smorgasbord of what I think are the best books and reference sources in the business.

Certainly the first that one would turn his attention to would be Bruce Babcock's Commodity Trader's Consumer Report.

Bruce is a compendium of market knowledge.

First, he publishes the widely respected Commodity Trader's Consumer Report, kind of a Ralph Nader's tracking service of all commodity trading services in the country. Here you can see how the pros are doing — which newsletters are hot — which are not.

Bruce, never one to rest on his laurels, also publishes a System of the Month, whereby he develops a commodity trading system and offers it for sale at a nominal fee.

While these systems may not be as good as some of the more expensive ones you see widely marketed, some of them are as good or better than some of the poorer, publicly marketed, high priced systems.

Beyond being a bibliophile of advisors and systems, Bruce is also a prolific writer, having written several manuals on commodity trading, and just recently has offered the Dow Jones Guide to Commodity Trading Systems.

For anyone who wants to see what systems and traders have been hot, and who was not, Bruce is the place to go. You can contact him at P.O. Box 254480, Sacramento, CA 95824. Other books on the list are:

<u>The Investor's Quotient</u> by Jake Bernstein
<u>Beyond the Investors Quotient</u> by Jake Bernstein

These books will get you looking more at you than looking at the market, which one simply must do to become a successful trader.

<u>The Mathematics of Gambling</u> by Dr. Edward O. Thorpe

While commodity trading isn't gambling, both rely heavily on money management. This book is a gem.

<u>Commodity Market Money Management</u> by Fred Gehm.

This is the backbone of money management books, one you definitely should read.

<u>The Money Motive</u> by Thomas Wiseman.

This will give you a psychological understanding of money and what it does to and for us.

<u>Behavior of Prices on Wall Street</u> by Art Merrill.

Though this is a stock market book, it gives you an understanding of how Art (who has been a real Rock of Gibraltar in market research) thinks.

<u>Opening Price Statistical Data on the Futures Markets</u> by Earl Hadady.

If you're as fascinated as anyone by opening prices, you can learn a lot from Earl's book.

<u>Stock Option and No Load Switch Fund Scalper's Manual</u> by Gerry Appel.

I don't know if this is Gerry's best book, but anything you can get by him should be read. He's highly technical, has a nice scientific approach, and while he writes and talks a good game, he trades and invests an even better one.

Also a "must read" from Gerry is <u>Winning Market Systems</u>.

<u>Technical Analysis of Commodities</u> by Perry Kaufman.

Kaufman, a consummate researcher and studier of other people's methods, reveals a great deal about how other people approach the market. This is good, basic technical reading.

<u>A Guide to Commodity Price Forecasting</u> published by the Commodity Research Bureau.

This is a definitive book that all good commodity libraries should have.

<u>The Big Hitters</u> by Kevin Koy.

You'll not learn much about the markets here, but you'll learn a good deal about how big market traders think and react. On that basis alone, it's well worth the money.

<u>Man and Cosmos</u> by Clifford Matlock.

This is probably the best book for those of you who think astrology has an impact on the markets. Get it. Read it over, then see what you think.

<u>How to Profit From Seasonal Commodity Spreads</u> by Jake Bernstein.

Most people focus on seasonal tendencies on just prices themselves. Jake's gone a step further here and looked at seasonal spreads, which are probably a more reliable approach to trading the market than just seasonal influences on price alone.

269

Beating the Street by Burton Fabricand.

This is an old book. If you can get it, read it. Otherwise, don't worry about it. But it will give you a good idea of how one can go about approaching the market on a more scientific basis and what does work, as well as what doesn't work.

How to Forecast Interest Rates by Martin J. Pring.

This is a good book on the fundamental understanding of what makes bond prices go up and down.

Anything by Marty Zweig.

You could start with New IRA's. But if Marty or Ned Davis write anything, it's been my experience (if you're a stock or commodity trader), you'd better read it. These two gentlemen have done as much work as all the rest of us together in developing workable trend-following methods. Their track record is excellent. Their advice has been superb. And, above all, they are two super people.

The Tunnel Through the Air by W. D Gann.

If you're into Gann, all those lines and astrological dates, this is probably the best reference point. Look at the dates Gann gives in his books of when things would happen and compare them to an ephemeris to see what was happening at those time points. You may then understand how Gann developed his system.

Stock Market Logic by Norm Fosback.

This is as good a basic reference as you'll ever find on the stock market.

The Professional Commodity Trader by Stanley Kroll.

Kroll writes well about the exciting life he's led as a commodity trader. It's one you should have for your library.

Astrocycles by Larry Pesavento.

Larry and Mason Sexton seem to have more scientific data going in this area than the other people that I've studied, with the exception, perhaps, of Arch Crawford. Anything by any of these three men is certainly worth reading, especially if this is your inclination towards the market.

Handbook of Commodity Cycles by Jake Bernstein.

This may be the definitive book of commodity cycles. Certainly Jake is the definitive commodity analyst of cycles. And if you're going to trade commodities, you'd better know something about cycles. Hence, Jake's book is a must.

Viewpoints of a Commodity Trader by Roy Longstreet.

This may be out of print or difficult to find. It contains reflections, as well as some applications, by a commodity trader of a generation or two ago. However, everything that is in the book is applicable to today's market, especially the psychology of the trader and the market, as well as the chart techniques discussed in the book.

Technical Analysis of Stock Trends by Robert D. Edwards and John Magee.

Complete coverage of traditional charting methods. I think this should be the starting point in any trader's education.

The McGraw-Hill Handbook of Commodities and Futures edited by Martin J. Pring. New York: McGraw-Hill, Inc., 1985.

271

The best treatment I've seen regarding commodity fundamentals. All the markets are covered — including the obscure (would you like to know why the Soviets sunflower seeds are more vulnerable to moisture and disease?).

The Elliott Wave Principle by A. J. Frost and Robert Prechter, Jr. Gainesville: New Classics Library, 1978.

Thorough presentation of an entirely different approach to chart interpretation. Like Edwards and Magee is to conventional charting, this one is "The Bible" on its subject.

The Haller Theory of Stock Market Trends by Gilbert Haller.

Excellent introduction to technical analysis. This book emphasizes the long term psychology evident in the stock market, and demonstrates how to objectively measure it using technical analysis. An absolute gem . . . this was my introduction to the market and systems.

Technical Analysis of the Futures Markets by John J. Murphy. New York: New York Institute of Finance, 1986.

Up-to-date, thorough examination of the multitude of techniques and indicators being employed by traders today. If nothing else, it will get the reader introduced to a broad spectrum of technical approaches.

Techniques of a Professional Commodity Chart Analyst by Arthur Sklarew.

This book picks up where Edwards and Magee left off.

New Concepts in Technical Trading Systems by J. Welles Wilder, Jr.

A good introduction to systems trading. Must reading since these systems/indicators, like RSI, have become household names in the technical analysis world.

<u>Reminiscences of a Stock Market Operator</u> by Edwin Lefevre.

Simply put, this is the best book to give you market "street smarts" that's ever been written. Every word is pure gold . . . if you don't have it — rush out and buy it . . . today.

<u>The Zurich Axioms</u> by Max Gunther

This is the 1980's version of "Reminiscences of a Stock Operator" by Edwin Lefevre. This book will give you the investment secrets of the Swiss bankers as well as exposing you to yourself. Once you read it, I'm certain you'll pass it on to others. It's just that good a book.

And of course no list of great market books would be complete without . . .

<u>How I Made a Million Dollars . . . Last Year . . . Trading Commodities</u> by Larry R. Williams. Brightwaters: Windsor Books, Third Edition, 1979.

Since I wrote it, what can I say?

FINAL AXIOMS

1. If it looks good . . . it isn't.

2. Big positions cause big problems.

3. No one absolutely knows the future.

4. When you are wrong, don't get even, get out.

5. Or, when the boat starts sinking don't pray, jump.

6. To average losses is to compound stupidity.

7. The majority is right in the middle, wrong at the beginning and end.

8. The majority rules, but it's a good rule to fade them.

9. You created the condition you are in.

10. Therefore, let's create some good times.